What Every Superintendent and Principal Needs to Know

School Leadership for the Real World

2nd edition, revised and updated

Jim Rosborg

Max McGee

Jim Burgett

For additional information about this topic and the authors, please visit our website at

http://www.superintendents-and-principals.com

ISBN 0-9708621-6-4

Cover design and layout
for both editions by
Douglas Burgett

Table of Contents

Dedications

Jim Rosborg

To my wife, Nancy, for her love, support, and being my right arm on every challenge I have accepted, and to my children, Kyle, Carol, Mike, and his wife Wendy for being the greatest joys of my life and bringing me an even greater understanding of the importance of family.

Max McGee

To Jan Fitzsimmons, an inspirational wife, colleague, and buddy, whose heart and hard work have closed the achievement gap and touched the lives of so many children and families in North Lawndale and beyond.

Jim Burgett

To my wife Barb, whom I have loved since I first saw her, and to our children, Stacey, Jennifer, and Doug; my two sons-in-law, Mike and Brian, our five special grandchildren, for making me proud every minute of every day, and to my "big" brothers Gordon and Bill for lighting the way throughout my life.

Introduction

When you want to know the best 20 steps to take to improve the work and learning atmosphere in your school or how to pass a bond referendum, build a business case (with forecasting and benchmarking), significantly raise your schools' reading scores, or wear the right shoes when the top school office is yours, then talk to top superintendents (and former principals) plunk in Middle America, like Illinois!

Our picks were Jim Rosborg, Max McGee, and Jim Burgett. Their biographies show why.

We gave them a dual mission: (1) Tell their colleagues how to be both effective leaders in a school setting and innovators with curriculum, and (2) Openly discuss every major problem facing in-the-field school administrators and principals today. The only guidelines were absolute honesty, clarity, real examples, and as little mumbo-jumbo jargon as possible.

The one area we couldn't adequately confront was finance, which in most states is relatively prescriptive. But we zeroed in on grant writing, collective bargaining, bond issues, foundation-forming, union-supporting, and technology—the kinds of financial things this book's readers can do something about.

We feel that learning from others who daily face the same headaches and hopes that you do is usually a whole lot more useful than trying to build a book around patched-up, outdated procedures templates. So we have tried to cram as much practical how-to stuff into 320 pages as we could, and then set up a website with even more follow-up info, plus the authors' photos!

While the pages in this book read conversationally, the advice is flat-out serious, because schools and teaching kids is about as serious a task as we face in America today. Nonetheless, fun somehow crept into the prose. But don't be deceived: Jim R., Max, and Jim B. are three decorated school dudes who care—and dare to share. They eagerly agreed to write this book because they want every one of you to succeed every time.

The Second Edition!

The introduction above, and the first edition of this book that it introduced, found such positive reception that we sold out three full printings, plus a fourth run solely made for an investment firm that wanted all of the administrators in its area to have a copy on their desk!

Now it's well into 2006 and rather than simply go to press as is again, I asked each of the authors to update his chapters (several were virtually rewritten with new material) and to provide us with five new case studies to add to the earlier ones, so we could keep the information current and immediately applicable.

They happily complied with this grumpy old editor's requests, although "happily" may be a tad exaggerated. That was a double good fortune because it makes this upgraded edition even better than the first, which has also been widely adapted as a textbook for graduate school administration classes across the country.

My requests were a real imposition because all three were at the same time writing the heart of a composite grand new book with a working title of *The Perfect School*, which ECU will release in November of 2006.

(See our website for the release date, ordering details, and two sample chapters: www.superintedents-and-principals.com.)

Another benefit has accrued since the release of *What Every Superintendent and Principal Needs to Know* in 2003. All three of the editors, by popular demand, are gracing lecture halls, educational conferences, and school administrator upgrade gatherings, building on the book's old and new contents, and sprinkling in up-to-date applications.

So here it is, what we call in-house "Supt #2," with new windows and repainted doors on a still-fresh foundation that we think will stand strong for centuries. Good stuff, with more good stuff.

Gordon Burgett, Publisher

Chapter One

School Leadership

Jim Rosborg

The greatest single ingredient to the success of an educational organization is still school leadership. Much has been written about it. The purpose of this book is not to debate the great theorists but to enhance their work with some practical insights that come from being a respected superintendent or principal.

We greatly appreciate the works of Amitai Etzioni, Fred Fiedler, Frederick Herzberg, Wayne Hoy, Douglas McGregor, B. F. Skinner, Ralph Stogdill, and the other great theorists. Yet many of their leadership theories were written before the development of unions, collective bargaining laws, email, and state standards. Times have changed. Our goal is to offer you modern-day suggestions for success in school leadership.

Effectiveness has to be the goal of school leadership. What is effectiveness? In school administration today, effectiveness is defined by the use of the qualities discussed in this chapter.

Effectiveness is a huge challenge, particularly since school systems have become easy targets in today's society. The general public hears about declining test scores, teacher discontent, and the lack of discipline in the schools. School officials must deal with decreasing parent support, declining enrollments, and more mandates unaccompanied by necessary funds. School leaders used to be able to focus on short-term individual student performance problems. Recent issues such as charter schools, vouchers, school choice, federal legislation, declining enrollments, and the consolidation of small schools present the leaders with long-term problems of survival.

As the school leader, you must attack these problems head on. You must face the reality that your success is going to be defined by your ability to reach objectives having to do with a multitude of sub-systems. Your job success will be evaluated by such subjects as physical facilities and equipment; the effectiveness of teachers; the school's curriculum; test scores; public relations; your effectiveness with the media, stakeholders, and politicians; collective bargaining; diversity; changing demographics; school safety; the perception of school discipline; and the monies available to fund programs. Add to this your need to have specific knowledge about transportation, special education, technology, buildings and grounds, food services, diversity issues, union organizations, health issues, and personnel. Talk about a challenging road to success!

This success has to be achieved in a time when control is continually being taken away from the local Board of Education. While the authors of this book disagree with the philosophy of less local control, it is a reality that all school leaders must face in the 21st century. Can a school leader be effective when confronted by all of these obstacles? Our opinion is that you can by putting together your own formula for success. Within that formula, we feel that, whatever your leadership style, the following 20 topics must be considered and included:

What is best for kids?

Many times superintendents and principals find themselves in a thankless middle position in conflicts between personnel. No matter what decision is made, at best there will be a winner and a loser; at worst, both lose. In part, that's because a successful school leader will not base his/her decision on the individuals involved but on the decision's outcome for kids. Often that is not the easiest decision, but it's always the right one.

Successful leaders work to maximize the academic success of students. They also find time to be with kids. How can you find that time?

1. Allocate 15 minutes each day to walk through a school in your district. If you have just one school, walk from one end to the other every day.

2. Start talking to kids two days a week as they enter school. If you are a building principal, make every effort to be out in the

hallways before and after school to converse with students, parents, and teachers.

3. Pick two events per week in your district to attend. If your schedule is tight, don't sit down. Circulate through the room. This makes it much easier to leave unnoticed.

4. Be aware of building and individual classroom calendars so you can attend special events such as grandparents' day, parent volunteer day, and other special awards days.

5. Send notes to kids who earn special achievements, even if the achievement is outside the school (like Eagle Scouts award ceremonies and scholarships). Attendance at these ceremonies makes the event even more special for the student.

Always be nice to students—one day they may be Board members! Once an administrator gets the reputation of being proactive for students, respect will be gained in every stakeholder circle.

Show a good work ethic

If you expect those around you to give maximum effort, then you as the leader must also be perceived as a hard worker willing to put in the time needed for student success. In an educational organization, everyone simply has to work hard. The example for this work ethic must start at the top. People will know how hard you work. There is no need to "toot your own horn." Hard work pays off for system success. You must be there for your staff. You must be willing to roll up your sleeves to get the job done. Many times I have helped my maintenance men and custodians. They ask if I'm concerned about getting my clothes dirty. My reply is, "If the cleaners can't clean my clothes after helping get a job done, then I need to change cleaners."

Be teacher friendly

Almost all school administrators were once teachers themselves. Sad to say, many administrators forget this. School leaders must not forget what it took to be a successful teacher. Teaching takes as much hard work and dedication as it does to be a school administrator. Teachers just have different responsibilities within the organization. No position is better than another. People have simply made different choices in what they want to be. Teachers are still the front line of defense for schools and the front line of success for students. The goal of school administrators has to be the removal of barriers that impede the teaching and learning process. If teachers are successful, there is a good chance the school administrator will be successful. Being supportive of teachers and being friendly with them not only makes good sense, it leads to better relations with the teachers' union, and that helps reach settlements in the collective bargaining process. How do you do it?

1. Strongly support teachers when they discipline students.

2. Work hard to help your staff be recognized for local, state, and national awards.

3. Meet monthly with district and building leaders to discuss problems and formulate solutions.

4. Attend events that involve faculty.

5. Write positive notes to staff members praising the great job that they do.

6. Support professional development activities. If these activities can be done in conjunction with the teachers' union, an even more powerful bond between the administrator and teachers will develop.

Grow mule skin

Mules are noted for their thick skin. A successful school leader needs the same. In the education business, administrators deal with many people, each with his/her own opinion about schools. Not all of those opinions concur. Consequently, there will be many disagreements about the decision a school leader makes. In addition, when we are dealing with children, emotionalism appears when there is a disagreement with the final decision and the philosophy supporting that decision. Nothing good is accomplished when both parties are in an emotional state. The school leader's responsibility is to remain professional and calm at that time. Leaders must look beyond the situation. Questions must be asked, like "Why is this parent acting like this?" "Is something else going on in his/her life that is dictating this behavior?"

For example, we have found that in districts where many families suffer economically, December is a particularly tough month for parents when dealing with their child's discipline. Once we get past the initial issue, we find that parents are experiencing extreme guilt for not being able to provide as they'd like to for their child's Christmas. So instead of backing the school regarding their child's discipline, parents feel compelled to come to the school and raise havoc with the authorities to show support for the child and the fact that they, as the parent, love that child. In reality, this is a very poor parenting technique that sends the wrong message toward helping the child achieve self-discipline. With these facts, patience, and professionalism, the school leader can help the parent work through the situation so that parent can help his/her child attain the needed self-discipline.

Diffusing anger is part of a school administrator's job. One way to get parents to calm down is to ask if they are mad at you, the leader, or if they are mad at the situation. Many times this will help the parents get out of their emotional state. When meeting with hot-tempered parents, never lose your temper. Whatever they say, don't get angry. Politely ask them to cool down. If they are swearing, politely ask them to stop, noting that you are not swearing and that nothing will be accomplished by swearing. If you cannot get the individual to calm down, ask him/her to make an appointment to see you later. If the parent does calm down (which happens 99% of the time), calmly ask him/her to continue. Take notes. Only interrupt for clarification. Wait until the person is done (or worn out), then restate what was said to make sure that both of you are in accord. From there, an opportunity to problem solve takes place. This makes you the leader, the problem solver. Most people are excellent problem identifiers, but very few are problem solvers. Patience and mule skin pay off in problem solving.

Be consistent in decision making

Individuals in the school arena expect leaders to be consistent. One of the greatest causes of school leadership failure, in our opinion, is that the school leader has mood changes depending on the environment. Parents, students, staff, and the community shouldn't have to worry about whether they are dealing with the Good Humor Man or Attila the Hun.

We have also observed many administrators letting one negative situation impact their decision making for the rest of the day. The individuals dealing with this administrator have no idea of the earlier negative situation. Their perception of the administrator is based upon the response to their own individual need, not on previous scenarios. For them, the most important issue is theirs. A successful school administrator always remembers that no matter how trivial the issue may seem, the issue is of great importance to the individual who has brought it. Consistency in the decision-making process is imperative to success.

Be a decision maker

As a superintendent or principal, you are in a decision-making position. Therefore, after seeking input from others and further researching the issue, make the decision. Many times a well thought out mistake is better in the decision-making process than no decision at all. You must expect to make some mistakes. The key is to learn from them, rectify them, and not make them again. The stakeholders associated with the school district want a decision maker. They want the school leader to consistently push a point of view and make decisions supported by that point of view. The general public still looks to the superintendent or principal to be the expert. They want decisions made.

Be consistent with discipline

A vast majority of administrative positions deal in one way or another with discipline, whether it involves a student or a staff member. Your reputation for consistency in this area plays a vital role in the perception of your success. This issue, along with zero tolerance, will be discussed in greater depth in Chapter 10, Successful Teaching and Learning.

Keep a straight backbone

In school administration, the individual leader is going to be attacked, criticized, and accused on many issues. When this happens, the administrator has to stand tall behind his or her own beliefs and value systems. In addition, an effective school leader stands behind the decisions of fellow staff members as long as they have followed school law, Board policies, and school procedures.

Recognize and respect diversity

As minority populations continue to grow in the United States, leadership in schools must adapt in recognition of this change. We believe that all children can learn no matter what their race, financial background, creed, color, or origin. What we do not believe is that all children can learn at the same rate. This learning rate is in itself a diversity that should be recognized. Not all children can be nuclear scientists, nor do we want them all to be.

For the most part, educational goals at the state level are set for the college-bound student. In 2002, the Congress of the United States followed suit with the passage of the No Child Left Behind Act. Our opinion is that the goal of 100% of all students meeting those state academic standards is a ridiculous expectation. This allows for no educational diversity and expects all students to achieve at the college-bound level. Yet consider the diversity in our society among service providers, skilled craftsmen, medical doctors, government workers, business leaders, educators, etc. For example, some career projections show potentially large shortages in service career positions. So let's cultivate the knowledge needed for students to be successful in those positions too.

While we agree with the stared goals of the No Child Left Behind Act and the emphasis on reading and math, we cannot forget the need for programs in the fine/practical arts, vocational education, gifted education, physical education, creative writing, and social studies.

Let's recognize differences in race, financial background, creed, color, and origin. As educational leaders, it is our responsibility to find strengths in each of our children to help them thrive as successful citizens in our society, no matter what occupation they choose. It is our responsibility to help each child be in an environment that secures his/her basic needs of food, shelter, safety, and clothing. When these needs are met, then we can begin to maximize their learning opportunities in reading, writing, and arithmetic. We must recognize that diversity is the biggest challenge we face, particularly in terms of the academic achievement gap. We will discuss how to deal with this gap in Chapter 9, which addresses overcoming the impact of poverty.

Collaborate, delegate

We feel that the day of the autocratic superintendent or principal is over. With the rise of state and federal mandates; limitations on discipline; and the increased influence of teacher organizations, parent groups, and the business community, autocratic decision making has slowly eroded. The authors do not necessarily think this is bad. Why not collaborate? Why not get a wide variety of opinions before making a decision? This greatly improves the working environment and gives more individuals a legitimate feeling of ownership in the organization. It also gives the organization a better chance of success. Many leaders fail when they want to take all of the credit for success but none of the responsibility for failure. Collaboration helps the leader find a greater middle ground of responsibility between success and failure.

Likewise, as a leader, we have to have confidence in the people that are part of the employee team. A confident leader empowers others by delegating. The responsibilities placed on superintendents and principals in today's society are extraordinary. Delegation helps relieve some of those stresses as it gives ownership to the fellow employee.

It is impossible to do everything by ourselves in today's educational environment. Celebrate and implement collaboration and delegation.

Recognize power brokers and stakeholders

For school leaders, the ultimate local power broker is the Board of Education. Likewise, each state legislature and state Board has direct impact on the local education agency, superintendents, and principals.

Let's discuss other power brokers. When it comes to voting, senior citizens are exerting more influence than ever before. Up to 65% of all voters in many elections are senior citizens. A school leader has to look carefully at the local community to see who else carries the greatest influence. This influence could be from parent groups, union leadership, a service organization, a wealthy landowner or businessperson, a local government official, a secretary, a cook, or a custodian from within the school system itself.

Working successfully with key stakeholders can also help us achieve our goals. These stakeholders change within the school community as different issues emerge. Sometimes a power broker and stakeholder can be the same person. This often evolves into a pressure group on the school system. The power brokers and stakeholders have to be identified and communicated with, hopefully in a collaborative way. Then a plan has to be developed to gain their support. Leadership is the will, sensitivity, and intelligence to put these pieces of the puzzle together to reach specific goals.

Accept change

Change is a reality in today's education, as it will continue to be in the future. In our opinion, change is good as long as it is research based. Too often, change is done for change's sake and is based on emotion rather than on research. Since it is going to occur, on which side of the spectrum do you want to be? Are you going to complain about change or are you going to cause positive, research-based change? Are you going to be proactive or reactive? Be a change agent rather than a change victim. Accept the change process and make life better for those around you. By accepting the status quo in education, we retard the potential of advancement. As leaders of education, we need to lead the change process by using research-based methods, like lesson designs by Hunter, higher-order thinking by Bloom, and cognitive growth by Piaget.

The principal or superintendent that stands in front of the staff and downplays the importance of a state initiative or federal legislation, like the No Child Left Behind Act in 2002, cannot expect the staff to maximize their efforts to make the school or district its best in the age of accountability. Successful leaders motivate acceptance of change and work towards accepting it. If the program has flaws, indicate what you as a leader think the problems are and what you are going to do to change those flaws. In the meantime, we have to do our best to implement the new programs. Successful implementation helps minimize the impact of the change and keeps the district from having to deal with further bureaucratic rules. Furthermore, local control is preserved when change is dictated through collaboration between the staff, parents, and community.

Get rid of the ego

Too often our ego gets in the way of leadership success. We feel that you should not be afraid to admit when you are wrong. It *will* happen! As a leader, you are dealing with people. And you are not going to know every aspect of the educational system. For example, if your background is at the high school level, you probably are not going to know how a first-grade teacher teaches reading. The solution is simple: ask a first-grade teacher to let you observe him/her teach reading. Ask the teacher to explain the difference between the phonetic, whole-language, and sight method. You will command more respect by admitting your weakness than by trying to cover it up. There will be times when you have to say, "I don't know the answer to that question, but I'll research it and get back to you." Take a good look at yourself. Know what pulls your chain. Look at who you are and what you want. Plan how you can coach your employee team to reach mutual goals for the benefit of your students. In the process, remember to laugh at yourself often!

Keep personal integrity and honesty

My father always told me as a child, "When in doubt, tell the truth." I would now say as a school administrator, if you want to survive in administration, always tell the truth. When you tell the truth, you are always sure of what you previously said.

As an administrator, you owe your fellow employees the reason for your decisions. They may disagree with you, but if you are honest with them, more often than not the employee will respect you for your honesty.

Likewise, personal integrity leads to long-term success. We truly do live in a glass house in terms of our employment. People know and talk about what we do. This "gossip" is the part of education that we have to live with but should never be part of. Many times the vehemence behind an issue is based upon how a person feels about the superintendent's or principal's personal integrity and honesty.

Continually maintain buildings and grounds

What does updating buildings and grounds have to do with leadership? A great deal, from a perception standpoint. More than 70% of the general population never steps into a school. Their perception of the school usually comes from the media or from driving by. Items that we may consider trivial are important to some community members. Is the grass mowed? The flag raised? Are the bushes trimmed? Is there evidence of vandalism? Does it look like a place where students learn? All are important to the success of school leadership. For school and leadership success, a good leader demands that any vandalism, along with broken equipment and furniture, are repaired immediately. Inside the building, stress pride and cleanliness. Don't forget the office, cafeteria, gym, computer room, and library since these are the most frequently visited rooms by parents and community members. Do you want to keep the neighborhood around the school looking good? Pride in the school grounds spreads to the community that surrounds and uses them.

Be media friendly

When a company buys ink by the barrel, be friendly with that company! A local newspaper can make or break a school district and its administrators. The school administrator must realize that the local newspaper's goal is to sell newspapers (and advertisements) for its profit. Sad to say, the media contends that negative stories sell more newspapers than positive ones. Consequently, the school administrator must spend a great deal of time helping the local media develop positive articles about his/her schools. This includes maintaining constant dialog with the local reporter. More will be shared about this subject in Chapter 4, Communications.

Be a visionary leader

Being a great visionary leader does not necessarily mean being a great innovator. Sometimes it means being able to assimilate earlier innovations that led to student success. A visionary leader develops a plan for success, sometimes by listening to other peoples' ideas and observing their accomplishments both inside and outside of the organization. The leader creates a leadership team with its major focus being the success of kids. From this teamwork philosophy can also come a collaborative vision that helps the superintendent and principal become visionary leaders.

Get out of your office

Because of all of the seemingly useless bureaucratic paperwork being thrust upon school administrators today, many administrators feel compelled to stay in their office to take care of the paperwork duties. This is a mistake. The students, staff, and community need to see their school leaders. If the school leader can find a couple of hours during the weekend to do paperwork, he or she might be surprised at how much faster and more efficiently it can be completed. This will create time to be with stakeholders outside the office complex. Despite the recent attacks on the American education system, people, overall, still respect school administrators and want to see them and gather their opinions. Chapter 2, Civic Leadership and Ethics, explores this topic in depth.

How a leader communicates with staff, students, parents, the Board of Education, and community members helps form the perception of the leader's job performance. Get out of the office and communicate positive happenings about the district and long-term needs to stakeholders. Here are some simple things an administrator can do to help manage the paperwork:

1. Have your secretary forward papers to other administrators that deal with their area of responsibility. For example, the business manager generally deals with all finance mailings from the state even though states generally mail all of their material to the superintendent.

2. Make use of email for communication. Develop lists on your computer so you can type the message once and send it to all those who are appropriate recipients, like principals, other superintendents, etc. The more that you as the school administrator can learn about and use technology, the better prepared you will be to handle the paperwork.

3. Develop a good filing system. Studies show that leaders waste a great deal of time looking for lost paperwork.

4. Don't procrastinate with paperwork. Clean your desk, organize your priorities, and get to it.

5. Find quiet time to get the job done. The concentration level must be high to manage paperwork efficiently.

Find time for family and friends

Successful school administrators have unbelievably time-consuming jobs. In fact, school administrators could work 24 hours a day. And while the job is important, it's not as important as family. Our family is our strength. Behind most successful administrators is a strong spouse who silently does things to make the administrator successful. Likewise, our legacy is borne by our children. Our children don't expect their school administrator parent to be with them every moment, but they do expect Mom or Dad to be with them and support them as much as possible. Being a good parent is also a great modeling role for others.

Friends are people the administrator can fall back on and who can provide support in times of need. They can be trusted and can provide an occasional laugh to help relieve the stress of the workplace. A friend is a person whom the administrator can disagree with on issues and still maintain the friendship. It works both ways: administrators can also help and support their friends. This concept is studied in depth in Chapter 12, Taking Care of *You.*

Be Prepared for Crises Situations

In every administrative career, there will be crises situations when you must react quickly, decisively, and effectively. Crisis procedures are needed so you and your staff can respond properly, especially during the first hour.

For example, when I served as superintendent in Belleville, Illinois District 118, we developed the following crisis procedures for:

* Death away from school
* Disaster or storm
* Fire or explosion
* Earthquake
* Student runaway
* Abduction
* Bus accident
* Suicide threat
* Death at or near school
* Serious injury at school
* Bomb threat, gas leak, or chemical leak
* Armed intruder
* Hostage situation

Immediate delegation is important in these situations. You and your staff need to know the chain of command for specific emergencies. An example: in a bomb threat, after securing students in a safe location, the administrator should turn the situation over to the police and fire department as soon as possible.

There are many ways you can create and implement a Crisis Management Plan. See if your state has a model plan. In Illinois, the State Board of Education and the Governor's office have made available a guidance template titled ***School Crisis Response Handbook for Education*** by Timothy J. Daley and Melissa Jamula.[1]

As a leader, you must have a plan in place. Part of your plan will be pre-emptive, to prevent crises. One such deterrent is having an effective discipline program with students closely supervised on campus. Other pre-emptive measures include:

* Setting up a crisis prevention and intervention team
* Having inservice for the team, then the entire staff
* Establishing communication procedures with emergency agencies such as the police, fire, and ambulance service
* Making sure first aid supplies are available for each class
* Identifying an alternate facility to house your students

---

[1] Reading, PA: New Century Solutions, 1998.

* Training some of your staff (if not all) in CPR, the Heimlich maneuver, and first aid
* Establishing emergency codes for the staff
* Preparing for the following events during the crisis:
    * Facility evacuation
    * Full- or partial-school communication: how and which students and staff will be warned
    * Emergency services notification
    * Student movement route to the alternate facility

The effectiveness of your crisis plan reflects directly upon you. It will be a criterion by which you are evaluated by your staff, peers, and community.

You can't pre-empt or plan for every eventuality, but having a Crisis Prevention Plan in effect will help you make better decisions to ensure the health and safety of your students and personnel.

Summary

Being a school leader has become an increasingly complex position to hold over the past 20 years. Our feeling is that school administrators can nonetheless be successful and effective. What leads to effectiveness? You have seen in this chapter that you need to care about kids, staff, community, family, and yourself. You need to work hard and have a passion for your job. You need to have patience with people and trust those around you so that collaboration and delegation can take place. You need to be organized and have a plan. The school leader also needs to be organized to deal with paperwork demands. The effective leader is visible in the school and community. The effective school administrator leads by example. The effective school leader recognizes that the job is still one of the most important jobs in the United States for the preservation of our society and the development of its future citizens.

"The buck stops here."

Harry S Truman

Chapter Two

Civic Leadership and Ethics

Jim Burgett

Do you think civic leadership and ethics are a strange duo? Unfortunately, many people do. They think that civic, especially political, leadership is missing a moral and ethical foundation. What a sad commentary on our world today! Civil leadership and ethics can be completely compatible.

The world is full of good leaders who are ethical and moral. It has been my experience that *most* leaders fall into this category. Most work hard at what they do, are respected and respectable, and follow their hearts as much as they follow their minds. How many civic leaders that you have worked with have had their ethical judgment questioned? But there are, as the adage goes, those few "rotten apples" who spoil the barrels. They make life hard not only for other civic leaders in general, but for you and me.

Whether you like it or not, you are considered a civic leader and a politician, and are subject to unwarranted criticism by many. That criticism escalates when they learn that their taxes went up, or they read about "overpaid" school administrators, or they disagree with something you support. If you doubt it, try to close a school, change school boundaries, award a contract to someone who has the lowest bid but isn't popular in town, or support the dismissal of a popular coach or teacher (especially when executive session discussion doesn't allow you to share the reasons why). If you are not the target of some criticism, you must live in Utopiaville. It comes with the job: school administrators' character is always open to attack!

So, how do we survive this inevitable questioning of our core values, our ethics, and our very existence? Better yet, how do we survive and grow from these situations? This chapter will offer some ideas and suggestions that work. How you make the pieces fit your own personal puzzle of success is also affected by the size of your district, the length of your tenure, the political structure of your community, and other factors like how much control you have *over yourself.*

Let's begin with a primer on civic leadership—getting involved as a civic leader, establishing relationships with elected officials, and empowering others. Then let's talk about ethics and how important ethical leadership is to being a successful educational administrator.

I understand what it means to be involved in the community. Currently I am a member of the local Lion's Club, chairman of the trustees of my church, a member of the City Library Board, president of the Community Foundation Board, and president, active in the Chamber of Commerce, and on the hospital advisory board. These are my "civic" jobs and do not include my professional association responsibilities.

These activities keep me busy, but they also provide a huge network of individuals who can be tremendously helpful with school-community issues. Civic involvement takes time but, if done well, pays great dividends.

Civic Leadership 101

Don't panic, this is not part of a college curriculum, just some common sense thoughts about how you can use the concepts of civic leadership both to be a successful school administrator and to improve student achievement.

Your mindset is important. If you think that the school where you work is an independent organization or that your district is just an arm of the state and not an integral part of the local community, you are in for either short-term employment or a miserable time. So basic tenet number one is to **view your school as only one component of a much larger political system.** You belong to a district, a neighborhood, a community, maybe a city or village, a township, a county or parish, and also a state and nation.

Any good administrator believes that the value of education is a top priority to anyone who can think. After all, did you ever meet a legislator who didn't tell you that education is his or her top issue? Is there anyone who doesn't know that a well-educated populace is the singularly most important factor to the success of a society? Or who can't comprehend that it costs less to send someone to Penn State than it does to the state pen? Well, here's a shocker, and tenet number two: **There are people out there who have agendas that don't include education as top priority issues.** And there are citizens in your community who couldn't give a hoot about the needs of your school, your kids, your teachers, and your system. There are taxpayers who think that you make too much, that teachers work too little, and that kids are all juvenile delinquents. Remember, in most communities 75-80% of the voters don't have a kid in school!

Keep that in mind, then ask yourself:

1. How do we get the word out?
2. How do we influence these folks?
3. How can we get the support from the citizens of our community?

The answer to these questions forms tenet number three: **To enhance ownership of the school by the community, you must be involved in the community**. Involvement in the community is the definition of civic leadership.

Does this mean you have to be the president of the Rotary Club? No, but it might help. Do you have to join the Women's Library Auxiliary? No, especially if you're not a woman, but if you are, it wouldn't hurt. Can you be a leader without assuming an office or committing to a lifetime of 50-50 drawings and raffle sales? Yes you can. We'll show you how.

Civic leadership, to me, is more than just involvement: it is being a *leading* citizen. To be a leading citizen means you lead others. You persuade them, challenge them, inform them, and educate them. It also means you become one of them. A lifetime membership helps, but it is not needed. In fact, no memberships are needed. The key word is involvement.

If you are a successful administrator, you will be known in the community. You will support your local government, local clubs and organizations, and local citizens. You will learn from them and they, in turn, will learn from you.

I know a high school principal who got involved with a local organization that wanted to use a "corner" of the high school property to plant and develop an arboretum. The community organization, let's call it a garden club, worked with both regional and state agencies to secure minimal funding. The group approached the principal, who approached the superintendent. The idea was sketched out and taken to the Board. The property was not essential to the operation of the school and, due to its nature, would never be considered for any facility expansion. The Board and central office gave the project its blessing. Even more, they gave it good publicity with *enthusiastic* approval, which set the stage for positive relationships with the garden club members and the community in general.

Think about that example. What groups in your community would be most associated with this type of project? Adults with little kids? Thirty-something-ites? Teenagers? Not really. Mostly senior citizens or adults with time to garden or enjoy an arboretum project. So, to expand the boundaries of this project, the principal involved the FFA and other high school students. He encouraged the garden club to include the city. Before long, a local merchant got involved, the city provided free mulch, and kids were planting trees. A local philanthropist offered to donate money. The garden club was awash in publicity and new members. What started as an arboretum was expanded to include a sculpture park—which sparked the interest of the high school art department, metal shop, and agriculture classes, and more interest from the community....

The story doesn't end there. The principal became the catalyst to this project. He didn't initiate it, but he certainly speeded it up. He never joined the garden club, but on one very hot summer day when the club had scheduled a day to dig around trees and spread stuff, the principal showed up in work clothes. He worked for about three hours, sweating, grunting, and getting dirty with the community volunteers, many in their sixties, and some way beyond. That three-hour investment may have been the smartest thing he could do. He didn't need to be a member to win respect and admiration. He put his muscles where his mouth was and invested some of his sweat in the project. They loved him for it.

That project is still being developed. It is now an official state arboretum site and a report is given to the Board on its progress every other month. Ownership has expanded, pride has developed, awareness has increased, and what was a modest idea has become a community-changing reality.

Let's analyze this example in terms of our three tenets of civic leadership. When the first call came to the principal asking if a community group could share "a piece of the school property," the principal's mindset was that the property belonged to the community, not just the school, so he thought, let's see what we can do. He was immediately acknowledging, in his mind, that the school is part of a larger community. Did he know at the time that he would be working with local, regional, and state agencies? Absolutely not. He initially thought that he was talking to a local garden club.

Civic leadership also requires that you must think before you respond because you never know how successful or how damaging your involvement might be. Imagine the negative message he would have sent if he hadn't returned the first phone call! Or had immediately said no, without giving a reason; or gave a response that sounded as if the idea was a bad one; or, heavens, had indicated he was too busy for one more project. Any of those responses would have been shared by the garden club (and probably six coffee groups) and damage, possibly serious, could have resulted.

Maybe the project couldn't be done, but just the willingness to consider it, investigate it, and support the concept are productive if done carefully and always from the perspective that the school is just a small, but important, element of a total community.

Tenet number two reminds us that not everyone thinks about the school or even cares about it. The garden club wanted land. They didn't ask for school involvement. I'm not sure if they even thought that school involvement was possible. It was the job of the principal to see the possibilities of a positive school connection within this community project. Remembering tenet number two helps educational leaders promote and involve the school with the community and, equally as important, the community with the school. It didn't take long before the principal actively involved several high school programs in this project, resulting in senior citizens working side by side with students and developing positive and productive bonds.

Tenet number three concerns involvement: To enhance ownership of the school, you must be involved in the community. Key words are ownership and involvement. Civic leaders lead, but it is essential to know where you want to go! As an educational leader, you want to spend your time on projects that enhance your domain, the schools. You can do this a number of ways. Let's say you become a Little League coach. Are you enhancing ownership of the school system? If you are a respected, fair, appreciated, and dedicated coach, you bet. People will know you are a school administrator before they know anything else about you. How you lead will influence what they think about the school system. They will value your judgment and your opinions. If you don't allow the parents to behave inappropriately at a game or the kids to compromise good sportsmanship, you are telling your "audience" that these are values you hold true, and they will be grateful you work for the schools. Knowing you will allow them to tell others that "our" school administrator is a decent person with good values. Thus, you have just promoted ownership of the school simply by your example and behavior!

If you spend three hours spreading mulch on a budding arboretum, you have shown by your multiple actions that this project is worth not only your leadership but also your direct involvement. By taking some ownership, you are encouraging others to take ownership. Again, if you lead, they will follow.

Every time you expand your horizons into areas of civic leadership, you also expand your network of associates. Whether you call them friends, coworkers, neighbors, or fellow club members, the title is far less important than the relationship.

If you are new to a school district, or new to the concept of civic leadership, here are some additional suggestions:

1. Ask to attend the community association of ministers or church leaders. Ask to sit in on a meeting. If the participants have questions about the schools, tell them you'll gladly try to answer them. Be interested in who they are, how long they have been in their positions, and what issues their churches have. Talk about growth, youth groups, and past relationships with the schools. Follow up your meeting with a hand written note to each person thanking him or her for sharing. Invite the whole group to tour your school and have lunch with you. (Make sure you have something to eat that day that is recognizable as food and appropriate.)

2. If you have a parochial school in your community, call the administrator and ask for a tour. Return the favor, telling the administrator that they can bring whomever they wish with them. If the school has an affiliated church, extend the invitation to its religious leaders as well. Exchange phone numbers and share mutual concerns.

3. Call the presidents of the local clubs in your community and ask if you can attend a meeting. Offer to give a presentation with a

Q/A session about anything relating to education—or offer to give a specific program on something of mutual interest. Most of these groups are begging for presenters. Be sure that you do three things in your presentation: be brief, be interesting, and allow time for questions. It always helps if you can bring a student or two with you.

4. If you have industry or large businesses in your district, call the presidents and ask for a tour. By taking an active interest in their world, you will more than likely find them willing to take an interest in yours.

5. Become a part of your Chamber of Commerce, Jaycees, or other highly visible and influential organizations in the community. By all means, get involved with any organization that donates a lot of time and money to your school or system. Here is a helpful hint: When you join, let them know that school administrators have a plethora of evening responsibilities. Name some of them (like supervising athletic events, curriculum meetings, regular and special Board meetings, open houses, parent-teacher conferences, state and district meetings) and tell them upfront you might not be available for every meeting. Make this very clear early in the relationship. They will understand and respect your schedule.

6. And, of course, get involved with your local community government. Your mayor, city manager, various department heads, and city council members are all extremely important people to know well and in a positive way. Ask their opinions, invite them to functions, give them tours of new improvements, and do whatever you can to help them feel ownership in the schools. If you reciprocate by being interested in community government, it will be very helpful as your bonds strengthen. If you see them trying to secure a grant for a park project, call and offer to write a letter of support. If you can share a playground or field for some city event or program and it might lead to a mutual-use agreement, be the first to make the suggestion. Don't forget the police, fire, and EMT departments. Trust me, an administrator's life is much easier if there are good relationships, mutual respect, and camaraderie between all elements of community government and school leadership. Nurture this relationship with time and energy. Letters to community leaders, boards, or to the newspaper in appreciation of improvements, projects, or just consistent good work are appreciated and help develop strong bonds.

Extremely important in civic leadership is visibility. Here are some tips to visibility that can save your sanity, and possibly your marriage or family life:

1. You don't need to be everywhere all the time.
2. You don't need to attend every game, every community function, or every meeting to be active and influential.
3. You do need, however, to attend some, and you do need to take a turn at working events or providing special leadership.

At one time I was a member of the local Optimist Club. It met every Monday night. I was also an employee of the Board of Education, which also held most of its meetings on Monday nights. And I also attended regular church business meetings on Monday nights. If you do the calculations, you can quickly see I was busy on Monday nights! How did I prioritize these meetings and remain a viable civic leader? (To be sure, I didn't miss school Board meetings since I had grown accustomed to eating.)

I asked the church if they would consider the second Monday for church meetings since the first and third were "normal" nights for regular and special Board meetings. They agreed. I informed the Optimist Club of my conflicts but also informed them that I would block out every Saturday morning for a month, between Thanksgiving and Christmas, to supervise at the Christmas tree stand, and that I would take a daily shift, for a week, at the pizza wagon during the County Fair in the summer. I also volunteered to take charge of the poster contest program. I then made it clear that I could never serve as an officer because of my Monday conflicts but that I would attend meetings when I could.

Did this work? You bet it did. It is a fundamental part of good civic leadership to be involved, be active, and be dependable. I am all three. The Optimist Club consistently pledges thousands of dollars for improvements to school programs. Involvement pays off.

Other helpful ideas about attendance:

4. If you need to arrive late, remember, that is better than not arriving at all. "Sorry for coming late, but I had a parents' meeting tonight." Translation: "Coming here is important to me. I am a busy person. I meet my commitments."
5. Another idea is to work the crowd and disappear. Show up for the concert or game and greet and meet people, but stay on

your feet or be on the move. Be seen, be sincere, be interested, and, when the time is right, be gone. Go home or to another event or meeting. There is nothing wrong with this; in fact, the more visible you are and the more interested you seem, the more effective you become.

Civic leadership also involves a positive attitude. Find the good in things and avoid the naysayers. If you suggest something, do it positively. Think about the ways you want to be approached about an issue, and follow these guidelines:

1. Don't give criticism without suggestions.
2. Don't dump the work on anyone without being willing to do your share.
3. Never be too good or too important to do anything.

Civic leadership works. It promotes ownership of the school by the citizens. It bonds the school with other organizations. It broadens an understanding of the needs of the school and the needs of the community. It promotes positive relationships. It takes time, dedication, commitment, and sacrifice, but it is worth it.

Business-Education Partnerships

Many schools and districts lack a specific partnership with their community, such as a partnership between business and education. If your school or district does not have an organization dedicated to this form of civic cooperation, consider starting one. You don't need a megabusiness in your community. You can form a partnership with any of the people or groups who serve your school, district, or community.

My concept of a business-education partnership is a regular meeting of influential civic leaders for the purpose of promoting both the business and educational aspects of the community. **It should *not* be a partnership designed exclusively to bring funds to the school**. It should be an opportunity for the school to work hand in hand with the local taxpaying businesses to promote their growth; respond to their needs; and to work cooperatively to enhance the mutual interests of the community, the school, and society in general.

What better way to display civic leadership than to be seen as one of the founders of such an organization! Let me briefly describe one such organization. The Highland Business Education Association meets five times a year, at 7:00 a.m., in various locations. Typical member includes the executive director of the Chamber of Commerce, a bank president, the CEOs or top-level executives of several companies, two school Board members, three school administrators, two teachers, the technology coordinator, and members of three service organizations. Attendance is usually 90% or better. The association holds no fundraisers, yet it generates about $20,000, or more, a year in revenue. It sponsors lunch-hour parenting meetings for business employees. We established an adult volunteer/tutor program that includes about 100 people each school year, many from area businesses. The association periodically hosts a local business fair and tours of area industries for students. We have an extensive job shadowing program and maintain a medical occupations partnership with about 15 local businesses. At each meeting they have a 20-minute program on some important issue in the community or school. The association proposed and supports a community-wide character education program that has become a national model. The association also provides mini-grants to teachers, and invites the local parochial school to participate in many of the programs. They formed an educational foundation that many of the businesses support with contributions.

Is this an example of civic leadership? Every month leaders from the community, local government, and the school work together for the betterment of everyone. And it works!

School Administrators and Political Leaders

We have talked about local civic leaders but not much about elected politicians. How does the effective school administrator establish and develop a relationship with elected officials? There is no pat reply to this question because of many variables, but there are a few fundamental rules to follow, such as:

1. Know who your elected officials are.

2. Communicate with them respectfully.
3. Work with them effectively.

Knowing who they are is the easiest. If you don't have a working relationship with your elected officials, at least have a list of them readily available that includes their names, the length of their terms, the boundaries they serve, their political affiliation, and communication data (address, phone, fax, email). Update this list and keep it close by. By each name add something specific they have done, like helping you solve a traffic sign problem, answering questions about a welfare issue, or supporting an educational tax issue.

Communicating with them respectfully is essential. "Respect" is key to successful communications. You may not appreciate, admire, or even like a certain political leader but to communicate with him or her disrespectfully will certainly not help your cause. Change places for a few minutes and think about the people in your district who attack you or your job without spending a minute in your shoes or have no idea what you deal with each day. Don't think for one minute that you understand the life of an elected official. Remember the second tenet of civic leadership? Surely, education is not the only issue elected politicians deal with, and even though we think it should be number one in their considerations, to many politicians it is just one of a dozen balls they may be juggling at any given moment. Remember that and think about the vast number of constituents that they must satisfy.

It is fine to respectfully disagree with any elected officials. I never hold back from sharing what I believe, but I always add a line or two, verbally or written, that in essence says how much I appreciate the scope of their job, the pressures they must experience, and the difference *they have the opportunity* to make. It helps and it works. Everyone likes to be appreciated.

Now that you recognize the need to communicate with respect, make sure you also communicate with efficiency. Make your comment short and to the point. Here is an example of an email to a state senator written on the district letterhead:

Dear Senator Rosborg:

I am asking you to consider voting in support of SB-505V which will allow school districts to modify the tax levy on heating costs. As you know, the variance in heating costs makes it difficult to budget these expenses at home, at school, and at businesses. We, in public education, have no extra funding source available when heating costs exceed the usual expected increase. Funds used to pay these increases often come from money budgeted to support normal operations and safety needs. Your expert review of this bill will see that it does not provide an open-ended tax, but one with reasonable limitations that protect the taxpayer and, at the same time, provide for efficient and safe operations of our school buildings.

I would be more than willing to discuss this issue with you in detail if you so desire. Senator, you have proven to be a fair legislator and I admire your willingness to support issues that are in line with your values. Thanks for all you do.

Respectfully,

James F. Burgett
Superintendent

Communications need to be short, sweet, and to the point. Legislators want to know the issue (or bill number), where you stand, and why. They like it when you offer to discuss the bill in more detail. Many elected officials don't pretend to know or understand each piece of legislation and will often call on you for help. If you offer help, however, be ready to provide it.

There is a second part. If the senator does vote for this bill, and even if it fails to pass, you need a follow-up letter or note. A handwritten thank-you note is more appreciated than you think. This action will distinguish you as a leader. Think about the effect that thank you notes have when you receive them.

Dear Senator Rosborg:

Thank you very much for your support of SB-505V. Even though it did not pass, I feel we sent a sound message concerning our needs. Hopefully, the bill will be reintroduced or another solution will emerge that addresses the concern. I want you to know that I have shared my appreciation for your support with our Board and citizens. Thanks again for all you do.

Respectfully,

James F. Burgett
Superintendent

Not only have you thanked him but you have also said that (1) you still need legislation and (2) you have given him positive support among a number of his constituents. Keep doing this, and elected officials will be calling you for your opinions. You will become a mover and shaker in political decisions. Boards like to know that your voice is being heard and that your opinion is important.

Written or verbal communications are the most common way to work with elected officials, but working with them directly is also important. Invite them to tour your school. Honor them when you have a chance. Support their campaigns if you so desire, but I suggest you do this on a personal basis and with care. I make it a policy to avoid bumper stickers, yard signs, and anything that might upset community members who don't share my political enthusiasm. When asked to display these things, I simply explain my policy to the askers and they understand. But I offer to help in other ways. The easiest is to write a check. Be smart when it comes to campaigning. Remember, though, that when you give elected officials a legitimate way to take credit or be recognized for the positive things they have done for your school, district, or community, you are building important bonds and strengthening your own civic leadership.

Don't forget visits to legislators' offices, both at home and in the Capitol. I remember the time when I really needed some consideration for a road improvement for an entrance to a new school. I started the process with a phone call to a state senator, inviting him to meet me at the site to look over a problem that he might be able to help me with. I followed it up with a thank-you note for agreeing to meet me that also reminded him of the time and place. I stopped in at his local office with a blueprint of the site and gave it to his secretary, indicating how much we appreciated what her boss did for our community. When he came for the appointment, I made sure I had a cold soda ready for him (it was a hot, hot day). I also drove him to the site so the mud and dirt were on my car, while he parked his in the clean lot. I was courteous, thoughtful, focused, and had all the visits and contacts well planned.

After his visit, I happened to be in the Capitol so I had a handwritten thank-you note sent to him on the floor of the Senate telling him how much I appreciated his prompt visit and how much I looked forward to finding out what the Department of Transportation had decided.

I didn't bug him in any way. I didn't call five times for a second appointment. One week after the agreed time for a follow-up, I called his office, left a message for him to call me back at his convenience, and told him that my secretary would relay the message immediately. I would return his call within minutes if I was not in, indicating that I respected his busy schedule.

The end result? I wanted help from the D.O.T. to move an entrance, and we ended up with a new road and a $750,000 grant. Does this work all the time? No, but I can guarantee that legislators like working with people who know how to communicate properly.

Finally, how do you encourage others to become civic leaders? First and foremost by example. When fellow administrators and educators see the impact you have on the school or district, they will realize the importance of your involvement. You must be proactive in this regard by inviting them to meetings, helping them compose letters to legislators, and training them in the essentials of both civic involvement and leadership. Asking and leading have different results. Lead them to civic leadership. I personally like it when superintendents strongly encourage their building administrators to be involved. Everyone wins.

Taking a few minutes at a staff meeting for administrators or teachers to talk about the many things that the local Rotary Club, or Representative Smith, or the Band Parents have done for your school or community is a good way to stir interest. Asking them to send a note of thanks to the local mayor for his/her support of the new community swimming pool only enhances participation and strengthens bonds. Asking them to join their school's PTO or Band Boosters is also a good idea. Seeing your name listed on the program at the next concert as a "Patron" also helps. Taking the time and exerting the leadership to facilitate *any* positive dialog is an example of civic leadership.

Ethics and Civic Leadership

Mahatma Gandhi once said that the things that will destroy us are politics without principle, pleasure without conscience, wealth without work, knowledge without character, business without morality, science without humanity, and worship without sacrifice.

If everyone would adhere to Gandhi's ideas, there would be no need for a discussion on ethics—but that isn't reality. And because it isn't reality, we need to list, discuss, check off, measure, and manage what should be the overriding parameters of not only our educational responsibilities, but also of our lives. Because ethical behavior, moral leadership, and political savvy are not inherited traits, we need to outline them and learn them. Because we know the "Golden Rule" but fail to put it in place at all times, we need to set standards and work toward realizing them.

For the purpose of our discussion, let's agree on some common definitions. Ethics can be defined as philosophy, beliefs, values, codes of conduct, principles, and morals. Morality is virtue, goodness, purity, and righteousness. Politics is best characterized by a shrewdness in managing, contriving, or dealing. Dealing with politics isn't always fun, but if you care about kids, you need to care about politics.

Ethical leadership may be the most important topic of all because without it, we can't be effective. With it, we will be respected, remembered, and admired for not only what we accomplish but, more importantly, for who we are.

There are many lists of the characteristics of leadership. On almost all of them you will find honesty, integrity, the ability to find the good in others, praising improvement, and encouraging coworkers to do what is right. They include ethical behaviors and moral attitudes. They are the essential characteristics of successful educational leaders.

Aristotle says, "Excellence is an art won by training and habituation. We do not act rightly because we have virtue or excellence, but we rather have those because we have acted rightly. We are what we repeatedly do. Excellence, then, is not an act but a habit." (When you write that well, you don't need a last name.) What he says seems to boil down to this: When we do what is right, we attain virtue and excellence.

Almost every professional organization has a written "code of ethics" or "code of conduct." Most of them say the same thing: Do what is right. Any administrator should know the specific "code" of his or her own professional organization.

Most textbooks on school administration contain "ethical checklists." They are more practical to me than formal "codes of conduct." Before making a decision, you simply ask yourself the following questions:

1. Is it legal?
2. Will this decision/act follow our policies or rules?
3. Would I feel good if my family knew about it?
4. Will this decision make me proud?
5. Would I like this decision if it were done to me?

If all of the answers are *yes,* then do it.

Does the topic of "ethics" really relate to our everyday job? More than you can imagine! An example: A man calls and says that he read in the paper that you are spearheading a drive to raise $50,000 for new lights for the football field. He then gives you one compliment after another about your leadership, the hard work you do, how great this project is, and how much he wants to help you reach your goal and save the taxpayers this expense. You aren't used to these types of calls, so naturally you are sitting tall in your chair enjoying every minute. He ends by asking if a $25,000 matching contribution would help the campaign. You're now ready to fall off your chair. $25,000? That would be the biggest contribution from one person you have ever received as an administrator. You immediately respond with a semi-intelligent, "Oh my, that would be wonderful." You can already picture the campaign for the rest of the money: "Every dollar you contribute will be matched up to $25,000!" What a way to raise money and to reach that goal much sooner than you had thought.

Then he hits you over the head. "You might not know me, but I am Henry Biltmore's grandpa. Henry is a junior on your JV football team. I'm really doing this because I enjoy watching him play football so much. Henry has played football since he was a little guy and he so wanted to make the varsity team this year, but he missed the cut. I thought you might want to talk to the coach and see if he could reconsider. You know, maybe he would 'get a bright idea' after he heard about the new lights!" And of course he follows this with a guffaw like he is a Jerry Seinfeld stand-in.

You don't answer right away. Then your administrative savvy kicks in: "Mr. Biltmore, you've given me a lot to think about. I'll get back to you no later than the day after tomorrow, after I look into things." (You need time to think so you buy some. Smart move.)

This is a good example of a decision that involves ethical leadership. Can you be bought for $25,000? If you ask the coach to do it, will he? If you tell him to do it, what will be the cost? If you decline and the coach is in favor, what will the after effects be?

You go to the checklist. If you agree, is this illegal? No, it isn't illegal. Does it follow policy? There is no stated policy against suggesting to the coach that you move a student from one level of play to another. Is this something you will be proud of? Yes! You would be mighty proud of the new lights. And no, you would not be proud to be "bought" by anyone for anything. Nor would you be proud to be part of a situation that compromises all of the reasons why students are selected for a certain team. And that's that. You answered no to at least one question on the "ethical checklist," so your answer has to be no if it is going to be the right answer.

You call the grandpa back and thank him profusely for his generous offer. You state that you cannot ask the coach to consider moving his grandson from one team to another because it would not be right. It would compromise the things the coach told every boy when he tried out. You try hard to point out that if he were a boy on the team and saw a teammate moved for reasons other than skill and ability, how would he feel as an individual? You try to emphasize that, as a grandpa, he understands that he wants to do what is best for his grandson, and you appreciate that. You remind him that the lights wouldn't be installed until summer and would be up for his grandson's senior year, and how proud his grandson would be of what his grandpa did. You try hard to make it work, but within the ethical and moral parameters that allow you to sleep well that night.

An administrator makes a moral decision when he or she drives after a drink or two, or walks into a tavern, or flirts with a fellow worker, or says something inappropriate, or swears, or gossips. If any administrator thinks those aren't ethical and/or moral actions, he or she needs a serious review of what people think of school administrators and expect from them. We are looked up to and expected to do what is right—always. It's that simple.

I think I could end this discussion right here with what has already been said. Ethics and morality boil down to four words—do what is right. It *is* that simple. And yet, in reality, it isn't. That brings in the third component, politics.

Politics seem to compromise our attitudes and behaviors. Right and wrong become less black and white and more a shade of gray or, more appropriately, mud. It's not easy doing what is right when there are two or three or seven opinions of what *is* right. That is where the term leadership comes into play. A good leader can convince, convert, compromise, explain, or justify decisions. A good leader can also accomplish goals and still end up doing what is right.

Even the words used to define ethics and morality make it easy to understand the difficulty in being considered an ethical administrator when politics are involved. That's because different people define the terms differently.

Politics is not a dirty word. Politicians are not criminals any more than bus drivers or cosmetologists. Politics is a way of life and a way of getting something done. As I mentioned before, the definition is "a shrewdness in managing, contriving, or dealing." Done right, it can be fun, exciting, and commanding. To be able to manage creatively and to reach positive results through compromise and dealing is exhilarating. Some are better at it than others. For many, it is too risky and too much work. Many administrators would rather be told what to do than figure out a way to get it done. A good administrator knows his or her strengths and weaknesses. If politics are not comfortable for you, stay on the sidelines. Be supportive, offer help, but mostly, keep quiet. If you are good at working with people, good at keeping and remembering your promises, and good at finding many sides to an issue, you will probably enjoy the fun of politics.

In my opinion, the best news is that you can balance ethics, morality, and politics—and do it well. You can reach a successful political solution while remaining moral and ethical. It takes skill, practice, and work, but it can be done.

A key word in education today is standards. The standards of the National Council for Accreditation of Teacher Education (NCATE), the National Association of Elementary School Principals (NAESP), and the Interstate School Leader Licensure Consortium (ISLLC) all tell the administrator to be ethical, moral, and deal with politics.

I think the standards part is best summed up in the preamble to the Illinois Professional School Leader Standards where it states, "We believe that we have a responsibility to bring the highest ethical principles to the process of administrative decision-making."

Strong civic leadership based on an ethical and moral foundation almost guarantees a system that will succeed.

There is no room in the schoolhouse, or in the community, for a leader who cannot be trusted, does not make decisions with the best interest of those he/she serves in mind, and is not honorable.

Summary

Let's tie all this together. Civic leadership is based on three tenets: (1) understanding that the school is just one part of a much larger political system, (2) remembering that education is not the top priority for everyone, and (3) realizing that if you want to increase positive ownership of your schools, you must get involved with community interests.

Successful civic leadership involves hard work, visibility, and commitment.

When it comes to dealing with political leadership, (1) know who your elected officials are, (2) communicate with them respectfully, and (3) work with them effectively.

Administrators encourage others to be civic leaders by setting a positive example, facilitating involvement, and helping others get started.

Ethics and civic leadership go hand in hand. Ethics are defined by educational standards, but are basically understood by everyone. Solid and strong ethical decision making helps define who we are, how much we will be remembered and respected, and the difference we will make. There simply is no place for unethical administrators. The lives of our students are too important.

Chapter Three

Business Basics for School Leaders

Max McGee

Let's begin eavesdropping on a conversation between a business leader and an educational leader.

Business Leader: The Business Community would like to give you some support to help you in your difficult, important job of improving the quality of public education.
Translation: You would never make it in the business world.

Educational Leader: Certainly, I would love to get some fresh new ideas, but please remember that we are not manufacturing widgets. We are dealing with the complexities of children, many of whom are quite challenging.
Translation: I would love to see you last one day in one of my high school classrooms.

Business Leader: Oh yes, we understand, but we have some experience that could help you operate more efficiently and have better results.
Translation: You need to stop wasting so much money and figure out how to improve test scores.

Educational Leader: I appreciate your insight but it is a little different in education where students come to us with diverse backgrounds and many do not have the background knowledge or skills they need to succeed, some have had little direction at home, and far too often their families are shattered and neighborhoods are dangerous.
Translation: I would love to see what you produced when you had no control over your raw materials or suppliers.

Business Leader: I understand, and we in the business world face difficult obstacles as well but our best leaders have found ways to make our businesses profitable and beneficial to our shareholders.

Translation: If you would stop spending so much time making excuses and start running your schools like businesses, you could turn things around.

Educational Leader: Yes, I'm sure that we can learn from you, but please understand that we have to do a lot more than improve test scores and really do not have access to profits or other revenue streams that business does.

Translation: So tell me again how improving state scores increases my schools' profit and assures that we can get more resources. Oh yes, and just where can I tap into some of your "venture capital" money to help me start and sustain innovative programs and services that will improve teaching and learning?

Business Leader: Well, it's really all about business sense, about fostering competition and assuring that you have the very best people working for you. We stand ready to do whatever it takes to help your schools succeed.

Translation: School leaders are clueless and overpaid to boot since they obviously don't know how to get results. They will never call and ask for help.

Educational Leader: Great, we welcome a sincere contribution, and I look forward to finding ways that we can partner together.

Translation: Business leaders are clueless and if they gave a fraction of their stock options, outrageous salaries, fat bonuses, and vacation homes to public education we could do a lot more for kids. They will never call to lend support much less a nickel of their precious bottom line to help our schools.

Sound familiar? The relationship between business and school is a rocky one and does not show signs of getting better anytime soon. Education continues to lag in international comparisons, an abysmal achievement gap exists, and most recently we have learned that we are soon to be quickly left behind by the scientists and engineers that the educational systems of China and India are producing. We take the blame from business, even though we do not have access to resources we need, we cannot raise venture capital, we cannot control the preparation of students who come to us, and we cannot divest unsuccessful divisions. Yes, no matter how "bad" that group of eighth graders may be, we just have to keep them.

It is tempting to dismiss most of the advice from business leaders outright. This is unfortunate because as we learned from Jim Collins' masterwork, *Good to Great,* business does have something to offer educators. Though schools and businesses don't always play well together, the superintendent who understands, appreciates, and practices the business side of leading his or her school district is a superintendent who will have far more impact than the pure educator.

Business leaders who take time to educate their workforce and superintendents who operate with basic business principles will serve customers and classrooms far better. This chapter explores the basic business principles of running our schools. We will share three different concepts that we have found to be particularly helpful in driving the improvements that have contributed to student learning and growth. Specifically, we explore the power of building "a business case" for innovation and improvement, forecasting finances, benchmarking and competing, and "bonding" your schools and yourself.

Building a Business Case

Building a "business case" is as important to a school leader as it is to a business executive. A business case is a formal presentation that engenders support for new programs, initiatives, or services. You have probably built many business cases in your Board packets. Some work, some don't. A solid business case can help convince reluctant Board members; it can also help gain broad support in the community and media. Building a business case takes time, hard thinking, and support from key staff.

Identifying the Problem

> Albert Einstein recognized the importance, and difficulty, of finding problems as opposed to solving them: "The formulation of the problem is often more essential than its solution."[1]

As school leaders, it seems we don't have to look too far for problems. They haunt us daily. (We could feed a third-world country with the leftovers from uneaten school lunches, and if we had a nickel for every voice mail or email complaint we received, we would be reading this book at our villa in southern France.)

The trick, however, is to identify the real problems that impede student learning, then find a way to solve them. Looking for patterns in the calls and complaints from parents, examining data, talking to teachers, and visiting classrooms all yield invaluable information for identifying critical, core problems. Consider this scenario.

For the past few years, the principal and superintendent have been plagued by phone calls from parents of students who are entering first grade as accomplished readers. The parents contend that their children are not challenged, the teacher isn't teaching them anything new, and the kids are getting bored. Test scores reveal that although nearly 50% of third graders exceed state standards, each year 12-20% of the class does not meet state standards. The problem begins to reveal itself after several visits to the classroom. The first-grade teachers are spending most of their time working with the six to ten students who are really struggling. Although teachers have classroom libraries for the more advanced children, they do not have the time to meet with them, thus the complaints. Moreover, only one of the first-grade teachers has special training in reading. About 20% of the students, then, leave first grade unable to read fluently or comprehend grade level material. The referral rate for special education is close to 15%, and the children continue to struggle into third grade and beyond.

The problem, then, is not just keeping the readers challenged but figuring out how to help all children learn to read by the time they leave first grade.

---

[1] A. Einstein and L. Infeld, *The Evolution of Physics*. New York: Simon and Schuster, 1938, p. 92.

Determining the Measures and
Stating the Goals

In this scenario, as in any business case you build, we suggest that before writing a goal, you first determine the measures. Though some would argue the reverse, we contend that until you can clearly state where you want to be, you cannot set your goal or develop your plan. When school leaders try to write goals first, the results are often in passive voice, cumbersome and vague. More often than not, they are a process, not an outcome. In the above extended example, writing a goal first could lead to these beauties:

- Interventions will be used to improve reading.
- Students will learn to read at grade level
- A plethora of resources incorporating direct instruction in phonemic awareness, fluency, comprehension strategies, vocabulary, and a value-added growth model of assessment will lead to improvement in student reading

Contrast these to goals in which measures were determined first:

- The percentage of students meeting state standards will increase 25% in three years.
- All students identified for reading intervention will make at least 18 months growth during the school year.
- Less than 5% of all "non IEP" students will meet or exceed state standards.
- All students will read with age and grade appropriate fluency and comprehension before they enter second grade.

The latter goals all have specific measures. The former do not. The latter are clear, the former are not.

Before turning to the next step of the business case, we want to emphasize the importance of having multiple measures. Multiple measures are valuable in assessing progress, in achieving buy in, and in explaining results. To determine progress toward the strategic goal outlined above, the team should be looking at results of both state and local assessments and norm- and criterion-referenced tests. We all know that educational testing is hardly an exact science, so it is important to use a variety of assessments as sources for gauging growth in student achievement. We have also found that it is important to include measures beyond assessment results. We want to know if we are providing the support that teachers need to achieve the goal, so we make sure that there is an opportunity for professional development. We want to be sure that we have the financial resources to achieve our goal, so we use budget figures and stick to them. We want to be sure that the children are challenged yet still enjoy school and find learning rewarding, so we write that as a measure.

We also find that if we use one measure—be it the state test, the Terra Nova, local assessment, grades, etc.—teachers rightfully complain about having to teach to a test. They have a legitimate beef. If only one measure is used to determine success, they would be foolish *not* to teach to the test. With multiple measures, however, they can focus on student learning and the assessment results will be what they are—which more often than not is superior to those when a teacher just attempts to teach to the test. Because there is more than one measure, any single test is not a threat.

To make a simple analogy, let's say that our goal is to get cool on a scalding summer day. We may not like what the thermometer says and we may curse the humidity index, but we know full well that they are not to blame for our discomfort. Putting the thermometer in the refrigerator and changing the THI scale is not going to help any more than replacing one state test with another to improve student learning. Until we do something—and probably more than one thing—we will be miserable. Cranking up the air conditioner, drinking a cold glass of lemonade, and/or jumping in the pool will work.

Multiple measures also ensure that your School Board and your public have good information and will make good decisions. Countless textbooks and curricula have been dumped because of lousy measures, not because they contained lousy material. We all have first-hand experience with Board members and administrators wanting to remove a series (or worse, a teacher) because too many kids did not meet one particular measurement. With multiple measures, they can see how curriculum and instruction may be strong in some areas and weak in others or how a teacher succeeds with some students but needs help with others. They have information they need to determine if supplemental resources are needed or if the program should be axed. In short, measurement takes opinion out of the process. As Admiral Grace Hopper once said, "One accurate measurement is worth a thousand expert opinions."

The use of multiple measures is an exemplary business practice that we should use in our schools. Despite the overstated contention of many business leaders, they know full well that the "bottom line" is not all that matters. Businesses spend considerable time and money measuring "customer satisfaction," equipment durability, market penetration, and the like. These measures matter because they are components of success as much as a profit margin is. Granted, they need to make money to keep functioning, but profits alone are not the measure of success. School leaders should use multiple measures to gauge school improvement, individual student progress, the building climate, and even their performance!

Finally, for each measure we suggest a specific deliverable: an actual product that the administration can use as evidence to show the extent to which each measure has been achieved. Here are examples:

- 95% of all first-grade students will have a fluency rate of 110 wpm on grade level material.
- 90% of all second-grade students will read at grade level or better as measured by the Iowa Test of Basic Skills.
- 85% of all third-grade students will meet or exceed state standards as measured by the state test.
- Special education referrals at the end of first grade will be less than 5% of the student population.

Because these measures and deliverables are so specific, they actually become the evaluation component. Success is gauged by comparing actual results to those targets. Other measures, such as the hours of training for the paraprofessionals who are delivering the instruction and marks on parent satisfaction surveys, could also be included to evaluate the success of the reading intervention. What matters most, though, is improvement in reading.

Once the leaders have written the goals and determined the measures, they have to make a business case for the intervention. The business case includes the goals and measures in a presentation that describes the program, weighs the costs and benefits, and enumerates the pros and cons for both the short-term and a three-to five-year horizon. It identifies sources of revenue to support the program and contains recommendations for short- and long-term funding, including an identifiable revenue stream, if one is available. The business case also identifies who is responsible for planning and implementing the intervention as well as who delivers it day-to-day. In short, it gives the School Board members the information needed to make a sound decision.

Planning the Intervention

Knowing that Board members have an annoying habit of requesting rationale before starting a new program, we need significant background support for sustained intervention. Books have been written about planned change, gaining staff support, shared vision, implementing innovations, and the like. Though we have too little space to cover it fully here, we advise you to work with staff to identify the best practices both in research and in actual school use.

Returning to the reading scenario, a planned intervention might entail 20 to 30 minutes of one-to-one tutoring in phonics, fluency, and comprehension. Trained paraprofessionals provide the tutoring, which is in addition to the children's regular classroom instruction. Those struggling most seriously work with a reading specialist instead of the paraprofessional. The classroom teacher administers assessments monthly to track student progress and the teacher, reading specialist, paraprofessional, and principal meet monthly to review the data.

The business case would include this description as well an appendix of research which supports it, examples of the assessment, and, if possible, data from another school or district which indicated its success.

Assigning Cost, Allocating Resources, and Showing Other Options

The next and perhaps most critical element of a business case is estimating the costs. For example, the reading intervention plan above might run about $2,000 per pupil. The business case, then, would need to show the "return on investment" in terms of both achievement and savings. Specifically, with the additional $2,000 per pupil spent on the 20% of students struggling in reading, one could show that in three years the percentage of students who can read when they leave first grade will have increased from 80% to 95%, that special education referrals (and thus special education costs) will be reduced by 40%, and that complaints about students not being challenged will be halved, thus saving the "soft cost" of administrative time in handling all the complaints.

The business plan, then, must show how you are maximizing the bang for the buck. Although not necessary for a business plan, we also recommend that you prepare a section, or even an appendix, that illustrates the costs and expected outcomes of two or three other possible interventions.

At this point you have a clear problem, a concrete goal, specific measures, and estimated costs for a sound plan that will maximize student gains. Your business case is almost complete.

Identifying Funding Sources

Because this program will cost money, you will need to get it somewhere, like from spending down a surplus, increasing taxes, or dropping or cutting back another program. As part of your business case, you must convince your Board that the returns are worth the investment. Given this example, the wisest course may be to spend down any surplus, knowing that by reducing special education referrals you will be saving significant dollars in the long run. It will take some very clear forecasting to demonstrate how spending a little more money up front will save you a lot more money in five to ten years. Assuming you can keep other revenues and expenses equal, you can clearly show how depleting reserves temporarily is a good business practice because you will get better learning and will rebuild reserves over time as you save money on special education and remediation.

Wrap it up

Because you have multiple and specific measures, you can now easily design your evaluation component since the measures are already incorporated into the proposal. (In our example, the principal used fluency rates, grade equivalency scores, and percentages of students meeting state standards.) You have identified problems, developed clear goals, shared supportive research or examples of best practices from similar districts, and provided real cost estimates. Using forecasting and scenarios, you have made a compelling presentation as to why your plan is the most practical. In short, you have created a convincing business case.

One of the positive consequences is that the time, effort, and energy spent garner public attention. The case will also garner broad buy in and create a sense of mission so that the children in question won't fail. It has become a priority and allowed you to focus. More importantly, by addressing an underlying problem, it will clear up other symptoms and issues that were eating into your leadership time.

The Board now has the information it needs to make a decision: clear outcomes, clear costs, and clear strategies. Your expert guidance will help lead them to the recommendation that you think is most appropriate. Moreover, better informed, they will feel even more confident about your leadership.

Building the business case is summarized in these seven points:

1. State the current and target levels of performance in specific, measurable goals.

2. Identify policies, programs, and practices—strategies and tactics—to get where you want to go.

3. Attach a timeline and cost estimates to the strategies.

4. Identify the person or persons responsible for successful implementation.

5. Include an evaluation component that has specific measures and deliverables.

6. Illustrate why your plan is more cost effective than other options.

7. Summarize supporting research and/or best practices.

Competition

The "C" word strikes terror in the hearts of many school leaders. They equate competition with winners and losers, and believe that if, God forbid, one school or district does better than theirs that their school will "look bad." What they forget is that competition enables all participants to improve. When all schools improve, students have more opportunities, they learn more and their communities get stronger. The phobia many administrators have of competition will ultimately hurt everyone and do nothing but further mediocrity.

Public school competition will ultimately benefit all schools, because we can learn from those who are doing the best, improving the most and trending upward.

Let me share a personal analogy. Since 1983, I have raced in triathlons. Throughout my 23 years of competing in four to ten events a year, I have made several new friends, but the two most memorable are my primary age group competitors, Randy and George. We always end up competing in two or three races each summer, and usually George wins, though Randy and I have picked him off a couple of times. Though we compete hard, we always share a few laughs and cold beers after the race and learn from each other. In fact, we have learned so much about swimming, cycling and running that our times are getting better even as we get older. One of the coolest benefits from the competition aside from improving our level of fitness and performance is that when we compete in races without the others, more often than not we win our age group.

A more relevant example comes from my most recent superintendency. Though we had a high achieving district, we were not a high functioning leadership team. The culture was "don't rock the boat" at best and CYA at worst. The shared vision was that the kids would continue to do well because they came from nice homes, and our district had money. In between pages of any School Improvement Plans was the safest place to put a $20 bill, because when you picked them up a year later, the money would still be there. In other words, status quo was the coin of the realm.

Transforming the culture to one of continuous improvement had to start with the leadership team, so who did I turn to for advice? No, not the other affluent districts; no, not the highest performing districts. I studied the practices of the Illinois "Spotlight Schools," the high poverty, high performing schools that had a history of exceptional performance and continuous improvement despite overwhelming obstacles. The competitive spirit of these districts to excel, their hunger to reach every child, their driving missions were inspirational and motivational. Adopting their practices to our team enabled us to develop a stronger leadership team and a close bond with the Board, the community and the staff around a common vision of continuous improvement.

Most educators disdain competition because they think that schools cannot be fairly compared, much less compete, based on the evidence that schools with more disadvantaged children do not do as well as schools with fewer children of poverty. Competition, they argue, encourages teaching to a test. We respectfully disagree and want to foster competition among similar schools and school districts because we think that way children benefit the most.

Yes, we actually think that competition among public schools and public school districts is healthy. Though we agree that schools with a higher poverty count do not do as well, we have evidence that disadvantaged children excel when given appropriate support. More importantly, we contend that they have a right to the very best education. We have found that the most effective ways to improve test scores are to have a rigorous curriculum, excellent teachers, and a host of student support services. In our experience, teaching to the test backfires. We believe that when schools compete, students benefit because leaders strive to improve programs and services to match the level of the competition. We do not apologize for wanting our schools to have the best test scores in our area, the highest attendance rate, the greatest graduation rate, the least number of teen pregnancies, and so on, because we think those measures are important for our children. When they have a quality education, they have more opportunities and choices than those who do not or those who drop out. Because staff members do not believe that competition is good for schools, building a collective vision will take time and real leadership.

As a quick example, one Illinois district used a team of Board, administration, staff, and parents to craft a mission statement that said the district would "deliver the highest quality of education to *all* students..." The lawyers cringed. "You cannot say that!" they advised. As the meter for billable hours clicked, they added, "If you commit to the 'highest'—not just high, but highest—quality of education, you will get sued by parents who think their kids aren't getting the very best. You can't say 'all students' because some students can't learn as much as others. Parents of special education students will be expecting a guarantee for college admission...." The list went on.

The School Board listened and weighed the advice carefully, but they stood by the mission. Their rationale was that if they did not strive to deliver—not passively "provide" or "offer"—the very best, they were not doing their job. They also deliberated the advice but included "*all* students," deciding that indeed they had to serve all students, including those with special needs. The staff responded with an ebullient collective commitment to help each and every child succeed. Yes, special education costs increased as the district hired more staff and paraprofessionals and, yes, funds were reallocated to assist struggling readers, but now, ten years later, the mission statement is still proudly posted in the Board room and the schools. The district may not be the best, but they are very close, with well over 90% of their students meeting and exceeding state standards while spending about 15% less per pupil than similar districts in their area.

Competition is not necessarily about "beating" other schools but about setting and reaching the high standards of student achievement, attendance, and graduation rates that make your district—and your students—among the very best. We contend that if you have 50% of your students meeting and exceeding state standards while similar schools have 40%, you have done well, but that 50% is not good enough for your students because that means half of them are *not* meeting state standards.

If the "C" word strikes terror into the heart of most superintendents, the "B" word wreaks panic. Real leaders, however, use benchmarking to learn from other school districts about how their educational programs, practices, and services can be improved for their students and staff. What is benchmarking? It is identifying similar schools/districts and comparing their level of performance with yours and then sharing the best practices within your benchmark group.

Benchmarking is something we do all the time in our personal lives. We all know where to find the best Friday night fish fry. (In our town, it's the Wool Street Pub, $10.95 for all you can eat, plus $2 beers. How do we know it's the best? We've tried the others within a five-mile radius.)

Now it may not be surprising, but the owners of the Wool Street also benchmark their establishment against others. They look at the other restaurants' menus, compare prices, eat their food, and even check their washrooms. They benchmark because they want to provide a better product and service. In schools we need to benchmark because we also want to provide better products (like curriculum) and better services to our children. They deserve it.

In choosing the benchmark group, you want to select competitors with similar demographics. Morton's Steak House would not be in the Wool Street Pub's benchmark group. Though both do a terrific job of serving their patrons, they are quite different. Likewise, when benchmarking select schools or districts similar to yours in percentage of low-income students, costs, and mobility. It's not always necessary to have an exact match. With an Excel spreadsheet, you can conduct simple regression analyses. What that means is you can choose any particular outcome measure and see if your district is above or below where you would predict yourself to be.

Graph 3-1 is an example from our benchmarking study in Wilmette District 39. With the assistance of Clay Graham and the Northern Illinois University Center for Governmental Studies (CGS), we compared Wilmette to seventeen similar districts. We compared test scores from the state test (the ISAT), homeowner's tax burden, and educational value. Knowing that the socio-economic status (SES) of a school district has an impact on test scores, we explored the use of several different variables to account for this effect such as median home values, per pupil expenditures, parent education, and family income. The best predictor of achievement was median home values, which we obtained from census data at CGS. Median home values, then, became our stand-in for SES. As the graph shows, we created a curved regression line to represent predicted third-grade reading scores for this sample of seventeen districts. Those districts that are above the line, like Wilmette, Hinsdale, and Avoca, are outperforming what one would expect based on the socio-economic status of the district. Districts below the line are not reaching expectations. The greater the distance is between the score and the line, the greater the over-or-under performance for the district.

Graph 3-2 puts the information from predicted vs. actual scores for third-grade reading into an easily read "over/under" chart. Though Wilmette did not have the highest score in terms of actual performance, the graph shows that in terms of beating expectations, it was the top district for third-grade reading. Other districts in the comparison group would be wise to explore what Wilmette is doing in the primary grades that enables their third-grade students to achieve beyond expectations.

The power of benchmarking is not to determine whether you are in first place or tenth place. Rather, its value lies in enabling the leadership team to identify similar districts that are providing an education that enables their students to achieve beyond what one would expect. District 39 will use the benchmark data for its strategic planning work. In fact, the next step is to send staff and parent project teams to the top districts to identify the most successful programs and services and evaluate if our district should try to replicate them. We are also developing a new benchmark group of districts from across the country.

Graph 3-1

Benchmarking Actual Performance (x)
Compared to Expected Performance (line)
2002 ISAT Results

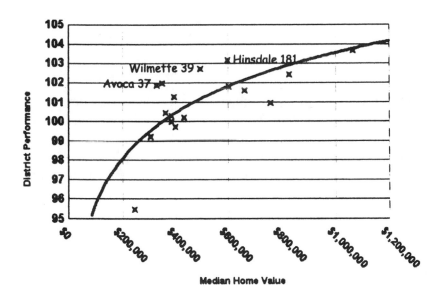

Graph 3-2

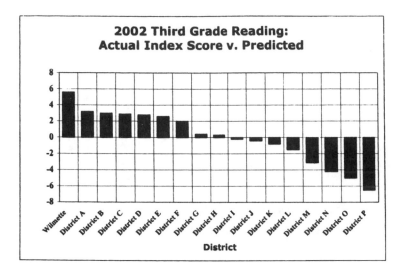

(To see the graphs in larger, reproducible format, go to
http://www.superintendents-and-principals.com)

To summarize, benchmarking and competing are common business practices that will improve teaching and learning and thus benefit students and schools. The first step is to identify comparable schools and districts. Benchmarking involves comparing both results and practices among these schools and identifying the programs and services that are effective in the best schools of your comparable group. Visit these schools and spend time with these teachers, then develop a plan to replicate what they do well. Competition is striving to be the very best school. Determine the measures you will use to gauge progress and success. Though we encourage competition among similar schools, competing to attain a high standard of achievement, attendance, or graduation is in itself a productive goal. Success will require collaboration and a collective commitment.

"Branding" our Schools

We know that the most successful businesses strive for a market advantage and that this advantage is due, in large part, to successful branding strategies. Though we are not necessarily competing for market share, as school leaders we need to market the success of our schools. Intelligent, active branding has enormous benefits including:

- Voter support strengthens

- Parent loyalty solidifies

- Home values increase

- Internal "school spirit" soars

- A shared commitment to the School Board's vision develops

- Schools attract high quality teachers and leaders

- Leaders become respected resources

- District identity emerges

- Stakeholders rally round you in tough times

In the school business, branding begins with a sound communications plan. Each day the leader should wake up thinking about how he or she is going to communicate the district or school's vision as well as particular matters of the day or week. In these waking thoughts should be how to touch all three components of communication:

Information—how will I share an important message and our vision.

Instruction—what can I do to teach parents, staff or some audience something important, e.g. what the state assessment results mean, the impact of obesity on teenagers, etc.

Interaction—what can I do to listen today; how can I gather information about our district/school that will help make it a better place for students and staff.

Branding your school or district involves a commitment that entails some simple, perhaps obvious steps, yet ones we find are too often overlooked or ignored. We need to think of how we communicate a simple message many times through many media. Too often, we rely on one media, the local paper, to reach our tax-payers. But they control the message, not us. To compensate, we may issue an annual report or even quarterly newsletters, even though many end up being tossed before they are read. Our challenge is to penetrate every home in our community. We must identify many ways to deliver our message repeatedly.

Identifying your main message. This is the most important and perhaps the most difficult step. Having read hundreds of mission statements, I am consistently baffled at how anyone can remember them, much less what they mean. Like weeds on a fairway at Augusta National, jargon needs to be pulled from them immediately, "self actualized," "intrinsic motivation," and even "lifelong learners" needs to go. They need to be short, pithy and in plain English. Why educators are compelled to write "utilize" in mission, vision and belief and goal statements instead of "use" mystifies me, but more importantly it mystifies stakeholders in the district who, when faced with rambling, stultifying mission statements, do not read them much less live them. New Trier High School has one of my favorites: "To commit minds to inquiry, hearts to compassion, and lives to the service of humanity." They have found this so powerful, that they have actually trademarked it!

In addition to a mission or vision statement, the school or district needs to have some succinct message points that speak to its beliefs. These message points should then be regularly embedded in every district communication. Here is what we use:

- We are "Teaching Tomorrow's Leaders"
- We are moving from "Great to Greater"
- District 39 will become the VERY BEST place for students to learn, teachers to teach and families to flourish
- We treat your child as we treat our own
- District 39 gives you the biggest bang for the buck

Developing strategies and tactics to communicate it. We recommend that each of the three components—information, instruction, and interaction—have specific strategies and tactics and that for each one you identify multiple media. For example, to provide information, we in District 39 use print media such as our Annual Report and quarterly newsletters (and many more), electronic media such as monthly television talk shows and our "virtual backpack," and "real time" media such as special presentations in the schools and throughout the community.

Here are some other examples of strategies and tactics we use:

Print media

External
- Press releases for papers
- Feature articles (e.g. required public speaking class, elementary foreign language)
- Guest essays/op ed for local papers
- Monthly columns for the PTA/O newsletters

Internally generated

- Annual report
- Long Range Plan trifold
- Topical trifolds (special education, curriculum differentiation)
- Quarterly newsletters
- Backpack reminders
- Internal email, handwritten thank you notes, bulletins, etc.

Visual media

- Ceremonial speeches
- Presentations at local, state and national conferences
- Panel participation at professional conferences
- Monthly cable television show—Update 39
- Televised Board of Education meetings
- Press conferences

Computer technology

- Website
  - o Hot topics
  - o Schools
  - o Clean and easy
- Backpack 39 (see what you've been missing)
- Forum 39
- Email list-serves
- Interactive surveys
- CD and/or DVD of meetings, presentations, etc.

Face to Face

- "Second cup of coffee" sessions with parents
- PTA/O circuit
- Instructional forums
- Legislative breakfasts
- Focus groups
- Casual contact
- Mother McGee's Book Club (The superintendent and some of the principals have staff and parent book clubs that meet every 4-6 weeks.)

Surveys

- Quarterly newsletter, "Opinion 39"
- Biannual telephone survey
- Target group parent surveys (gifted mathematics, new first grade parents, etc.)
- Harris Interactive Staff Survey
- Student surveys

Attending to internal communication. The single most important component in your communications plan is informing your staff and getting them on board. You need to explain in detail the rationale and benefits that will accrue for staff and students. You need to get their input into developing the plan and incorporate their strategies. Most importantly, you have to provide training, especially for your leadership team, in how to communicate effectively in speaking and writing. As we all know, most adults fear public speaking more than spiders, snakes and Great White Sharks so you will need to give them the skills they need to deliver message points concisely, how to use nonverbal techniques and how to answer difficult questions. Let your staff know how you will measure success and how you will keep them informed as to the success of the efforts.

Choosing the best messengers. Most of you have probably had occasion to say, "Don't shoot the messenger." If not, we are sure that you have heard it more than once. The best way to assure that your message is communicated effectively is to have a messenger that people love and would never think of shooting, ever. In delivering a message, be it through a presentation to the School Board or a greater community, an op ed column, or an interactive forum, the leader needs to consider who will be the most credible messenger. More often than not, it is not us. Usually the messengers that everyone embraces are teachers or parents and not administrators. As Malcom Gladwell reminds us in the *Tipping Point*, public opinion and public action depend more on who communicates the message (the salesmen and mavens) and to whom (the connectors) than the content of the message.

I learned this lesson as State Superintendent. Whenever I really needed a piece of legislation passed or an increase in appropriations, more often than not I found articulate teachers, passionate students or concerned parents to testify at Committee Hearings. Although I enjoyed a fine relationship with the legislators, it was much easier for them to deny my requests than to give bad news directly to parents, teachers, and students. In fact, when a high school student, who told the Senate Appropriations how he bought his first suit for $8.00 from Goodwill in order to look nice to testify about the need for funding Jobs for America's Graduates and shared how the program had kept him in school and prepared him to be a productive, responsible citizen, even the grizzled committee chair nearly melted and was ready to write his own personal check to help fund the program.

In addition to selecting the best messenger, it is important to provide them the training and coaching they need to be effective messengers—in both speaking and writing. One of our principals has joined Toastmasters to improve her public speaking skills, our new teacher orientation includes public speaking practice, and I run a writing workshop for our principals. Moreover, we rehearse every Board presentation and practice every presentation. For new superintendents, we strongly recommend formal media training so you can learn how to deliver your message clearly and powerfully, how you can skillfully answer difficult questions and how you can communicate what you want to say under the most threatening, hostile conditions.

Choosing the best media. As with choosing the best messenger, choosing the most effective media is of critical importance. Although we firmly believe in repeating the same message many times in multiple media, a message will be more effective in one than another. With the proliferation of web sites, it is easy to over rely on using it for all messages and even as the primary portal for communication. We have found that our district's web site is good back up, but broadcast telephone messages, group email, newsletters and personal presentations have far more penetration and impact.

Finally, remember that the adage, a picture is worth 1000 words, is both accurate and profound. Too often, school and district leaders fill their newsletters and annual reports with text and more text. Less is more, and a good graph, a touching photograph or even a colorful graphic can more effectively communicate your message than a page of text, which most will not read regardless of how sparkling your prose is.

Measuring your message. We advise you to find ways to measure the impact of your message. We actually ask parents and teachers if they can state our mission statement, if our district is delivering on the promise to be the "very best place for students to learn, teachers to teach and families to flourish." This question from our parent survey turned out to be especially helpful:

5.
A. District 39 uses several methods of communication between school and home. As I read you each method, please tell me whether or not you have received or participated in that particular method of communication.

B. Now I would like to have you rate (INSERT ITEM) in terms of its effectiveness in keeping you informed of District or school activities by using the 4-point scale of Excellent, Good, Fair, or Poor.

District newsletter, "School News 39"
Articles in the *Wilmette Life*
PTO or school newsletter
School Board meetings
Special informational meetings
Update39 on cable channel 6
District or school website
Teacher communication
Backpack Express
School Weeklies (weekly bulletins)
Connect Ed broadcast telephone calls
Email messages

We learned that what parents read most frequently as well as what was most effective was our PTA/O newsletters! I had assumed it was our community's weekly newspaper or our school district newsletter, but they lagged well behind the PTA/O newsletters. As a result, the principals and I both write monthly columns for these.

Creating a crisis communication plan. The best school leaders are the best communicators and they are at their best in a crisis. No matter how bad the situation may be—and we have faced some bad ones including student and staff deaths, staff arrests, students being taken in handcuffs, bomb threats, hazardous material spills etc.—it is of critical importance that the leader remain in control and appear to be a tower of strength. The best, and perhaps only, way to be the leader your community needs in a crisis is to be well prepared. We recommend you develop a crisis communication plan that specifies who carries the message to the various stakeholder groups, how it is delivered to them, how the media is notified and managed, and the like. As the business world has told us, a crisis can either crush a product or make the brand stronger. Tylenol's response to the poisonings and the Lexus recall of their first luxury model illustrate how leaders managed their crises to benefit both consumers and the brand.

Consider the experience of Lexus. In 1990, just after Lexus first introduced its line of luxury cars in the United States, the company realized that it had two minor problems with its LS400 line that required a recall. The situation was, by any measure, an awkward one. Lexus had decided, from the beginning, to build its reputation around quality workmanship and reliability. And now, within little more than a year of the brand's launch, the company was being forced to admit to problems with its flagship. So Lexus decided to make a special effort. Most recalls are handled by making an announcement to the press and mailing a notification letter to owners. Lexus, instead, called each owner individually on the telephone the day the recall was announced. When the owners picked up their cars at the dealership after the work was completed, each car had been washed and the tank filled with gas. If an owner lived more than a hundred miles from a dealership, the dealer sent a mechanic to his or her home. In one instance, a technician flew from Los Angeles to Anchorage to make the necessary repairs.

Was it necessary to go to such lengths? You could argue that Lexus overreacted. The problems with the car were relatively minor. And the number of cars involved in the recall—so soon after Lexus had entered the marketplace—was small. Lexus would seem to have had many opportunities to correct the damage. The key fact, though, was not the number of people affected by the recall but the kind of people affected by the recall. Who, after all, are the people willing to take a chance and buy a brand-new luxury model? Car Mavens. There may have been only a few thousand Lexus owners at that point, but they were car experts, people who take cars seriously, people who talk about cars, people whose friends ask them for advice about cars. Lexus realized that it had a captive audience of Mavens and that if they went the extra mile they could kick-start a word-of-mouth epidemic about the quality of their customer service—and that's just what happened. The company emerged from what could have been a disaster with a reputation for customer service that continues to this day. One automotive publication later called it "the perfect recall."[2]

---

[2] Malcom Gladwell, *The Tipping Point*, New York: Little, Brown and Co., 2000. pp. 277-8.

"Branding" is hard work, but it is one of the primary responsibilities of the school, district and business leader. It is a principle that has proven enormously effective in the business world, and one which would serve schools well. Schools who successfully brand their schools and districts as magical places for students, families and teachers to learn and grow will enjoy far more support, successfully pass far more referenda, have a much smaller mobility rate, and most likely enjoy better student performance than similar schools who do not attend to making every day a great one for communicating.

Walking the Talk

Though we may be disgusted by cuffed corporate leaders, publicized dalliances, and perceived arrogance, the fact of the matter is that most CEOs are honest, responsible, and hard working. They got to where they are because they are their company and they conduct themselves like leaders. You are your school district. That means you must dress and act like the boss. To paraphrase Thomas Watson, former Chairman of IBM, "We need to have our heart in the business and carry the business in our heart."

Let's close, then, with some simple "helpful hints" which may be more appropriate coming from your mother than us. Still, they may be some of the most important advice you will glean from this book.

* Look good when you go to the office. You are a model for staff and students. If kids see their parents leaving the house in business clothes, dress like them or better.

* Use proper grammar; ending sentences with prepositions is not where it's at.

* In social situations with your staff or your Board or at functions in your community, limit yourself to one or two drinks—two max.

* Keep your cool at all times—and don't swear.

* Don't do anything that would embarrass your family.

* Make sure you retain your credibility by having everything you write carefully proofread. (Or is that prooofred?)

* Don't say or send anything in an email that you would not want to read in the newspaper.

* Get out of the office and into the classrooms—show them how much you care.

* Conduct your Board meetings like business meetings.

The main points of "branding" are:

1. Write a communications (aka marketing) plan.

2. Wake up thinking about communication.

3. Tap into your key internal and external leaders to develop concise, inspirational "mission" and "main message points."

4. Disburse short and simple messages many times by multiple media.

5. Be sure to build internal support prior to launching an external communication/branding initiative.

6. Market yourself in words and action.

Summary

Though we do not recommend running schools like businesses where the bottom line is profit or loss, we have found that successful, effective school leaders incorporate some business practices that can help improve teaching and learning. They know how to write a business plan to achieve specific goals for their school and district. When proposing the addition or major revision of programs and services, they make a strong business case. Forecasting enrollment, revenues, and expenses is an important planning tool for these leaders. Benchmarking your schools against similar schools, competing with them, and competing for achievement of high standards enable school leaders to identify and replicate successful programs and foster a collective commitment to improving teaching and learning. Marketing your school entails communication of short, simple messages. Showcase your successes, publicize your school improvement plans, and share good news with a common theme—our schools care about teaching and learning. Finally, market yourself through your actions and words because the public, the staff, and the students see you as the embodiment of your schools. Hard work, heart, and integrity are what people expect, and need, to see from their leader.

Chapter Four

Communications

Jim Burgett

Nothing is more important to success in the school administrative world than communications. So, in this chapter, I want to share a few thoughts about the topic in general, then zero in on specifics that can make your school jump to the head of the pack, like newsletters, a speakers bureau, a "Senior Citizen Prom," news releases, the school marquee, memos, a "homework hotline," websites, notes, and placemats.

Also crucial to your success will be communication with the media, so I'll spend some time there too. Some skills, I should mention, are vital to communication success—like trust and tact—plus three other elements worth sharing—disclaimers, rewards, and sufficient background. Each will get its due. I'll end with 14 effective communication ideas.

How important do I think communication skills are? A graduate student working on his administrative certification found out recently when he interviewed me. He asked lots of questions but the first may have been the best: "What is the most important skill for a new administrator to learn?"

Without a moment's hesitation, I said, "The ability to effectively communicate."

That's why I was eager to write this chapter.

Think of the many aspects of communication. Writing and speaking are the most obvious, but there's also body language, smoke signals, a wink, silence, apathy, a grunt, action, and inaction.

We are communicating right now. If I am doing so effectively, you will understand what I'm saying and will learn something from it. If you say, "I already know this," then my message is confirming. If you leave this chapter with usable ideas, my message will be informative. If you're in the middle of this chapter, and you throw it down and rush off to do something new because of it, my message will have been motivational.

In education, we communicate many times a day.

Most of us began our careers as teachers. There, we survived by our command of the spoken word. As an administrator, however, we no longer have that captive, can't-leave-your-seat audience. Now our speeches are to the Board, the PTO, and the Buffalo Club.

The higher we rise, the more the written word becomes key—reports, grants, thank-you notes, memos, and e-memos. It's a grand balancing act and one goof can badly hurt our kids or our schools or even cost us our jobs.

The Written Word

We have a real advantage when communication is written. For example, I have written this chapter a dozen times. I wrote it, rewrote it, read it, reread it, sent it to Jim and Max for their review and suggestions, rewrote it again, and then submitted it to the book editor who will probably rewrite it again. (Editor: Yep.) But by the time you get it, it should be easy to understand and ready to apply.

The written word doesn't disappear either, unless we inadvertently pop the "delete" key before we hit "print." It's convenient too. You can read it when you want, or read some of it now and some later. You can reread it, underline it, scan it, or copy any part of it. You can outline it, comment on it, or even email it to a friend or to one of us for further discussion. (You could even ignore or shred it.)

It is great for me too. I can doodle with it, move the words around, call to check the facts, and get it in the exact form I want you to see. That's why I think the written word is *the most important* form of prepared communication we use. But it carries plenty of responsibility because in print it *is* what we meant to say. So we are forced to get the job done right. In other words, as educators we have no excuse for not doing so.

In Defense of Noise

Then there is the spoken word. It is surely the most frequently used mode of communication since we engage in dialog virtually every time we encounter another person. One of my former secretaries even talkcd to plants! Another person in our office talked to herself. (We didn't interrupt her because she seemed to enjoy the conversation!)

Speaking is quicker than writing and is widely used: prepared talks, salutations to people we know and others we don't, telephone exchanges with people we can't see, "filler" talk without much substance, in-depth conversation on issues of importance and urgency, lectures given to full classes or to a daughter or son, good-byes, hellos, arguments, "I'm sorrys," eulogies, love babble. The number of times we talk is truly scary.

And most of the commentaries are important because they reflect directly on you and your schools. So it is important that we think before we speak. The only saving grace is that once it's said, it is lost sound (unless it's done on the air, on tape, or in front of a crowd). There is no waving paper with the injustice captured forever in type!

A Last Thought before the Specifics

Communicating is, without doubt, the most important skill of any administrator.

However, you will recall that I have emphasized "effective" communication: words shaped to create the result you wish. That is the core of leadership—to determine that effect, then shape the words and ideas to make it happen. Orally, that's on-the-spot stuff that comes from years of building the experiential base to draw from. Written, it's a slower crafting of words to paint the picture and prompt the action.

Effective communication, to me, is the presentation of well-planned information.

The nature of your job, and position, has prepared you for a thousand situations. Even in an impromptu conversation, or when being yelled at by a half-crazed parent, or being questioned at a Board meeting, you must present well-planned information. You should know your subject, and thus know what to say. You must respond like a professional, keeping your cool and sharing the right stuff at the right time.

Writing and speaking effectively are like driving your car to a set destination. The preparation is figuring out precisely where you want to go, then using a map to choose the roads that will take you there. If you're a superintendent or principal, you already know how to drive. You can steer your car—and your career. You've got a good sense of direction and have taken the right roads before. But I'm also quick to pull over and ask for help—because I hate driving in circles. That's effective communication in a nutshell. Set your target, plan your route, ask for help if you need it, and arrive safely and on time.

The three of us writing this book—Max McGee, Jim Rosborg, and I—have over 250 years of educational administration experience. (Well, it seems like that much. Actually, it's about 100.) Collectively, we have lots of miles on our cars driving toward many goals. We learned a lot on the way. Mostly, when we get together and share stories of success and disaster, we usually end up laughing the hardest at the latter. We've made some big mistakes over the years, but we've learned from them too. We've all driven into the ditch occasionally and needed to call a tow truck to save our mission and our dignity. Given a chance, it's better to do it right. So there is some trial and error as you work toward being a successful and effective communicator. The extra work and attention to what you say and write is worth it: effective communication is the single most important skill you will ever need.

Tools and Traits for Effective Communication

Develop Trust

If you want to be an effective communicator, the first thing you need to develop is *trust*. In fact, it is so important that the next chapter is totally dedicated to that subject. You can earn trust by sharing information that is valid, timely, tactful, and honest. When people learn to "believe you," you are halfway to your destination. Soon they will also learn to "believe in you." Once this happens, you can almost put the gearshift in neutral and coast the rest of the route.

Once, I met a man who immediately told me he couldn't trust me. I asked him why. He replied that I was a school superintendent and "not a one of them" could be trusted. I never did earn his trust, although I tried. A school superintendent had fired him, so he considered all of us derelicts. The point? You can't win everyone's trust, no matter how hard you work at it. Some won't like the way you talk, that you are thin or bald, or that you dress nicer than they do. They don't like taking advice from the opposite sex. They won't like how much money you make or the kind of car you drive. My advice is to keep trying anyway, but also keep driving toward your goal. Don't let those you will never win over cause you to take a detour. I've spent too many sleepless nights over things that should have been put in the "no matter how honest and effective you communicate, not everyone will believe you" file.

You win trust by consistently providing honest and fair communications. Never make up information. Never fear saying, "I don't know that answer. Let me research it for you." Never hesitate to say, "Bill, our auditor, has that exact number. I'll find it and get back to you as soon as I can." Never fudge or lie or slide past the right answer. Honest communications are not an option; they are mandatory for successful administration.

Use Disclaimers When Needed

Don't report or state things you "think" are right without a clear disclaimer. It's okay to say, "As best I recall, the enrollment in our district peaked in the late 80s." If you are writing this information, you have the time to verify the facts, but if you are asked, you need to communicate some type of disclaimer if you are not totally certain of your information. I often add something like this: "My memory isn't too sharp on this topic, but it seems to me that...." Then I add that I will double-check the information and get back to them if I am wrong. In reality, I get back to them if I am right or wrong, just to assure them that providing the correct information is important to me.

Quantity *and* Quality

Sometimes the quantity of your communications is as important as the quality. For example, you spend hours drafting and preparing a short, concise, accurate description of your escalating problems with increased enrollment. You know that you will refer to this prepared document many times to plant seeds for a future referendum or bond issue. You submit it to the *Town Blab*, your local weekly newspaper.

Three weeks later, you give an annual report on school issues to the local Buffalo Club. You talk about the enrollment issue, assuming everyone is up to speed on the facts. Instead, all you receive are glassy stares. You are not communicating effectively because you have erroneously assumed that your audience knows the background information. Worse, you have to interrupt your speech to answer several questions about the very information you had outlined in a newspaper article only a few weeks before. You ask yourself, what is wrong with these people? Don't they care about the school? Why don't they know that the average class size has risen 37% in the last five years?

After the meeting, you share your concerns with the club president over a buffalo burger. The president informs you that half of the club lives in the country and they probably subscribe to the *County Crier* rather than the *Town Blab*. Oops. No wonder they didn't know. Then you wonder how many of those in town even read the town paper.

If you had a district-wide newsletter that went to every home, and if you had submitted the article to both the town and county newspapers, and if you had sent a special letter home with each student, and if you had asked the PTO to include your article in its monthly report, and if you had accepted that invitation by the local radio station to be a part of this month's "Community Issues" show, maybe 80% rather than 30% of the Buffalo boys would have been able to follow your presentation. Lots of lost "ifs."

That's why communicating effectively sometimes requires quantity as well as quality. A good understanding and careful development of effective delivery systems in your district and communities help here. More about those in a moment....

Tacky or Tactful?

Let's add tactfulness to trust and quantity. If you want your communication to be effective, be mindful of the audience. You can do major damage if you don't think before you speak, write, or send smoke signals.

I attended a meeting where high school students were recognized for their leadership. It is a wonderful program put on by our local Optimist Club. The program builds trust, respect, and pride in our students and school. The man who does all the work for this program and makes it an outstanding event is a local funeral director. During the meeting, one of the guys at my table made some humorous remarks to the funeral director about his vocation—all in fun and appropriate under normal circumstances. But because one of the other members had tragically lost a son two weeks earlier, many members were upset with the comments. Damage was done that night. So we must be particularly careful with humor, sarcasm, or any type of communication directed toward a person or their occupation. Almost all of us will make mistakes in this area. When we do, we need to immediately call or send a note of apology to try to undo the damage.

Being tactful is a twin to being thoughtful. If in doubt about the appropriateness of a comment, a joke, or an example, avoid it. Better to err on the side of caution than to take the risk of hurting someone or permanently damaging your relationship with a person or group. Reread everything you write. Reconsider everything you plan to say. Think twice and give your communications the "tacky or tactful" review before you proceed.

Make Your Communication Rewarding

Finally, to make your communication truly effective, make it rewarding. A quick note to someone who won an award might mean more than you know. A letter sent home to students, and their parents, recognizing students' induction into the National Honor Society may become a treasure they keep forever. It doesn't need to be long, but you do need to personally sign each letter. I always sign in blue so they realize it isn't a computer-generated signature. Telling the students you are proud of them and thanking their parents for their help and support along the way is greatly appreciated.

Letters to senior citizens who volunteer their time or are recognized for something they did in the community strengthen the bond between them and the school. I send birthday cards to every current and retired employee. We buy them in bulk. One of my secretaries addresses the cards and writes the birth date in little numbers on the back corner of the envelope. She gives them to me in a big bundle, once a month. I work on them as time permits. I always write a personal message on each card. I thank them for their many years of dedicated service, the difference they've made, their dedication to the profession, their love of students, and then I wish them a happy birthday. If I don't know anything special about them, I ask a principal or an office worker who remembers them. Many times I write something like, "I am told you not only kept the grade school sparkling clean but you always had a smile to share with others. I wish I would have had the opportunity to work with you." Don't think that doesn't make their day? Effective and important communications? You bet. I send over 500 cards a year. Yes, it takes a lot of time, but it builds a network of appreciative people and also fortifies their trust.

Honest, timely, tactful, personal communications make a difference. When you have an important message to share, consider quality first, then go for quantity. Remember to think before you talk, plan before you write, and research before you respond. Learn from the mistakes you make, and when you make them, apologize and move on. Remember, you won't win everyone over, but by developing strong communication skills, you will make a difference.

Examples of Effective Communication

Let me share some of my favorite examples of effective communication. (This is not intended to be a template for your school or district, just a summary of things that have worked well for us and may be worth considering.) Each of these ideas is a way to share a message or to increase understanding of and support for your school or district.

Newsletter

Develop a district newsletter. Include information from each school and department as a regular feature, like food service, transportation, guidance, senior citizen news, and community service projects. Have regular articles from the FFA if you serve a farm community, from the Vocational Center if you are in a blue-collar area, from business classes if you are mostly white-collar, or a combination. Recognize school, staff, and community award winners. Make the lead story positive; highlight success. Be sure to distribute this newsletter to *every* family in the district by some means. Often local papers or "shoppers" have some vehicle to get into every home and will print or include your newsletter at a lower cost than if you did it yourself. Make this newsletter something to be proud of.

Speakers Bureau

Develop a "speakers bureau" from the community. Invite, secure, and share local speakers. Give them an option to talk for 15, 30, or 45 minutes. Many will prefer 15 minutes, but some will opt for 45. Once you have the list, use them! Offer to preview their comments and to coach them on how to present to students. You will be surprised at how much people like this idea. You can even provide a short, bulleted list of suggestions on giving a speech to students. A good suggestion is to schedule your speakers at the end of the hours (perhaps the last 30 minutes) so they get to the point and don't get "windy."

Communicate with Senior Citizens

This is a must. Our local high school has a "Senior Citizen Prom" every year, funded by our townships and hosted by the school (FFA, SADD, and National Honor Society). The students come in formals and suits and dance with the senior citizens, help serve food, provide assistance to and from cars, and perform other services. The cost is free but a reservation is needed. We have a "live" band of mostly older musicians playing really corny songs, as well as the high school's own jazz band; both take turns playing. The "prom guests" love it. They crown a King and Queen (from a drawing of names) and give away donated door prizes throughout the evening. "Tickets" are sold out soon after the date is announced. Doors open at 6 p.m. but the oldsters start arriving at 4:30! The dance is over at 10:30. The rewards are many. The school shares lots of information that night with a few short speeches (none over three minutes), some written literature, and much conversation. Add this to "Grandparent's Day" at each grade school, Senior Citizen tours, and various coffee hours and soon you will have a strong network of support from the older folks.

News Releases

Provide frequent news releases to the local, and not so local, newspapers. Write as much of it as you can and provide digital photos. It is easier than ever to do this over the Internet. Newspapers love to receive school news and you get great press on the issues you want reported. It also builds that strong bond needed between the school and the media. I'll discuss working with the media in the next section of this chapter.

School-to-Home Communications

Send home frequent calendars and parent-teacher handbooks, and encourage newsletters to be sent home by teachers, schools, and administrators. These are forms of school-to-home communications that families come to rely on and truly appreciate. Clear and concise information about field trips, school lunches, bus routes, school closing procedures, and so on are *very important* and need to be written well and shared widely. Internal communications can be enhanced with in-house calendars that outline school events, end-of-the-quarter requirements, Board meetings, PTO/A meetings and events, etc.

School Marquee

Communicate effectively with a school marquee. What a great communication tool the school signboard can be! Nothing makes me crazier than driving by a school in March and seeing "Happy Holidays" on the signboard! Or, "Drive Safely—Students are Back!" in the middle of October. I want to get out of my car and rearrange all the letters to say something absolutely unforgettable, but I give this action the "tacky or tactful" test and just keep driving![1]

---

[1] It wouldn't be the first time. Art students in a district where I was first an administrator never failed to change the early September "Arts and Crafts Show" to the "Farts and Crap Show."

Think about all the opportunities a signboard provides: daily messages that keep the public's interest, announcements of school events, scores of last night's game, congratulations to the victorious opponent (a message of good sportsmanship), announcements of award winners, recognition to senior citizens or parent volunteers, booster club news, and thanks to the community for buying miniature cans of popcorn for 900 times the store value. Signs like:

"WE THANK OUR BUS DRIVERS FOR GETTING US
TO SCHOOL SAFELY EACH DAY!"
or
"THANKS, TAXPAYERS, FOR PROVIDING
A QUALITY EDUCATION FOR OUR KIDS!"

I love signboards! Why not let your special education class put up the message each day, then give them public credit for the job well done? Why not let your technology classes design a software program that tells you if your message will fit your board and if you have enough letters for it? By doing these few things you make the signboard a shared responsibility with positive outcomes and lots of ownership. (Just make sure the spelling is correct and the letters are not upside down or backwards or you will surely see a large photo of your marquee in the next issue of the local newspaper!)

Memos

Write memos that are meaningful. Memos are an especially important form of communication. I remember one that went out about a staff party. It read, "We are sharing gag gifts at the party. Be sure to bring one so that every person gets a gift." Some brought one gift while others brought one gift for each of the 20 people at the party! They had each read the memo differently. So effective communication here, as always, means accurate and clear memos. It should have said, "We are sharing gag gifts at the party. Be sure to bring only _one_ gift _so_ that everyone will go home with something funny to remember the evening."

To avoid misunderstandings, reread them and have them proofread. I like to write them, read them, have them proofed, go back to them, clarify them if needed, and then send them. Adding clip art, at times, might make them more readable or enjoyable.

And always remember to write memos on a simple level, avoiding long and complex sentences that might be easily misunderstood. One of my high school English teachers used to remind us frequently that the most effective written communication is "a short, concise, simple, and proofread sentence." (Bless him. He lives in my mind forever.) This applies to memos as well.

Homework Hotlines/Mass Message Systems

Use "homework hotlines" or the new systems that send hundreds of messages at the same time for school announcements, weather bulletins, and school closings. These systems can be used to announce the estimated arrival time of band or field trip buses. Teachers can call on a cell phone and record when the bus will arrive at the school, saving parents hundreds of wasted hours parked and waiting. You can even give your parochial school, service organizations, churches, sport clubs, police, and other organizations free extensions on your homework hotlines. Talk about positive community relations!

Websites

And of course post classroom, school, and district websites with *current* updates and relevant information. There is no excuse these days for not having a classy and informative website to share facts, test scores, and other information. But old news is bad news; you must keep website information current!

Teacher-Home Communication

Encourage positive communications between your teachers and the home. Purchase school "thank-you" notes. Offer to have a staff person address and stamp them. Ask the teacher to write a sentence or two of positive comments when appropriate. Encourage the same with administrators and district personnel. Personally, I wrote thank-you notes to almost everyone who came to me with a complaint or concern. I thanked them for giving me the opportunity to discuss the issue and invited them to call or visit again if the problem was not resolved. Probably 90% of those who shared concerns received a note. For some, a note was not appropriate, but, for most, it was an excellent form of effective and appreciated communication.

Share School News Widely

Share positive school news whenever possible. Offer to speak at service or church organizations. Call them and ask them if you can be put on their speakers' list. Then prepare a low-key, short, snappy presentation. Bring a student with you, if possible, to thank the organization for what it does for the community and school. Distribute handouts (but never gifts, not even pencils or other inexpensive items, since many consider this a waste of taxpayer money). If you can bring a short video of school activities or programs, consider doing so, but always make sure the proper equipment is available and *always* have a back-up in case the equipment doesn't work or can't be found. If the group gives you 15 minutes to talk, talk for 12 and ask for questions. Never exceed your time limit. Practice your presentation in front of a group of peers and brainstorm possible questions you might be asked. Remember, to make your communication effective, prepare, practice, and produce.

Placemats

Develop a placemat with the school calendar and some interesting facts on it, the kind put on a tray at fast food restaurants. "Did you know...?" items are always of interest and easy to read in small bites. Here is one example: "Last year 95% of all third graders in our school met or exceeded all _____ (insert your state) reading standards! The average in our _____ (state) is 66%." Be sure a sponsor pays for the placemats and have that clearly noted. It's a win-win situation for the sponsor and the school. Give the placemats to churches and other organizations for community dinners and potlucks.

There are at least 9,567 more ways that you can effectively communicate with your public. One good way to come up with a few thousand more that fit your school or district is to gather a group of educators and parents and do a brainstorming session on what are the best and most effective ways to share your message in your community!

Communicating with the Media

"Never argue with someone who buys their ink by the barrel." I've heard that one a thousand times. I have no idea if anyone in your town buys ink by the barrel. I know I buy it by the cartridge, and I can't believe the cost of just one plastic container of the stuff! The point is: Don't get the mediafolk mad at you. They have the power to retaliate big time! Frankly, I can't imagine any paper or radio station not wanting to have a positive relationship with the local school system since we provide a lot of information that helps keep them in business. On the other hand, I do know of some newspapers that are nasty to schools and seem to like it that way. The best advice when working with the media is the same I'd give about any type of effective communication: be honest, be fair, and be timely. If you treat other forms of communication this way, the media shouldn't be any different. But there are some "special" rules:

Get to Know Your Reporters

Get to know your local reporters. Offer to spend time with them going over things. Never tell them you are too busy for them unless you really are, and then make sure you get back to them ASAP. They work on tighter deadlines than you do. If they call when you are out, don't count your blessings because you missed them. Call them back as soon as you can and offer to help them. Other rules:

1. Never go "off the record" unless you have built a very trusting relationship with that individual, a relationship you know they will not compromise. If you don't know the reporter or don't have this type of relationship, never, ever, go "off the record."

2. Remember that the reporter has space to fill. If you respond with, "no comment," they will find someone else who will gladly give them one, right or wrong.

3. Encourage your administrative staff to submit positive happenings even if they don't get published each time. Keep sending and sending and eventually the reporter will get the point.

4. Make sure you have a policy or procedure about what is sent to the paper and who sends it. Many administrators want to preview or approve anything sent to print.

Schools often get the rookie reporters. The newcomers mean well but their ignorance, often total, about school issues such as finance, law, taxes, employment obligations, union agreements, salary schedules, and assessments can be devastating if they file an inaccurate report or misquote you or someone else. Young reporters need, and usually want, some on-the-job training. An hour spent giving a primer on, say, tax rates and levies will be an hour well invested in the future.

Never Guess!

Never guess an answer you give to the media. If you don't know, give them the name and number of someone who does, or get the information for them pronto. If you refer them to someone else, call that person *immediately* to give them fair warning. If the reporter asks for an unreasonable amount of information in a short amount of time, simply tell them that their request is unreasonable. If the reporter calls you and wants to talk just as you are about to enter a disciplinary hearing (with two parents, their kid who brought a gun to school, and a set of lawyers), refrain from telling the reporter why you can't talk at that moment. Just tell the reporter when you hope to be able to return the call. Be honest, but don't give anything away that may haunt you later. It would be foolish on your part if the reporter called to find out when the Christmas concert was scheduled and ended up getting a story about "Guns in the School!"

Don't Let the Interview Intimidate You!

When you are interviewed, ask the reporter to repeat what you said to make sure they understand the context and subject matter. If you are being interviewed for a taped TV spot and you think you made a mistake, don't delay but immediately turn away from the camera and say "I'd like to repeat that statement, if you don't mind." (Don't give them a pause before you ask because they may be able to delete your request and use the mistake.)

Never fear asking for a second chance to answer a question when you are being taped. If you are going to be interviewed live, ask the reporter what questions will be asked before the camera is turned on. Remember, you *don't* have to be interviewed, so don't be afraid to state some terms of your own. Never let the reporters (or crew) intimidate you. Remain calm and in control. Since you only have a few seconds to communicate effectively, use the time wisely. Even if they ask you questions for 10 minutes, the TV spot will still probably last 20 seconds.

We strongly urge any administrator to attend professional development workshops on working with the media. You never know when you may be the target of a story, a tragedy, an event, or a situation. Having some basic training in media communications is extremely helpful.

Remain Calm and Cooperate

Finally, when working with the media, don't be nervous. Be calm, be yourself, be firm, and be kind. Remember that they have a job to do and if you help them do it, you will all be pleased with the results. Try to know the deadline and help the reporter meet it. Understand that you cannot control the media but you can make it a positive part of your job. If you feel you have been treated unfairly, call that reporter and share your concern. Ask what you might do to ensure an improved relationship in the future. If you write a letter to the editor, remember it may be printed as a "Letter to the Editor." I have found that most media people want to like you and build a relationship with you. They are hard working and usually under a lot of stress, just like you. Letting them know that you understand the difficulty of working under a deadline and a budget helps. Thank them when they report a story fairly (even if it didn't support your position), and thank their supervisors as well. Be considerate and cooperative. It usually pays huge dividends.

Effective Communication Ideas

Here are some additional lessons we have learned the hard way, as well as some things that have made our lives easier.

1. When you use email, *always* check to see who is copied. Most people get in trouble when they reply to someone's email and fail to realize that 10 other people are going to get the same response. Been there, done that. Double-check *every* email and *every* recipient!

2. Be smart when you use email. You can save lots of time by using list serves that send one email to a set group of people. Learn how to use the "automatic reply" so that when you are gone, the sender knows that you will not be able to respond immediately. I usually indicate when I will be back and apologize for missing his/her email. A typical automatic response would be, "This is an automatic reply. I am unable to receive emails until Wednesday at which time I will respond as soon as possible. Sorry to miss your message." One more thing, be sure to remove the automatic reply on Wednesday!

3. Don't gossip. Ever. Don't tell inappropriate jokes, never put them in print, never send them via email, and never share them with anyone you don't know. Better yet, don't tell them at all.

4. Never, never, never send, share, or copy anything that is pornographic. One time can cost you your job.

5. Remember that employees do their best work for bosses who lead by example, are ethical, clearly define expectations, speak kindly, care about work and home, communicate with integrity, and are enthusiastic.

6. Employees are less likely to do their best when their boss is disrespectful of their time, is never wrong, speaks in circles, writes sarcastic or negative memos, is cynical, or is unfair and inconsistent.

7. Send lots of positive, constructive, complimentary notes, letters, cards, and memos. Don't send them if you aren't sincere.

8. Always have at least one person proofread anything you plan to share in writing. It is best if two people proof your work by reading it aloud to each other and jointly make corrections. (But don't use illiterate people.)

9. When someone talks, listen. Don't look around the room—look directly at the speaker. Don't talk on the phone when someone has made an appointment to speak with you in your office. Either disable the phone when they come in or, if you have to answer, tell the caller that you will have to get back with him/her later. That person must feel that he/she has your undivided attention.

10. Use spell checker and grammar checker for even the shortest and simplest memo. Always try to make every written communication as good as possible.

11. Read the section in Chapter 13 about how to communicate assessments. This is an extremely important job for most adminis-

trators and one where effective communication is essential. The tips about assessments in Chapter 13, written jointly by my writing partners, is probably the best outline of this type you will find anywhere.

12. When faced with the task of giving a speech—regardless its length—make sure that you prepare your information well, practice the speech several times under different circumstances, and deliver it using all that you learned in speech class. Stand tall. Don't have your hands in your pockets—give all your loose change to poor people before you start speaking! Remember that notes are not bad, nor is a prepared script, as long as you know the content well enough to be able to have *lots of eye contact* with the audience.

13. If you delegate the job of writing your speech or article to someone else, before you say a word be absolutely certain that you know and understand what he or she wrote and that you agree with the content. And practice, practice, practice.

14. When communicating with legislators, be concise, clear, and complimentary. Hand written thank-you notes are much appreciated. Many times the legislator will read a summary of your communication rather than the actual message. What he or she may see is a summary that says this, "Supt. Jones does NOT support HB56, complimented your work ethic, thanked you for your previous help." Or the summary might say, "Supt. Jones does NOT support HB56, was abrupt, had nothing positive to say." Which way do you want your legislator to remember you? It also helps to send positive press clippings with notes written in the margins, to make short and unscheduled visits to his/her office just to say thanks, and to personally share with the legislator that you recognize the difficulty of his/her job.

Summary

My goal in this chapter has been to emphasize the importance of effective communications, plus share some examples and tips. Communication is the presentation of well-planned information. The more trusted you are, the easier it is to communicate effectively. All communications should be based on honest information presented in a tactful manner, always respectful of the receiver. To effectively share a message, you need to understand that the quality of the communication can be secondary if you don't have enough ways to get the message delivered and read.

Never be afraid to admit you don't have all the answers, but always seek to find them. Never fail to apologize when you make an error in information or judgment.

There are many ways to share a message, report a finding, give a compliment, or report an event. Be creative and look for the best vehicles possible.

The media, more often than not, is a friend of the public school. A good administrator builds a strong relationship with reporters and mediafolk. Offer to help them remain honest, understand the reporters' stress and responsibilities, and work toward meeting their objectives as well as your schools'. Training in media relations is a must for all administrators.

Keeping track of what works for you and what does not work is a good idea. Brainstorming with others in your community about the specifics of a particular situation is also a good idea. One of the best recommendations is to proof what you write, prepare and practice what you say, and always think before you engage in any form of communication.

"Trust men and they will be true to you; treat them greatly and they will show themselves great."

Ralph Waldo Emerson

Chapter Five

Building and Sustaining Trust

Max McGee

One can rarely pick up a paper without reading about corrupt leaders in government, the private sector, and even in church. The headlines are so incredible that even the supermarket tabloids cannot match those we read in our trusted daily newspapers.

At the time of this writing, the former Governor of Illinois was just found guilty on 27 different counts in federal court and the Chief of Staff of the former Republican Illinois House Leader is also in jail.

Chief Executive Officers and Chief Financial Officers from top companies such as Enron, World Com, and Tyco fabricated financial data. "Cooking the books" made them millions but left thousands of employees and investors without a nickel.

Stories of sexual misconduct by priests filled headlines across the country in 2002.

Even a widely-read and respected newspaper columnist, who wrote compellingly about abused children and crusaded to change the outcomes of child abuse cases and the underlying child welfare laws, resigned because of a past dalliance with a teenager.

In times like these, you may wonder why someone should trust you. Or if anyone will. Our answer is that you are one of the few people left to trust. If parents and taxpayers can't trust their teachers and administrators, there is hardly anyone left. How can children learn to be trusting and trustworthy without models? They cannot.

In this chapter, we explore four elements of trust: actively earning trust, being a trusting leader, recovering from loss of trust, and the ethics of leadership.

Actively Earning Trust

Trust does not automatically spring from the ground like crocuses in April. It must be actively nurtured. To earn trust, you must work at it every day. Here are a dozen tips:

1. **Make minimal promises**, but keep those you make. This is much easier said than done. We all recall times when we were confronted with requests and we said maybe, not yes. We might have phrased our response "I will look into the matter" or "I don't think I can help you but let me see what I can do." A few days later, we hear from the requesting party that we have gone back on our word because they heard that we said yes or that we had even promised to grant the request.

The message we say is not always the message they hear. To avoid falling into a trap, it should be your stated policy not to make promises. Phil Rock, a legendary president of the Illinois Senate had a saying on his desk, "No one stops by just to say hello." That is good advice for school leaders. As witty and charming as you may be, most people come to see you because they want something.

When people make requests of you and are looking for definitive commitments, we suggest three things. First, insist that any request be made in writing. Second, at the conclusion of the meeting, have them repeat what you said, and third, follow up the meeting with a quick written note. Though momentarily time-consuming, it will ultimately save a great deal more time, enhance your credibility, and increase respect for you.

I learned this lesson the hard way. During the three years I served as State Superintendent, not a day went by when people didn't ask for money for some special program. Often I felt that I was perceived more as a venture capitalist or an ATM than a State Superintendent. One very talkative and incredibly well-connected woman asked for an additional $800,000 for a teacher education program. I definitely told her no for the current year, but that I would consider putting it in a future budget. A month later, she came with her legislator looking for her money. When I told her no again, she claimed I had promised her the money and went to the governor and chairman of the state Board claiming that I broke a promise. Knowing she was an individual who could talk nonstop for 30 minutes and seldom, if ever, listened to anyone else in the room, I was foolish not to follow up the meeting with a written memo stating my definitive denial of her request.

2. **Develop a small set of goals and priorities**, let everyone know them, and show what you are doing to accomplish them. The key word here is small—like two or three. By focusing on two or three top priorities, publishing these, discussing them in speeches and presentations, reminding your staff of them, and engaging others in helping you achieve them, you build support for your vision—and trust. Without this set of goals, your time, energy, and effort will be needlessly diluted. You will probably be doing a lot of things, but none of them very well.

For example, each year my goals, along with specific measures and deliverables, are published on our website found at www.wilmette39.org. As you can see, they are quite ambitious. Seldom, however, does a day go by without parents, staff, Board members, or legislators coming up with new goals, additional projects, and other demands—98% of which are both reasonable and good. The challenge, however, is to stay focused on your "mission critical" goals and projects and find ways to support good ideas worth pursuing while not making them your own work. An advantage to published priorities is that it gives you cover to say no firmly and politely, then point out why the other goals are of a higher priority. Though others may not always like the answer, the recipients of the response respect the honesty and, in most instances, have been more than willing to assist me in addressing the key projects. willing to assist me in addressing the key projects.

3. **Return all phone calls and answer your emails**. People who contact you have something important to say. You need to get back to them promptly. Brevity of response is important. When returning calls, stick to the point and be brief. When responding to emails, if you cannot respond in three sentences, use the phone or dictate a response. I am always amazed that people have the time to write me two- and three-page emails, frequently packed with questions. More often than not, I pick up the phone and in five minutes answer the questions that would have taken me 45 minutes to type and send.

4. **Be punctual**. Nothing erodes trust like showing up late. People don't assume you are busy. They assume you don't really care, or you are arrogant, or that you have become "too high and

mighty." People trust people who respect them. Showing up on time is a sign of respect.

5. **Avoid over-committing yourself**. I learned this lesson the hard way. As a true extrovert comfortable with ambiguity and a doer who thrives on change, I tend to commit myself to far too many projects. For example, this month I had a book chapter and two articles to complete, three major speeches to give, a Half-Ironman Extreme triathlon to survive—all with a district to run, my garage to clean, and my family to love. The articles still aren't done, one of the speeches was truly lousy, and my wife is aggravated because the garage remains a disaster. But everything else actually went well! It is safe to say that those expecting the articles are far less likely to trust me than they were a month ago, so my credibility with them is damaged.

On a more serious note, as State Superintendent I worked hard to keep every commitment that I made, like being out "in the field." Yet, while crisscrossing Illinois with speeches, visits, and meetings with legislators, I neglected my duties as an agency manager. Though I didn't intend to let the agency run itself, there was simply not enough time—or a competent assistant—to take care of business at the office. Many of my staff felt abandoned, others were angry, Board members were peeved that legislators and superintendents got more attention than they did, and even a couple of my top assistants "went off the farm" complaining to the Board about being ignored. Credibility with my own staff was stretched to the breaking point because I had made too many commitments to the field and to legislators.

It was a painful but important lesson. As a chronic over-committer, I have to remind myself that trust is far more important than saying "yes" to every interesting project or than trying to be everything to everyone. We all trust individuals who are "men of their word." These are people who have learned to make a manageable number of commitments.

6. **Under-promise and over-deliver**. This has worked well in the corporate world for Intel and others with multi-year track records of success. In reverse, individuals or companies who over-promise and under-deliver are not around long. They are the Professor Harold Hills, the con men, and the "slick Willies." They leave dashed dreams, crushed expectations, and faded hopes in their wake. Aside from outright lying or criminal offenses, nothing

destroys trust faster than falsely increasing expectations. Superintendents who have learned to set just a few goals, talk about two or three expectations, and then deliver on them are trusted. We believe that lack of trust is the greatest reason for short career tenure and that trust is usually eroded when performance does not match expectations.

Again, we have found it easy to say "no" when we consider the value and importance of trust. For example, this year, a Board subcommittee and I worked on my performance goals. At the end to our sessions, we had more goals than the Old Country Buffet has dishes. There were nine goals, each with four or five deliverables. Needless to say, I expressed my discomfort verbally and also in writing to the entire Board, noting that "the scraping sound you hear is Max being spread too thinly." The Board president jumped in and within a week I had a manageable number of goals and a very doable set of deliverables.

7. **Know the names of most of your staff**. One of the most effective ways to enhance your credibility is to learn those names. People will respect you more and will work harder for bosses who care about them. If they know that you take time to learn the names of your teachers—and especially the support staff—you will be trusted far more than if you do not. Remember, you do not teach kids; the teachers do. Your success depends on those teachers, so learning their names should top your priority list. If you are not particularly "good at names," take a staff list with you when you visit a school; have a building administrator send you the staff group picture, with names written on them; or just walk around the school with a building administrator who will whisper names to you as you pop into classrooms or meet someone in the hall.

8. **Treat *every* member of your organization with dignity, respect, and cordiality**. One of the best ways to build and maintain credibility is to be courteous and considerate of everyone—especially those well down the "corporate ladder." Respecting hourly wage earners by spending time talking with them not only enhances credibility throughout the agency as the word quickly spreads, but it also gives you the chance to learn things about the "real world" of your organization. The maintenance employees will love it when you show up with donuts at the beginning of the day and talk about projects they are doing. Nor does it hurt to roll

up your sleeves occasionally to shovel snow, pick up trash, or pol-
ish a mirror.

Other successful superintendents are good about sending a
personal handwritten note to a lunchroom worker, a playground
supervisor, or a similar type of employee who has gone "above
and beyond." Too often, the "big boss" is perceived as someone
who at best patronizes the "worker bees" but more often berates
them. Not a day goes by that I don't spend a few minutes with a
bus driver, a custodian, a building secretary, or a teacher's aide. I
enjoy it immensely and usually learn something. Moreover, my
credibility as someone who sincerely cares about people has been
enhanced.

9. "**Do not distort the facts with your own biases or agendas**," advise top management consultants Susan H. Gebelein, Lisa
A. Stevens, Carol J. Skube, David G. Lee, Briann L. Davis, and
Lowell W. Hellervik in *Sucessful Managers Handbook: Development Suggestions for Today's Managers*[1]. That is good advice.
People are wary of those who appear to distort arguments in order
to win them. Use accurate facts and ask others to discuss them. A
superintendent's sin of omission will create as big a problem as his
or her sin of commission. For example, when summarizing comments from a community survey, we need to present both the positive and the negative points. When using educational research to
support a proposal, we must at least acknowledge contradictory
research, if it exists. It will enhance others' trust in us and we will
more often get what we want if we present data objectively.

10. **State your personal agenda on an issue openly**. Effective superintendents are first and foremost leaders. As leaders,
they have strongly held opinions and educational agendas. They
have strong beliefs about where to put the "first dollar" of their
budget. The public and staff trust and respect leaders who advo-
cate an agenda and build a shared vision. They do not trust or follow individuals who try to get what they want through "back
door" or political means. As State Superintendent, I believed that
the most effective way to close the achievement gap at the upper
grades was to ensure that all students had the opportunity to participate in a core curriculum. Knowing that "what gets tested gets
taught," I worked hard to incorporate a college entrance examina-

---

[1] Minneapolis: Personnel Decisions International, 2000, p. 567.

tion, the ACT, into the statewide high school test. Though many local superintendents and not a small number of legislators— including the Senate president—disagreed, they respected my conviction and energy as I stumped across the state. Eventually, my efforts were successful and my credibility as a leader who put the needs of kids first flourished. Now many more students in Illinois are eligible to go to college because they did better on the ACT than projected. New opportunities came to their lives because of this change. These results have made my efforts worthwhile.

11. **Avoid the use of sarcasm**. People respond differently to sarcasm—some think it is funny while others think it is hurtful. Few, however, truly trust a sarcastic leader because they realize they may be the next victim. Remember, you are the professional; do not get caught up in the trap of sarcasm.

12. **Be careful about public disagreements**. As a leader, you are under an electron microscope. Public hearings and Board meetings are a favorite place for community members to launch an attack. Though tempted to reduce them to a sniveling mess with your quick wit and skillful repartee—or else clobber them with a verbal Louisville Slugger—why not use confrontation as an opportunity to build trust in you by being an active listener, keeping a cool head, and responding in a measured manner?

It is all right to disagree, providing you do so civilly. It is important, however, to respond. Not doing so fans the flames and can give the impression that you are concealing something. So it's important to respect the dignity of the loudmouth, to acknowledge that you have heard him, and to express your disagreement in a straightforward, rational manner. This is easier said than done. When confronted, we instinctively move into the "flight or fight" mode. It is important to realize that this is an automatic response, but one that can be controlled. Resist the temptation to fly or fight. Take time to gather your thoughts. Repeat the gist of the comment. Turn it into a question. Make one or two key points, then move on. If nothing else, have him leave his phone number and call him first thing in the morning.

I remember very clearly being confronted on a radio show heard by millions of people. The caller was livid; the State Board had done some horrible thing that affected her family. My response was to restate her problem, "Let me get this straight. I believe I heard you say that…" I continued, "I need to look into this and will give it my personal attention. Please give me your number—or better yet, here is mine. Let's talk once we get off the air and solve this problem." I could almost hear the applause while the morning radio personality complimented me on being forthright before several hundred thousand listeners.

Trusting

To be trusted, you must be both trustworthy and trusting. If you don't trust others, they won't trust you. This means that you trust people to do a good job and help them if they falter. You trust others to complete delegated tasks and point out problems if and when they occur. You trust your Board members to read their packets and not to surprise you at meetings. You trust your spouse and your kids to tell the truth and to support you.

This sounds naïve to many leaders. Unless you know the people with whom you live and work, it probably is. Trusting others is built upon relationships. When you have a close relationship, trust follows. The key to being a trusting and trustworthy leader is the power of relationships. Here are some questions to ponder:

1. Does your staff know about your hobbies, your children, or a book that you have read? You build trust to the extent that you are willing to share a bit of your personal life. Your staff wants to know you, and they will trust you more if they believe they have a personal relationship with you. Think about peers that you trust. You are much more likely to trust what you hear from a colleague whom you know well. Sharing personal information shows that you are trusting.

2. Do you have a reputation as a good listener? Good listening shows others that you trust them. Trust is strengthened through relationships, which, in turn, are built on active listening. When someone talks to you, put everything else aside. Eye contact, nodding, summarizing key points are all indicators of being a good listener. Taking notes is not as important as intently focusing in on what a person is saying.

I learned my greatest lesson in listening from one of my teachers when I was a principal. Susan never said or heard a word without eye contact. Even when taking a class of kids to the gym and passing other teachers in the hallway, she maintained eye contact for every hello and good-bye. The eye contact made the staff and students feel that she listened to every word and that they were important to her. She was also a favorite of parents because her eye contact sent a non-verbal message of understanding and reassurance that they were partners in their children's education. Without question, she was the most trusted and credible staff member. Contrast this behavior to those of other colleagues who, while shaking your hand, are looking over your shoulder to see who else is in the room, who finish your sentences, or who glance at their watch or the clock.

3. Do people share confidences and do you keep them? Do you, in turn, share confidences? Protecting confidential information is extremely important. You must learn to keep secrets and to never, ever break a confidence. Information is power these days, and confidential information is big currency. By trusting others not to share confidential information you give them, you demonstrate that you trust them. The most successful leaders are both trustworthy and trusting about protecting and sharing confidences.

Trusting, like trust, is built on consistency between words and actions. "You are judged by your actions, not your intent."[2] People admire those who keep their word and "walk the talk." Actions do speak louder than words, as does demonstrating that you trust people. You can give them responsibility for presentations to your school Board and community. You can publicly recognize their accomplishments and achievements. You can delegate meaningful leadership opportunities.

Recently, a fire consumed a home across the street from the front of an elementary school just as students were arriving there. The principal and staff handled the emergency with calm and concern. They rerouted buses around to the back of the school, met the children walking and being dropped off in cars and escorted them to the back of the building, and found creative places for classrooms when smoke blew across the street. When the four major networks arrived to cover the blaze, the superintendent chose not to have the district spokesperson speak with reporters or to do it himself. He let the principal have the limelight, trusting that she would communicate how well her staff handled the situation. She

---

[2] Ibid, p. 574.

did better than the others would have, and what could have been a tragedy turned into an opportunity to strengthen the community's faith in the school leaders and staff.

Give full and honest answers to tough questions. In this day of the "sound bite," people seek short, meaty answers. More often than not, however, tough questions require elaboration. To be trusted, be sure to answer tough questions thoroughly and completely. Do not reach for facts or cite statistics that you can't back up.

A good example concerns a top official's responses to questions regarding teacher shortages. Depending on the day of the week, we hear that 30%, 33%, 40%, or 50% (choose one) of teachers in their first, second, third, or fourth (choose one) year of service leave the profession because they were not mentored, not paid well, or had poor principals (choose one). Needless to say, her penchant for throwing out numbers has reduced her credibility with superintendents to zero, none, or *nada* (choose one).

Here are a few other helpful hints. Do not waffle. If you must change your mind, explain the reason for it. Elaborate on your thinking. Bullet-point your reasons and speak with conviction, and do *not* change your mind on this same issue again.

When giving out information, distribute it to as many people as possible. This shows you trust them. All people want to hear from you so give them the opportunity to. If you make a presentation or hold a forum, tape it and give it to your public access cable station to show. Put your overheads on your website for people to view.

Be personally accessible. For the last twenty years, I have given everyone my office and home phone number. I also publish my office and personal email addresses. Get out of the office and meet people. Remember, people trust those they know. They need to meet you and see you in action. Stay for faculty meetings, attend lunches, and teach a class now and then.

Avoid playing favorites. If you play favorites, you are in effect saying that you trust some staff but not others. One of the quickest ways to undermine trust is for members of your team to think you favor others more. (Sibling rivalry is a close second to administrative and staff jealousy.) Being human, you will like some people more than others. You will also rely on some more than others. As a leader, however, you aren't allowed that humanness. You cannot show that you favor, listen to, or reward one more than another.

I guarantee that, although you think that you treat everyone equally, you probably don't. A 360 evaluation is a good reality check. It will give you the information you need (but probably don't want to see). It's not for the thin-skinned because it enables your school Board *and* your staff to evaluate you. I recommend that you do not try to use your own instrument but contract with a firm that does this sort of evaluation with follow-up assistance. You will learn how others perceive your leadership and whether or not they trust you. It will reveal the extent to which you play favorites. In my case, I learned as a principal in 1981 that some staff trusted me more than others, and that the staff thought I played favorites. Based on their feedback, which as a first-year principal was extremely hard to swallow, I changed my behavior. As State Superintendent in 2001, I learned that I had a similar problem with some State Board members who felt they were not getting the amount of attention they needed. Needless to say, the sirens rang and I changed my behavior immediately. For example, I had assumed they all read my weekly email updates. I discovered that two never did and two only did occasionally. I decided that they needed phone calls instead of emails.

Seek out feedback and pay attention to it. People trust those who care enough to ask for opinions and then do something with the information they receive. Please read that whole sentence again. Too often, we ask for opinions but then go right on behaving as before. If you are not willing to change, do not ask.

Recovering

This section is for those who have or may soon lose the trust of their staff, their Board, or their parent community. Loss of trust is one of the most serious problems we can face.

Why does it happen? Because school leaders are human too. Not only do we look remarkably like the photo on our driver's license, but we can be jerks or lose our composure just like anybody else. Still, we are properly held to higher expectations, to be civic models.

Although difficult, recovering that lost trust is not impossible. But it is time-consuming and must be at the top of our agenda every day. It also requires an observable change in our behavior. How much time, how much effort, and what kind of action is necessary to restore the trust are determined to a certain extent by the degree of the loss and how it occurred.

Before understanding how to rebuild trust, let's look at the most common ways that school leaders can create mistrust. They usually fall into one of four categories: misspeaking, misusing company time and materials, alcohol or drug abuse, and sexual misconduct.

Misspeaking

Misspeaking usually means lying. But breaking a confidence, over-promising and under-delivering, and even failing to share important information can also fall into this category. Overinflating results, overstating a problem (or a solution), exaggerating the impact of an event, and "stretching" individual accomplishments are other examples. Leaders who engage in these activities quickly lose credibility no matter how likable they are or how honorable their intentions.

Misusing Company Time and Materials

Misusing company time and materials is, sadly, too common a charge. School districts are beginning to restrict Internet access because they are finding staff (primarily administrative and clerical) spending too much professional time on personal business: checking their stocks, sending personal emails, and dabbling on E-Bay. School computers are school property and should be used solely for school business. When staff gets word that an administrator is spending personal time on the Internet, trust is compromised. Likewise, school leaders with an active consulting business, or any other independent business, need to be cautious that they relegate time for pursuing these interests to personal days, holidays, or weekends. Be upfront and forthright with Board members and staff about your consulting business. Remember that if they perceive that your heart and head are in other pursuits, some of your credibility as a school or district leader will be lost.

Alcohol and Substance Abuse

Alcohol and substance abuse is too often found in individuals with high-pressure jobs. Even when administrators don't drink on the job, their social misadventures can create serious professional problems. Parents and teachers expect their leaders to set examples for children, so a DUI ticket or being apprehended for marijuana can create a breech in trust that may be irreparable.

Sexual Misconduct

Sexual misconduct—viewing Internet pornography, sexual harassment (like telling off-color jokes to members of the opposite sex), or having an affair—causes much mistrust. As examples for children and teachers, school leaders simply cannot dabble in sexual misadventure. One incident may be all it takes for them to be sent packing, whatever success they had known in the past.

Though some of these categories are far more serious than others, most can be fixed (provided you still want to be a school leader who can make a positive difference in the lives of children). If you are trying to recover trust to keep your job until retirement or for financial gain, our recommendation is, find another job.

How does one recover?

We recommend prevention as the first step. Recognize your foibles and resolve them. If fatigue is causing you to misspeak, forget promises, or impair your judgment, you must get more rest or learn a way to keep yourself organized and on track. This book has an entire chapter called "Taking Care of YOU." Following its recommendations may help in that prevention.

If you have a consulting business or are involved in another venture, schedule time off to work on these projects—and keep your Board and staff informed. When you are with them, be 100% there. When you are working on your other job or project, stay away from the school or office. Most contracts provide plenty of vacation days and personal days to take care of other business.

Having willpower is the best prevention for the other behaviors, from too much Internet browsing to sexual misconduct. Recognize that these are addictive behaviors and learn how to control your actions. Changing your behavior is not as easy as it sounds. There are many "self-help" books on the market that can be useful. Most emphasize the need for assistance from a significant other such as a spouse, relative, friend, cleric, or support group. Changing potentially destructive activities may take professional counseling or some other intervention, like medical treatment or a dietary adjustment. Whatever the case, denying that a behavioral problem—or even a potential problem—exists can cause you much pain while others' trust erodes and your job is in jeopardy.

The strongest leaders know when and where they are weak, and they solve those problems. President Bush is a good example. Early in his business and political career, he was an admitted "partier" and drinker. Realizing that even his social drinking was a problem, he quit. During his presidency, he has also fought fatigue and stress with rigorous exercise.

If prevention fails, you will need to work long and hard to rebuild trust. The first step will be to stop denying or trying to rationalize what you did wrong. Though denial is *always* the first stage in response to questions about your integrity or an addiction, it is just a first stage. "It is critically important that you really hear how the other person was affected. To rebuild trust you need to hear and understand what you did from the other's point of view."[3] That means admitting to those affected that you have made a mistake and that you are going to change. They will be hostile and skeptical for a long time and will watch you very, very closely; your actions will truly need to speak louder than your words.

It will take a long time for your new actions to have an impact—a very long time. The time will be measured in years, not weeks. You will get over it far more quickly than the affected parties. Realize that, be patient, and keep acting in trustworthy ways.

As you strive to rebuild trust, focus on rebuilding damaged relationships and strengthening the strongest ones. As noted above, you will need support from important people in your life and you will need to spend time with those whose trust you lost. Seeking outside assistance is not an indicator of weakness, rather it is a measure of strength. Although the process is long and painful, the recovery will make you a better leader and a better model.

Our final piece of advice is to simplify your professional life. If rebuilding trust has become a top priority, you have to delegate more responsibilities. Not only will this give you more time to renew relationships, it will also show others that you trust them. Delegating important tasks will actually help speed the rebuilding process.

As a final observation, we have found that when trust issues arise, leaders tend to move or be moved. If you have lost or are about to lose trust, we encourage you to stay in your situation. Your students and teachers need consistent, strong leadership.

---

[3] Ibid, p. 579.

Having the courage to remain in your position and grow as you address your problems will be an important example for them.

Ethics

One of the positive results of rampant corruption in corporations, churches, and government is an increased need to discuss ethics. You must lead this discussion and constantly be the ethical "watchdog." You need to point out when any staff or Board member is behaving in an inappropriate or unethical manner. First and foremost, it is your job to point this out to that person in private. You need to explain your thinking and provide help for them. If you don't do something, you are supporting it. Silence means consent.

What constitutes a disruption in ethics? Of course, there are the obvious cases like lying or submitting false reimbursement claims—even taking home paper clips, toilet paper, and supplies. None of those is acceptable, and it may well be worthwhile to point out that the consequences are severe.

Consider this true story from the early 80s. A superintendent decided that ditto fluid (in that murky past before copiers and computers) would also make good charcoal lighter. He took a can home and sprayed some on the charcoal. Lo and behold, it worked! The charcoal burst into flame. Deciding that a little more would get the coals glowing even more quickly, he held up the can and shot out another stream. You guessed it! The flames shot back into the can and it exploded, leaving the superintendent with excruciatingly painful injuries.

Other current and common unethical behaviors are inappropriate Internet use, accepting favors from vendors, and racial and ethnic jokes. What can you do about them?

1. Remind your staff that school computers are your school's property and that you can track every keystroke that comes in and every keystroke that goes out.

2. Forego invitations and gifts. The old days of long lunches, an afternoon of golf at a swank club followed by a big steak dinner, box seat tickets, and the like are long gone. Favors from vendors did, and still can, influence your decisions, and it takes a strong will to simply say "no thanks" to generous offers. Board

members, your staff, and the public expect that you will make decisions based on merit and not on favors. Though you may have made up your mind long ago not to let an afternoon of free golf influence a decision, no one else will see it that way. Perceptions and appearances are the reality of credibility.

During my tenure as State Superintendent, Illinois actually had a law—the Gift Ban Act—that prohibited public officials at a certain level from accepting gifts over a minimum value. If I attended a vendor-sponsored dinner, I paid for my own meal. If I went to a ball game, I paid for my own ticket. Though the law is now off the books, it became a valuable habit and, to this day, legislators and other leaders still comment publicly on my ethical credibility in that office.

3. Don't tolerate . My father was a social activist long before it was fashionable; I got into teaching because I liked working with poor, minority students. My wife has spent nearly two decades working with students in one of the toughest neighborhoods of Chicago, North Lawndale, about which Jonathan Kozol wrote in **Savage Inequalities**,[4] which was the subject of another great book, Alex Kotlowitz's **There Are No Children Here**.[5] Needless to say, we do not think racial or ethnic jokes are funny.

We suggest that you make it clear that you do not tell or like racial or ethnic jokes—and there is a penalty for telling them at or through your school. They are demeaning; there are plenty of other ways to create laughter. Be assured that if you tell one or even pass one along via email, the word will be out in a matter of minutes. That laugh may well cost you your reputation, possibly even your job. Whether or not you are racist, you will be quickly labeled as one.

The bottom line is that the best defense against unethical behavior is a good offense. We recommend effective written policies that are clear and specific. We believe that you should have guidelines for dealing with vendors and that you should have written standards for Internet use, for using company property away from the school site, and for accepting gifts that parents give to schools or staff members.

---

[4] New York: Harper Perennial, 1992.
[5] New York: Anchor Books, 1992.

Summary

To be an effective leader, you need to be trustworthy and trusting. "Trust is built on fulfilled promises."[6] Keeping promises, consistency between words and actions, and attentiveness to relationships are critically important. Remember that actions do speak louder than words, so taking time to learn staff names, listening carefully, and demonstrating ethical behaviors go a long way in building trust. If you violate trust or lose credibility, you can recover. The process is long and often painful, but quickly moving from denial to action, immediately curbing the behavior that got you in trouble, and rebuilding relationships can work.

---

[6] Gebelein, p. 575.

**"The first step to leadership
is servanthood."**

John Maxwell

Chapter Six

Planning

Jim Burgett

*A plan is an organized and scheduled approach
to reaching a goal.*

In the Beginning

I'm sitting in a hotel room in Peoria, Illinois as I begin to write
this chapter. It is a suite, actually, and a fairly nice one to boot. I
arrived here last night—in truth, about 1:30 this morning—having
driven directly from a school Board meeting 150 miles away. I'm
here because in a few hours I will be addressing principals, assistant principals, and aspiring principals on the topic of ethics. Tomorrow, I will lead a full-day workshop on effective leadership.
My schedule in the past few weeks has been horrendous. I have
been speaking "on the circuit." Before the month is over, I will
have logged more than 2,000 miles in the car, plus jaunts to
Washington, D.C., and Arizona, all while putting in my normal
60-plus hours per week as superintendent of my district. Successfully accomplishing all this requires the work of a master planner.

Sounds good, doesn't it? But I'm not really a master planner
at all. I've become fairly good at it, but planning takes both a lot
of thinking and a vast amount of, well, planning! If I were a true
master planner, I wouldn't have had to call my wife a few minutes
ago and ask her to overnight me a videotape that I need for the
meeting tomorrow. I would also have called the hotel late yester-
day afternoon and "reminded" them of my very late arrival last
night, so they would have tagged a room for me. As it turns out,
tomorrow I will be forced to move from this luxury suite and oc-
cupy my more normal nonsmoking, one-bed digs a few feet from

the only noisy air conditioner in the hotel. Master planners don't waste time and energy repacking, relocating, unpacking, and re-booting.

Planning Comes in Two Sizes

Planning comes in two sizes, which I will simply call the Big Plan (like a strategic plan) and the Day Plan. Doing both at least adequately is essential to becoming a successful school administrator. I'm much better on the Big Plan—and I'm getting better with the Day Plan. At least I now have my $29 roll-around suitcase packed with all my materials for my presentations. I have double-checked it and feel confident that everything that I'm in control of for today and tomorrow is ready, except, of course, that missing video. I even double-checked the request form I submitted months ago to make sure that I asked the organization for exactly what I need for my presentation. My Big Plan is in place and the daily stuff is in control. How I got it done is something I will share a little later.

In this chapter, I will focus much more on the Big Plan than the Day Plan. The Big Plan is breaking the large-range strategies and dreams that you, your Board, and scores of others involved in your enterprise want to put in effect, in manageable parts, in the coming days, weeks, months, and years.

Superintendents are school generals, and it's up to them to get the goals, troops, equipment, morale, and whatever else they need into some marching order. But we don't want the cooks lined up in front of the artillery or one battalion attacking tonight and its flanking support rallying to its defense next June!

Principals are the captains and majors, with their own Big Plans too.

So, as a school leader, you make the Big Plans, design the orders, prioritize, rev up the troops, and give the command to go. (Generals also reject, defer, phase out, and share with other divisions.)

Some generals (and some captains and majors) have others who design their Day Plans and see that they stick to them. Here the analogy breaks down. In your school-based world, you are your own daily planner! Yes, life is unfair. (But at least you don't have to wear a uniform or salute. I hope!)

I am about to discuss the two most important things school generals must do: deal with plans that make major changes (like building a new school, raising cumulative test scores, meeting AYP, and much more) and implementing the School Improvement Planning (SIP) process. I will walk you through each process, showing you what works best in each.

Then I will return to this breathless example in Peoria and the many ways that others also set up their Day Plans. I'll even offer a process for faking it when you goof.

The Big Plan

Don't bother to hunt for the terms "Big Plan" or "Day Plan" in those academic tomes about the planning process. I've simplified the terms because I think we make too big a deal of the process and at times get caught up in rhetoric and redundancy. Planning is really quite basic and logical. The Big Plan is merely a term that covers planning for something that you won't accomplish in one day. Call it long-term planning, strategic planning, planning for success, developing a life-plan, plan of attack, five-year plan, corporate plan, or whatever your heart desires. It all boils down to this: a Big Plan. What you do daily is the Day Plan.

Analyzing the Big Plan

To analyze the Big Plan, we need to return to the basic definition of planning: "An organized and scheduled approach to reaching a goal." The pivotal words are "organized," "scheduled," and "goal." Logically, then, the first thing you need to develop in a plan is a purpose. The purpose itself helps define if it is a Big Plan or a Day Plan. Building a new school, raising cumulative test scores, expanding the science curriculum, writing a book, investing for retirement, and improving the school's public relations program, all reek of long-term consideration and fall into the Big Plan category. They take longer than a day.

Big Plans require a bigger everything: More organization, more schedules, more details. By their generic nature, they usually scream for more participants, so planning becomes a shared activity. It's not more difficult, just more work.

Why is Planning Such a Challenge?

For some, planning seems impossible. Some of those who have a problem planning may have minds that are not well organized, or they can't visualize the steps needed to accomplish things, or perhaps they lack "go-do-it" leadership. Some simply may not care. We have all been in a group where a certain person raises his or her hand and says, "I'll take responsibility for that activity!" We sit back and say to ourselves, "With that person in charge, this activity will be a success!" But when someone we know, who is a card short in organizational skills, offers to take responsibility, we fear total disaster. We pray that another soul might rush in to help, just to prevent total mayhem.

If you are in the latter group, then say out loud "Planning is *not* difficult." Keep saying it to yourself as you craft a chart, write down goals, prepare timelines, build support, and work toward implementation.

Components of the Big Plan

Since much of the planning for the school administrator, who is responsible for running a building or district, falls under the heading of a Big Plan, let's look at some key concepts that will lead to success. These concepts are included in most school-related plans *except* the School Improvement Plan, which I will explain in detail later.

Clearly understand the goal

Here are some goals that administrators usually need to deal with at some point in their career: listing the needs of the school or district, providing more space for students, developing a breakfast program, increasing writing scores on the state test for third graders, and increasing attendance at parent-teacher conferences.

It may take a group to define the purpose and capture the specific goal in a concise and well-crafted statement. (Note that these sample goals are clear but they are not quantified. That comes later in the Big Plan process.)

Determine who will help develop the Big Plan

The Board may state that it wants certified teachers to help develop a plan concerning the third-grade writing scores. You may suggest that a broad-based committee needs to work on the list of needs for the district. You might ask the food service director, a representative sample of building principals, and two PTO members to help write the Big Plan for a breakfast program. The goal or purpose of the plan often determines the participants, but when in doubt about who should help, ask those who will most benefit once the purpose of the plan is understood.

Set a tentative timeline

For a truly Big Plan, you might want to state very general timelines. Here are some examples:

1. We will establish a planning committee within the next thirty days.

2. We will meet within a week of the committee being named.

3. We will meet every other week until a plan is agreed upon and finalized.

4. Our goal is to have this plan presented to the Board of Education no later than six months from today.

Plan to plan

Some administrators bristle at the thought of "planning to plan." They want definitive, time-referenced, action goals and aren't patient enough to realize that the bigger the plan, the greater the need for taking the time to establish *appropriate ownership*. Getting the right people working on the Big Plan may be the best reason for its ultimate success. Time spent planning the plan is time well spent. Sitting down and writing out a plan to plan, having it reviewed by others, and then moving on it is a good way to begin a Big Plan process.

Learn from others

Who said you have to reinvent the wheel when it comes to writing a Big Plan? In fact, why not pick the brains of someone who has had experience with successful planning? I have been asked by many organizations (schools, districts, professional educational organizations, churches, etc.) to help facilitate the development of a Big Plan. In no case did I help write the final plans. I merely facilitated the *process* and shared a "third party" perspective. Did any of these "planners" research a planning model? Did any of these "planners" come to the table with a format in mind? In most cases, the answer was no. They realized that if a person can facilitate a successful process in one place, that person can usually transfer that knowledge to another. Thus, they used my expertise to help them facilitate a process that let them develop their own plan. How did I learn the process? I watched someone else facilitate a top-notch Big Plan. Then I reviewed a couple of books, filtered out what I thought was excessive, and created a simple process that fits most situations.

Developing a Big Plan

To show you what I mean, let's walk through the development of a Big Plan for a school district. Let's say, "The Board of Education wants a long-term plan to identify and address critical issues in the district." Notice that the Board doesn't list the critical issues, the length of the plan, nor does it include any restrictions. This is a good foundation for a traditional Big Plan, one that's strategic in nature and long-term in duration. And this represents the actions of a good Board, one that allows the administration to do their jobs without micromanaging.

Who will develop the plan?
The answer to this question often sets the tone for success and should be related to another, more fundamental question. Who will be responsible for accepting and implementing the plan? If the City Council plans to build a new pool for the community but finds out after many months of planning and expense that no one in the community sees a need for the pool, the project is sunk. If, however, the planning process includes representation of pool planners, city fathers, *and* the potential users and taxpayers, the plan is more likely to succeed (or drown in apathy) before it gets work intensive. To best know if the plan has a chance, involve those who will be asked to work for and support the plan at the start. Therefore, the answer to "Who develops the plan?" is best answered by asking a more fundamental question, "Who will pay for and support the plan?"

In the school example, we are using the planning committee which usually includes a nearly equal number of consumers and educators.

How many should be on the Planning committee?

Ask yourself, "How many committee members will it take to provide adequate representation?" If you want community involvement and have 10 communities in your district, it seems like you might need 10 individuals, one representing each community. Understand that you can take those 10 and also use them to represent other segments of the population. For example, a farmer might represent Farmsville, while Pikestown might have a foreman from the Pike Valley Piston Company as the rep, thus giving you a secondary blend of agriculture and industry on the committee. You might also conclude that since demographics show 81% of your voters are 55 or older, you should include three committee representatives who are senior citizens.

You need the same careful consideration when picking the educators for the committee; for example, they may represent the Board, various grade levels, buildings, staff, administration, and unions. It pays to spend time carefully finding the representation you want.

Who makes the decision about who actually sits on the committee?

A select group usually makes that decision. You, the leader, pick that group. I would suggest that you choose two or three people to work with you who know the community, support the process, and would be willing to work on the committee. Then, before you actually contact the folks your group suggests, run the list by other people you trust (but who won't be on the committee), to see if there is another perspective or idea you have missed. It is also suggested that you specifically ask for names from the president, chair, or head of the interest groups, unions, or associations most likely to be involved or affected by the outcome of the plan. This, I highly recommend.

Do you just pick people who will support the plan?

You need a committee that will be viewed as representative of the population most involved with the plan. If a specific group of voters will have questions about this issue, include some people whom those questioners will respect. Some administrators have no objection to having "flaming radicals" on the committee, feeling that the others on the committee will tame them in the long run. Most often you will be most knowledgeable about the potential members, so think through the membership carefully. But if you pick Ned Negative or Carol Complainer, make sure they are in the minority. Speaking of minorities, include them too, plus folks with disadvantaged kids and important small group you hear from regularly. If you don't do a good job of getting adequate representation on a Big Plan committee, you may pay for it when you seek approval and support for the final product. Again, it pays to spend time on this part of the process.

Your final planning group needs to be open-minded, interested, willing to attend meetings regularly, and committed to helping you reach your goal. I give all prospective committee members a list of these expectations before I ask them to agree to serve. The list also includes an estimate of how many meetings it might take, probable meeting length, and where the meetings probably will be held. Then, I invite all potential committee members to ask any other questions before they commit.

How does my planning committee learn "how to plan?"

The answer depends on the nature of the project. If you are planning for a review of the science curriculum for grades 6-8, it will be much less involved than discovering the major issues facing the district. The procedures are similar but the process is shorter. In all cases, your planning should include the following important steps:

1. **Share and discuss your mission statement.** If it needs revision or replacement, make that the first step of your Big Plan. Nothing is more important than making sure that what you are doing is in line with the organization's mission! Unfortunately, some schools or districts do not have a mission statement. So if a mission statement is not in place, stop. Do not pass go. Write a mission statement! The very exercise of developing a mission statement is in itself a valuable experience. It results in the development of core beliefs and in a clear, concise statement of what the school and district value.

2. **Review the value or belief statements for the organization.** If it doesn't have such a list, one must be developed. This is critical to understanding the direction the district is headed and essential for establishing the foundation for successfully implementing any action resulting from this plan. A clear understanding of the assumptions of the plan and the core beliefs of the school or district are very important components of any Big Plan.

3. **Follow any parameters that have been established.** If other groups in your organization give you specific parameters to follow, be sure to share and review them. Examples might be: "All facility issues will be handled by the facility committee," "Revenue issues will not be part of this planning process and will be handled separately," and "All committees must have representation by the teachers' association."

4. **Review any research, data, or information that has been provided for the committee.** This has usually been done before the committee is organized. Demographics, legal documents, curriculum guides, statistical reports, financial documents, and historical background are examples of materials frequently assembled and given to the committee members days in advance of their first formal work meeting. These materials may be distributed at a preliminary, "get-acquainted" meeting. You must be aware that many people will not understand the data or reports given to them, and some will simply disregard them or, even worse, misinterpret them. Plan to spend some time in a session dedicated specifically to outlining the information and explaining it in detail. Make this learning session mandatory. (Some administrators include a "data class" at every Board meeting. It is not listed as such, but during the course of the meeting the administrator will take a few extra minutes and review numbers, terms, or other "data-like" material. The Board [and public] are being instructed and don't even know it.)

5. **It is imperative to set aside time to list and review the strengths and weaknesses of the organization**. Don't start from scratch with this process. The following recommendations come from experts in strategic planning about how to conduct this review:

* Small groups *brainstorm* perceived and real strengths and weaknesses of the organization, writing down lists of everything discussed. Consensus is not involved in this process. All ideas

during this session are listed and none are rejected. A specific amount of time is given for this process, usually less than an hour.

* The small groups immediately meet as one large group and each small group posts and shares its list, reading its items but not explaining them in depth. This is not a time for discussion, just sharing.

* After all the groups have presented their findings, the facilitator leads a process where the general similarities are listed, again not discussing the issues in depth, but in general. The facilitator circles those items on the lists that represent common strengths and weaknesses. No record of this process is kept, and all papers used are collected and destroyed. No names or specific situations are listed or discussed. That is a firm rule. Participants are told in advance how this process works and that the process is an "in-house" review, not for publication or sharing.

This process is excellent for developing strategies or specific goals because it addresses both the strong points and the needs of the organization. It helps everyone seek the good things that will serve as a foundation for improvement as well as for the areas that need strengthening. Most groups focus more on the good and this tends to bind the committee members together. While some find this exercise risky, if done the right way it is usually very, very beneficial.

6. **Write your strategies**. The next step is to combine all the previous information and form strategies or general goals, which defines the Big Plan in writing. It is important to note that different formats of the Big Plan define terms differently. You need to agree on the definition of "strategy" and "goal" for your situation. Many consider a strategy to be a process and a goal to be an outcome, yet others define strategies almost the same as goals. It is important that you have a clear definition of these terms as you work on your Big Plan. At this point in the process, it will be very easy to see the strategies that have evolved. Every step of the way has helped refine and define what your "Big Plan" should be.

The Planning Checklist
A quick review should indicate that you have done the following:

1. Carefully formed the group that will help select the members of the Big Plan Committee according to agreed upon parameters such as size, representation, and timelines.

2. The Big Plan Committee will review the assembled data and information sent to them before their first meeting (this may require a special "training session") so that when they start their formal meetings, they can intelligently discuss the data.

3. The Big Plan Committee will consider the organization's mission statement. If it needs revision, rewriting, or any changes, that will be considered and accomplished.

4. The Big Plan Committee will review the organizational value statements and parameters of their task. If none are available, they should consider taking the time to write some.

5. The Big Plan Committee will participate in an exercise listing and discussing the common strengths and weaknesses of the organization.

6. The Big Plan Committee will take all the information they have discussed and gathered and will use it to formulate goals or strategies.

General comments on procedures: All the steps listed, except for reviewing the data and research materials, are usually done in small group formats first, followed by a large group review of the small group's findings. During the large group review, consensus is reached on the specific items: mission statement, value statements, parameters, and strategies. A good facilitator is very important. The facilitator should be someone who is detached from the organization, familiar with leading this type of Big Plan process, and able to keep people on target.

Consensus is defined by the group and agreed upon in the first stages of planning. It usually means that the group has "agreed to agree" on the findings. Not everyone has to be able to embrace the findings, but everyone has to at least be able to live with the findings. If anyone can't or won't support the findings, you will not have reached a consensus.

Once the strategies or goals are agreed upon, you move into the second part of the Big Plan process: the Action Phase.

The Action Phase

The Action Phase is a more quantitative process. Let's take our Big Plan example of finding issues within the district and suppose that one of the eight goals or strategies that emerged was the following: "Strategy #3. The district will consider air conditioning all schools in District 5."

The "Action Plan" phase of the Big Plan will establish an "action committee" to deal with each strategy. Anyone interested in serving on these committees is invited to register as a potential committee member. Typically, prospective members are asked to list two or three committees (each representing one of the strategies) that they are interested in, from which a selection committee makes the final assignments. Recruitment of Action Plan committee members is usually done through a variety of sources such as newspaper articles, public meetings, and fliers. The Big Plan Committee may establish guidelines that each "Action Plan" committee will consist of approximately 50% community and 50% internal (school) members. Big Plan Committee members may be asked to volunteer first for specific Action Plan committees. Usually they are limited to serving on only one Action Plan committee, and usually only a few Big Plan Committee members are allowed on any Action Plan (1-3 is a good number). At this point in the planning process, you want widespread involvement to develop broad ownership.

The Action Plan committees set meeting times, deadlines, and procedures that fit their task. They do not follow a "standard format" but operate more as the task dictates. They may need to travel to see other schools, collect data, talk with experts, interview administrators, or perform a variety of unusual tasks. For the example given, the committee may invite several contractors, the head of maintenance, or an engineer to the meetings to learn more about their related areas of proficiency.

Many times sub-committees are also used to investigate specific issues or topics.

Action Planning Requires Action!

After the study/learning process is over, the Action Plan committee agrees on the steps of action, decides who is responsible for completing the steps, and sets specific deadlines. In many cases, they are also asked to develop a budget. This is optional for many plans.

An action plan for this strategy might look like this:

Action	Responsibility	Deadline
Identify and analyze the costs and benefits of air conditioning (AC)	Architect	1/5
Estimate capital and operating costs when AC is added	Architect Engineer	1/5
Review existing electrical service	Engineer	1/5
Review current AC and electrical reports, as listed above	Committee	1/15
Present AC options	Contractor	1/25
Draft of AC needs	Committee Architect	2/15
Review reports and draft	Committee	2/25
Prepare report for Board	Committee Architect Engineer	3/15
Present to Board	Committee	4/10

In this case, the Board will review the Action Plan. It may accept it or reject it. In most cases, using this type of process, the Board does not alter the plan. If it feels an alteration is needed, the Board shares its concerns and questions with the committee, rejects the plan, and lets the committee meet and present a revised plan. This helps develop ownership and cooperation; it also helps secure support.

School Improvement Planning

There is a special type of Big Plan that involves school improvement. This is a site-based process used to help schools look at their strengths and weaknesses in a systematic way and then find ways to improve any number of identified functions, processes, and environments.

A team approach is used to create the improvement plan. Just like other Big Plans, the planning team needs to represent all facets of the school, including teachers, students, parents, community representatives, support staff, and the building administration. The entire learning community needs to be involved. Teachers need to represent the fine arts, physical education, industrial or vocational education, and the academics. Many schools utilize volunteers for the School Improvement Planning (SIP) process, and committee members generally serve for a set period of time, often three years, before being replaced.

It is also important that the principal or appropriate administrator attends all SIP team meetings, but not as the team leader. The SIP team leader should be a teacher. Although the school improvement process is site-based, the goals of each building should be shared with district administrators to help set common goals that form the district's improvement plan. Key areas frequently considered by school improvement teams are academic achievement, teaching/learning strategies, resource/ technology deployment, family/community involvement, professional development, and partnerships. School Improvement Planning takes place year-round, but many schools make a special effort to utilize the summer months to facilitate concentrated and focused planning sessions. Teachers often feel less pressured and more inspired during the summer. When possible, it is recommended that school staff members be compensated for working on SIP teams.

The first task of the SIP Team

The first responsibility of the SIP team is to collect data. This data should include district demographics such as: the attendance rate, mobility, free and reduced lunch participants, ethnic background, special education students, gifted students, and any other special program data that needs to be identified. Other data that could be included in the team's study might be nationally normed achievement test scores, state assessment scores, building climate surveys, parent surveys, student surveys, and peer teacher observation data. Reviewing this type of data gives participants a broad overview of the district.

Another item collected could be "A Day in the Life of YOU-NAME-IT School." This data consists of each teacher's lesson plans and activities for one specific day. The goal is to look at the variety of teaching strategies being used in the school in one day. To get a true picture of the teaching and learning in the school, this activity should be done at least once each semester. This type of activity generates interesting school perspectives.

Analyze School Improvement Plan Data

The next step for the SIP team is to analyze the data collected. Data is very important for reviewing trends, to see what is working and what is not. Data gives the team facts rather than opinions and should lay the foundation for quantitative measures of improvement. It is worth the time and effort to train the team on the use of data, how data is collected, and how important it is to the process of school improvement.

Begin the process by searching the data for "what's working." The team may need to desegregate the data, looking for trends. For example, it can look for program strengths and weaknesses by reviewing student achievement data for each subject and learning standard. The purpose of this is to find what's working and build on it as well as to strengthen where there are weaknesses.

It is important that each member of the SIP team be involved in the analysis of data and that they also involve the teachers the data represents. Therefore, the SIP team member takes the student achievement information for his or her grade level or department back to the group of teachers that he/she works with. It would be the responsibility of each SIP team member to lead his/her grade level or subject matter team to look for additional strengths and weaknesses based on learning standards, to plan ways to address the weaknesses, and to set measurable goals for improvement. This grade level or subject matter team then writes an improvement plan for its group and submits it to the SIP team. The SIP team leader, the principal (or appropriate administrator), and a subcommittee of the SIP team organizes and summarizes the data collected so it can be presented to the entire SIP team for consideration in the plan. This information should all be analyzed using a uniform format. In many states, the State Board will provide help with this process. In Illinois, the State Board of Education website provides a format that is very user friendly (see it at http://www.isbe.state.il.us).

Writing the SIP

Now it's time to write the plan. Each grade level or subject matter team leader presents the information he/she has analyzed and summarized regarding student achievement in the agreed upon format. The survey analysis subcommittee also reviews these findings with the entire SIP team. The team uses all of the information gathered to set priorities and establish three to five building-wide school improvement goals. The number of goals is important. Too many and the work becomes less focused. It is better to have fewer goals and concentrate on real efforts to make solid improvements than to have too many that don't get the attention needed to make a difference.

Remember, the overriding goal of this Big Plan is *positive change*. Once the goals are identified, plans for activities must be put in place to address these goals. The plans must include a timeline, how the plans will be measured, the person responsible, the population served, and the budget necessary for implementation. The most expedient way to make this happen is to have the entire SIP team involved in establishing priorities and setting goals. Finally, the team and administrative leaders become the writing and editing team to compose the final school improvement plan for the year. Before it is turned in to the district office, all SIP team members must have an opportunity to review it and make corrections and suggestions. Each district handles the SIP process differently. Some require district review and approval before implementation. Knowing the district "rules" and processes is important.

SIP Success Based on Follow-Up

Once the plan is written, its success depends on how effectively and thoroughly the SIP team follows through. The SIP team should establish a calendar of monthly meetings at the beginning of the school year. These monthly meetings should be used to monitor the progress made toward accomplishing the goals and completing the activities addressed in the plan. The SIP teams discussions might also include plans for implementation of professional development activities, success of student help sessions, or programs or events to address school culture and climate issues. The time may also be used for evaluation of the success of activities that have been completed and suggestions for improvement of similar activities in the future.

As the goals are revisited each month, the budget also needs to be reviewed. It is important to have a report from the SIP team at each faculty meeting. This keeps the goals before the entire faculty all year and provides information about the progress being made toward reaching the goals. Often, a school-wide goal can be addressed in a faculty meeting through "mini" professional development sessions presented by the SIP team or individual faculty members who might have information to share that helps address the goal.

The key is to keep the goals and vision for improvement in the minds of the entire learning community *all* school year. If the entire staff has been involved in the analysis of data through its grade level or subject matter teams, and it is reminded of the goals regularly, it is more likely to "buy in" and help work toward the goals.

SIP Plans are an Ongoing Process

When SIP teams begin their work, they must realize up front that school improvement is an ongoing process. Sometimes school improvement goals take several years to be accomplished and to be reflected in data. It is also important when looking at student achievement to look at the scores of cohort groups. If you just look at grade 7 scores each year, you are comparing apples to oranges. You need to follow the *same* students from grade 6 to grade 7 to grade 8 in order to compare apples to apples and see if the students are growing.

The school improvement process can be a way to move your school toward a "professional learning community" model similar to one described by Richard DuFour and Robert Eaker in their book *Professional Learning Communities at Work: Best Practices for Enhancing Student Achievement*.[1] In this book they describe professional learning communities as having these six characteristics: (1) Shared mission, vision, values, goals, (2) Collaborative teams, (3) Collective inquiry, (4) Action, orientation, and experimentation, (5) Commitment to continuous improvement, and (6) Results orientation.

The SIP team becomes a collaborative team that shares the characteristics of the professional learning community. The grade level and subject matter teams that analyze data and plan for improvement in their area are also collaborative teams. These teams are all working toward common goals and are collectively seeking continuous improvement. In the book *Getting Started: Recultur-*

---

[1] Bloomington, IN: National Educational Service, 1998.

ing Schools to Become Professional Learning Communities[2], Eaker, DuFour, and Burnette share how the school improvement process can be used as the basis for building a professional learning community.[3]

The Day Plan

The Day Plan has a smaller compass—getting you through each day. It is an always-on "action plan" based on good organizational and thinking skills rather than a long list of processes and procedures.

I'm good on the big stuff, but I'm so-so on the Day Plan.

You've got to bat 80-90% every day with your Day Plans to stay in the academic big leagues, and bat even better with the Big Plans. Both are patched together with details and relentless organization.

I rely on instinct too much with the daily details.

I needed to wear my black belt the other day at another speech. But why worry—I always have one in my suitcase. Except that as I unpacked and began to dress an hour before my talk, it dawned on me that I'd switched suitcases! No black belt. So I winged it. For what seemed like hours, I kept my blue suit coat buttoned so nobody could see my brown belt. (Everything has a bonus: I think I lost nine pounds that day!)

I would say that one of the best steps to successful daily organization is a good night's sleep. Really. Coming to work energized and ready to make a difference is a huge first step to a successfully engaged and fully functional Day Plan.

---

[2] Bloomington, IN: National Educational Service, 2002.
[3] Each district has a talented person who can facilitate or inspire the development of School Improvement Plans. I have been fortunate to work with Miss Pat Schwarm, who shared her expertise with all of us in the previous section on School Improvement Plans. They don't come much better than Pat. Her leadership, vision, motivation, and "push" has helped the Highland School District become one where students learn well in a caring, successful, learning community. I also know that Jim Rosborg feels the same way about his Assistant Superintendent, Bill Porzukowiak, and Max McGee, about Mike Dunn. We are all fortunate to work with exceptional team partners.

There is no Day Plan cookie cutter

Another key element is what you did the day before to prepare for today's Day Plan. Please understand that there are, at last count, 1,467 different procedures for organizing your day's activities. Some administrators love the "post-it-note" process where you take a manila folder for each day and put post-it-notes inside the folder for things you must accomplish that day. When the item is completed, you throw the post-it-note away or keep it in a "done" folder with the date of completion written on it until it is be tossed after an appropriate amount of time. Proponents of this organizational tactic like it because you can put the post-it-notes in a priority arrangement, changing them at will, adding or subtracting as your needs change. Some people use different color post-it-notes for different tasks with colors deciding priority, such as orange (get it done today), yellow (it can carry over), or blue (make daily progress on this task).

Some administrators use formal "planners" and take great pride in following a well formulated plan of "to-do lists," calendar entries, time arrangement, and structured record keeping. Still others use the pile approach: the stacks on your desk indicate the tasks for the day arranged by priority, stacked by deadline, feared by height.

Jim Rosborg shares something he does to organize each coming week. On Sunday night, he reviews his calendar for the major events for the next week, then reviews the events with his wife, and they discuss the nights he will not be home. They coordinate joint calendars and both have a good handle on what the week will be like.

Another suggestion has to do with meeting with your associates. One thing I have found to be both helpful and time saving was meeting during lunch with my two assistants. We alternated between various restaurants in town, brought a clipboard of notes, and talked and planned during lunch. Our Subway has a nice side room that is usually great for discussions. Dairy Queen has a table near the back that we frequented as well. It killed two birds with one stone: a needed planning meeting and nourishment. We also enjoyed the time together, and it never hurts for the public to see the administrators working and available for a comment or a simple hello.

As I mentioned, organizational skills can be coordinated in a thousand ways, and calendars, Palm Pilots, computers, notebooks, and secretaries must fit the user to be successful. The *key* to all of this is the mental discipline to stick to your program, to plan the day efficiently, and to review your success. If you are never reaching the goals of your Day Plan and feel like a set of tires spinning on ice, you need to step back, review everything you do, and *reorganize* your approach.

A few years ago, I asked my secretary to open and stack my mail. We worked it out so that she stacked the items that needed immediate response on top and the garbage on the bottom. I asked her not to open what looked confidential—but if she accidentally did, to keep it confidential! I asked her to forward mail that was not for me and to toss the goofy stuff, like invitations from the Czar of Croatia to attend a conference that cost $23,000. I trusted her judgment. Over the course of several months, we even listed items she could copy and forward, dispose of, file, or stack on the bottom of someone else's pile. This one change in procedure probably saved me 30-45 minutes *each day*. I could go on and on with ideas and tips that save time and allow you to arrange your day, meet your goals, and go home feeling like you have completed your Day Plan successfully.

Fit the Day Plan to your work schedule

The Day Plan can be more effectively executed if you fit your work to your schedule. If I am going to a meeting that requires a 45-minute drive, I might make five phone calls during the car ride. Often times, I shut off the radio and just think. It is not uncommon for me to pull over to jot a note on my clipboard, to dial and leave a message for myself at home, or, when I was still a super, to call Marie, my faithful administrative assistant, and ask her to do something, write something down, or check something. No time is wasted. If I am going to be in a motel overnight, I bring a laptop and a briefcase full of papers and set up a mini-office. I can get more work done in four hours there than in ten hours at the office. I do email, write letters, organize papers, write, think, prepare, plan, and feel good about what I have accomplished. Sometimes I can even do it with a basketball or baseball game on in the background. Again, no time is wasted if you plan your days to the max.

Faking it

Can we talk about the art of faking it? No matter how good you are; no matter how well you fill in your $75, leather bound, zippered planner; no matter how detailed that Day Plan is, you will forget something, be late to an appointment, forget that someone is coming to see you, miss a deadline, or just simply mess up with some area of responsibility. Even the best-trained and most experienced planner is still a frail and imperfect human. When you mess up, you have several options: fake it, admit it, learn from it, or a combination of the three. I encourage you to fake it during those times when no one will know. If you are busy writing a report and your secretary calls you to announce that your ten o'clock appointment is here (and your calendar is as blank as your brain for a ten o'clock appointment), merely ask your secretary who is waiting and if they he or she is alone. When she says the name, your brain will engage quickly. Arrange a chair for the person and invite him or her in. All you need do is indicate that your schedule has been a little tight and invite the person to get comfortable as you get your papers ready for the meeting. There is no need to say you forgot. Just work through it as best you can. Faking it is not illegal or immoral; it is just a fine art form refined with experience. After the person leaves, ask yourself why you forgot to write down the appointment—and learn from the mistake.

One point is important here. Don't lie. If asked why you missed a deadline or didn't show up at a meeting, sometimes an honest "I forgot to make my calendar" will be best understood. Honesty helps when the human side of you takes over and organization takes a back seat. Just work twice as hard to fix the problem. No one admires a person who is always late, misses deadlines frequently, or plans poorly. One more thing: if you keep people waiting for you, like staff members at a meeting, begin the meeting by saying, "I'm very sorry to be late. Your time is valuable and I feel badly that I made you wait. Please forgive me." Then get to work. My best guess is that 99.5% of those hearing this apology will forgive you immediately *if this is not a frequent occurrence.*

Summary

Big Plans, like strategic planning, corporate planning, financial planning, and extended planning take organization and work. It is as important to "plan to plan" as it is to present a final plan document. Who serves on the planning committee is exceptionally important to the plan's overall success because widespread ownership of the plan is necessary for it to work.

There are many steps to developing a plan that need to be followed, including a clear understanding of the plan's objective, complete data collection, appropriate data analysis, a serious review of strengths and weaknesses, group plan writing, and a professional plan presentation. Strategic plans are general in nature and pave the way for follow-up action planning.

Action plans follow strategic plans and are equally dependent on the right mix of committee members. Action plans require an understanding of who does what, when, and how. Action plans are specific and time-related.

School Improvement Plans (SIPs) are specific Big Plans that relate to school issues. They follow the Big Plan format with some special modifications for the school environment. They are key to successful growth in any school.

The Day Plan is really an exercise in organization and mental thought. What works for you is the format to follow, but continual review of efficiency and success on a daily basis is critical to successful administrative leadership.

Finally, understanding that no administrator is perfect is imperative to becoming more successful in the quest for being a master planner.

Chapter Seven

Expert Knowledge

Jim Rosborg

When you shoulder a leadership role like principal or superintendent, many people working with you assume that you are an expert. They also depend upon you for support and knowledge.

While it is important for an effective administrator to be respected for his or her knowledge, it is just as important for that person not to feel that he or she must be an expert in everything. It simply isn't possible.

We are stressing in this book the importance of collaboration and using the knowledge of those around you. By using the shared knowledge of those people and expanding on your own knowledge base, your leadership will grow, as will the respect for you by those individuals associated with your leadership. Collaboration and expanding your own expert knowledge are the foci of this chapter.

You can develop expert knowledge by keeping current with teaching and learning. That development also includes your professional development and your involvement with your staff's professional development. There are other components to this success. You, as the leader, must network with universities for staff development, personal development, and program development. In addition, you must develop critical technology capabilities for yourself, your school, and your school district.

Malcolm Baldrige Act

One way to keep current with teaching and learning is to make yourself aware of the quality school expectations established by The Malcolm Baldrige National Quality Improvement Act of

1987, Public Law 100-107. Awards are given yearly to businesses and school districts as a result of this act. The award name honors the U.S. Secretary of Commerce who served from 1981-87.

The Baldrige Act established criteria that evaluate components common to all systems. It is a *blueprint* for building good, well-connected parts that can help make schools capable of high performance. It also is a *measure* of these parts and connections. How effective are the parts of a system? How effective are the connections linking those parts? The criteria established by Baldrige force us to assess our system and determine how well each of the elements of that system is working to achieve the district's goals. Baldrige is also a powerful *process* for organizational self-assessment. Which connections and which components add value and which do not? To have an effective school district, we must answer these questions.[1]

The Baldrige law includes seven categories which show the school districts how to evaluate their own performance so that each district can create its own plan for improvement. The exciting thing about Baldrige is that it provides a common ground of criteria for business, industry, and education. These criteria must be satisfied to receive the Malcolm Baldrige National Quality Award. They are also important for effectively managing schools. The seven categories of leadership established by Baldrige are:

1. **Leadership**. This category shows how you as the school leader can set the district's goals so that high performance standards supporting student learning are established. This area also looks at how schools are viewed in the community.

2. **Strategic Planning**. We dealt extensively with this in our last chapter. While we referred to it as our "Big Plan," both strategic planning and the "Big Plan" fit into the Baldrige criteria. Both establish long-term goals; both seek input from parents and other key stakeholders. Both establish short-term and long-term action plans along with needed resources to meet goals.

3. **Student and Stakeholder Focus**. What do students and stakeholders expect and need from our schools? How does the dis-

---

[1] Shipley, Jim, and Marilyn Caldwell Wescott, "Baldrige Education Criteria: 'Flavor of the Month' or the Road to World Class Schools." *Quality Network News*. Vol. 10, No. 4, September/October 2000. This is the full text of an article related to Baldrige and Quality Improvement in Education published by American Association of School Administrators Quality Network.

trict meet those needs? Are all of the stakeholders satisfied with the schools' performances? Building from these questions, this category establishes a plan to build good relationships with stakeholders.

4. **Information and Analysis**. This area looks at the strategic plan, evaluates data, and identifies strengths and weaknesses so that student, school, and district performances can improve.

5. **Faculty and Staff Focus**. Here the act concentrates on the design of the various staff positions within the district. How well is the staff paid? Are staff members recognized for their performance? Does the district provide adequate resources for professional development? Does the district provide a work environment that is conducive to personal and professional fulfillment? The Baldrige's goal is to create ownership by the faculty and staff so that everyone can work toward common goals.

6. **Educational and Support Process Management**. This is the programmatic area of Baldrige. Do schools design classes and programs to satisfy student needs? Do faculty and staff receive sufficient classroom resources so they can teach to high standards? How do the schools evaluate their programs? Are the results of these evaluations used to improve student performance? The Baldrige framework provides a systematic method of improved performance.

7. **School Performance Results**. In the award criteria, this area counts for 45% of the total. How are the students performing academically? Are the students and key stakeholders satisfied? Does the school provide a good educational environment? Does the operating cost per pupil align with student success? The goal is to increase bottom line results in students' achievement and behavior so that they come to understand and value their learning opportunities to become successful citizens in our democratic society.[2] This bottom line revolves around the collection of hard data. Anecdotal data gets a zero on the Baldrige evaluation system.

If you want more information about Baldrige, you may wish to visit these websites:

> http://www.quality.nist.gov
> http://www.baldrigeineducation.org

---

[2] "Business, Educators Find Power In Baldrige to Improve Schools." *Work America*. Vol. 15, No. 4; April 1998, p. 2.

There are many other worthy ways to assess an organization, like state and national accreditation, state and national awards or incentive programs, and even partnering with a local corporation in a quality-improvement effort. Because the Baldrige Award Program is quite labor intensive, it may not be achievable for all school districts. You may choose to adapt some of the Baldrige principles and mold them for your own district.

Personal Professional Development

Another key component of your own personal professional development is networking with your local and area community colleges and universities. I have worked with higher education administrators and professors on a variety of topics that have proven richly beneficial to our district. Some of the topics that we have successfully collaborated on with a university include:

* State accountability initiatives
* Mentoring and induction for beginning teachers and administrators
* Off-campus courses
* National Science Foundation grant on math problem solving
* Placement of student teachers
* Development and implementation of the Reading Recovery Program
* Complex-generated testing development for higher order thinking
* Legal workshops and consultation
* Americorp support program
* Instructional support of reading and math
* Health support for indigent areas

Of particular value to me was the National Science Foundation grant for math problem solving. This $2,000,000 grant was written with the much-appreciated assistance of Professor Jerry Becker of Southern Illinois University at Carbondale. He developed this teacher inservice to use math problem-solving techniques to develop higher order thinking skills in students and to make mathematics less instructionally threatening to elementary and junior high teachers. Its success has been phenomenal. Through the efforts of Dr. Becker, Teacher Leader Mike Koenig, and the staff at Belleville, Illinois #118, the student math scores in our district have continued to improve even though our poverty level has increased for the past five years. They now have some of the best overall math scores in the state of Illinois, despite the fact that nearly half of the students live in poverty.

There is an interesting side note to the grant application. The first time Belleville #118 applied for the grant through the National Science Foundation (NSF), the application was rejected because the readers of the grant felt I was being too aggressive in stating that 80 of our 106 teachers involved with teaching math would participate in the six-week inservice and the year-long support groups involving mentor teachers and modeling behavior. When the district applied the second time, the teachers' union president wrote a letter stating that there was no administrative pressure and that he also felt that at least 80 teachers would be involved in the program. Belleville #118 got the grant. But the NSF was correct: the district didn't have 80 teachers involved. They had 102! What a testimonial to the professionalism of the teachers in the district.

At this printing, I am in my 31st year in education with the past 18 years in administration. During every one of those 31 years I have taken a class, attended a major professional development seminar, observed another school and district, or taught a graduate-level course. My feeling is that if we as leaders let our professional development stagnate, we slowly die internally. We are alive physically but we are shrinking developmentally.

Many of my colleagues say to me, "I am not going to this seminar (or class) because nothing will change in education regarding the public's perception." I totally disagree. We owe professional involvement to ourselves and to our key stakeholders. I get frustrated like any other administrator or teacher. I get upset when I see money freely flowing to failing districts while successful ones are financially punished for doing a good job. For example, Belleville #118 is not eligible for summer school monies from our state because their test scores are too high!

Are we the only profession where one gets financially rewarded for doing a bad job? I get frustrated at bureaucratic mandates that are placed on good schools. Why make everyone go through the same red tape if they are successful with students? I get frustrated at special education rules and mandates that are hurting children and financially strapping schools. The district I retired from, Belleville #118, is presently at $4-million dollars in expenses over revenues in special education (with a $30-million budget). I am bothered by test score requirements that state that 100% of all students will meet state standards when we know this is not possible, given the environment some of our students come from, along with other factors that negatively impact the learning process.

We may be the Rodney Dangerfields of society when it comes to getting no respect. But we can't stop working for positive change. Much of this has to occur through our own professional development.

The Interstate School Leaders Licensure Consortium (ISLLC) developed some outstanding professional development guidelines to be merged with the district's school improvement plan and goals. Their "Propositions for Quality Professional Development for School Leaders"[3] are listed below:

Proposition 1: Quality professional development validates teaching and learning as the central activities of the school.

Proposition 2: Quality professional development engages all school leaders in planful, integrated, career-long learning to improve student achievement.

Proposition 3: Quality professional development promotes collaboration to achieve organizational goals while meeting individual needs.

Proposition 4: Quality professional development models effective learning processes.

Proposition 5: Quality professional development incorporates measures of accountability that direct attention to valued learning outcomes.

The ISLLC goes on to emphasize that professional development goals should emphasize teaching and learning, which still must remain the most important function of administrative knowledge. All agree that administrators should be involved with curriculum. The successful administrator is not just satisfied with managing the school, he or she has a passion for curriculum and student academic improvement. Long-term professional develop-

---

[3] Keenan, N., and others, *Collaborative Professional Development Process for School Leaders*. Washington, DC: Council of Chief State School Officers, 2000, p. 3.

ment needs to focus on aligning curriculum with several other aspects of the overall educational program, such as:

* State standards
* Reporting instruments to parents: report cards, continuous scale (1-100) for assessment, etc.
* Grading scale
* Honor roll
* Core subject matter taught
* Time allocation given to core subject matter

This alignment helps lead to improvement in your professional development foci of teaching and learning. You must also acclimate yourself to learning styles. What method does a student need to maximize learning potential? Become an expert in student learning by making professional development a career-long process. Also consider these 13 suggestions to enhance your professional development:

1. Join Toastmasters to develop your speaking skills. Every administrator has to speak to educational and community groups. Self-confidence in your speaking skills helps you to organize better, think on your feet, and to remain calm when tough questions are placed before you. Good speaking skills also enhance your reputation with major stakeholders.

2. Keep yourself in tune with advancements in technology. There are many sources available for inservice, including your local community college. (See the discussion later in this chapter.)

3. Know the principles of effective instruction. The Hunter model is still a viable source for outlining an effective lesson. This includes the anticipatory set, objective and purpose, input, modeling, checking for understanding, guided practice, and independent practice.[4] Many, including me, feel that "closure" should also be added to the lesson so students can see what has been accomplished in the lesson.

4. Go to yearly legal workshops. Many school administrators considered going to law school while in college. Little did they know that they would have to be so knowledgeable about educational law and its constantly changing procedures.

5. Improve your psychometric skills in the interpretation of tests. Your staff will gain more respect for you if you have the

---

[4] Hunter, Madeline, *Mastery Teaching*. El Segundo, CA: TIP Publications, 1982.

knowledge to analyze data so that an effective school improvement plan can be established. You need to know what is and what isn't significant data. What statistics are meaningful to determine student improvement?

6. Understand portfolios. How is a portfolio developed? What kinds of portfolio? Is it a best practice portfolio, an assessment portfolio, or an improvement portfolio? Finally, does the portfolio show all of the student's work? Many of those strongly supporting portfolio use don't know the differences between the types of portfolios or how they can best serve as a continuous assessment tool.

7. Go to school finance workshops. The dollar is still the bottom line for school effectiveness. Make sure you maximize the resources available. In lean financial times, a strong leader strives to preserve proven programs at all costs.

8. Know the fundamentals of reading development. Reading is still the key to student success at all grade levels. Know phonetic, whole language, and sight instructional methods.

9. Take time to go to positive mental attitude seminars and stress workshops. Chapter 12 expands on this point.

10. Pursue your professional development on an individual basis. The effective school administrator best thinks strategically by being well read and current. For example, scan professional journals every month. Look at the tables of contents and find articles that fit your district's or your own needs. (In my case, other administrators also send me articles they think I could use. Often we discuss the most applicable articles at our monthly administrators meeting.)

11. Continually enhance your skills with teacher's issues like collective bargaining, teacher recertification, and special education laws.

12. Stay current on cultural issues. Strive to properly communicate with kids regardless of their race, creed, or color.

13. Keep up to date on current issues such as character education, violence prevention, and crisis intervention.

Bond Issues and Referenda

Another important professional development area outside of teaching and learning is how to get bond issues and referenda passed. You will be unique if you do not have to face this challenge in your administrative career. What should you look for in a professional development seminar on tax referenda? Minimally, it should include these topics:

Fund Raising
In most states, it is against the law to use tax funds to promote a "yes" vote. Private donations must be secured for pamphlets, brochures, and newspaper and other media advertisements.

Brochures and Public Relations
What is a good brochure for bond issues and tax referenda? Which should you distribute them to? How are you going to promote the issues and the district?

Get Out the "Yes" Vote
The best way is to network with your parents. Get them involved. We set up district chairpersons, building chairpersons, and classroom chairpersons. We then identify others who have been supportive of the district. We also work with other special groups to gather their support for the issue. These might include:

* Parent-Teacher Organizations (PTA/PTO)
* Music Club
* Sports Booster Club
* Father's Club
* Mother's Club
* Special education groups
* School volunteers
* Local churches
* Civic clubs
* Government officials
* Labor unions
* Senior citizens

Also, make an appointment with your local congressperson or state representative. I guarantee you they will give you a great in-service on how to get out the vote. At our last election, we would not have been successful without the efforts of our Congressman, Jerry Costello. His knowledge of how to get the "yes" vote was simply amazing.

Another person you might visit is an administrator in your area who has recently worked a successful referendum. What worked in that election? What didn't? You would be surprised at the information and clues that are shared. For example, you may discover that people in your area don't like yard signs but prefer handbills in car windows— or vice-versa. Other sub-committees need to be involved with getting out the "yes" vote, such as voter registration committees, transportation to the polls committees, and poll-watcher committees.

Employee Committee

This committee should have representatives from all employee groups in the district. The purpose is easy to understand. By being knowledgeable of the issue, the employees will get ownership. Use the fact that teachers, custodians, secretaries, lunch supervisors, bus drivers, and paraprofessionals all directly talk to the key district stakeholders who vote in the election. Three points of caution here:

1. Don't involve staff members in any organized activities during the contractual school day.

2. Most successful school districts keep students out of the political agenda and direct campaigning.

3. Acknowledge the fact that not all employees will support tax increase efforts. You must never force or require employee participation.

Kindergarten Committee

These are motivated parents who want to ensure the long-term quality of the district. They will be involved with the district for the next 12½ years. Many of these parents' own parents live in the district. Use this networking opportunity.

Legal Committee

This committee monitors laws affecting school finance referenda, timelines for election ballot submissions, campaign committees, voter registration, and poll-watchers. It generally overseas the smooth running of the election process.

Principal Tasks

The principal coordinates activities at the building level. The principal must:

1. Work closely with the building and classroom co-chairs and make everyone feel needed in the campaign.
2. Become familiar with proper and improper campaign techniques.
3. Encourage staff members to make sure they keep a positive attitude in conferences and other dealings with students and parents.
4. Make sure that no major changes are made while the campaign is going on. This is not the time to raise people's emotions. Remember, the word "change" is threatening to many people. Change threatens their security and makes them question the future success of the district.
5. Provide staff members the necessary background information to answer questions.
6. Distribute specific duties to all committees and individuals involved with the campaign.
7. Develop a list of potential "yes" voters.
8. Use parent meetings to disperse the message about the positive happenings in the district. Go over major facts about the district and the referendum.

The principal is a key component to the success of the issue.

The Board, superintendent, and principal must have the issue plan, the facts behind the issue, and the strategy ready to go when the campaign kicks off. Those in need should go to seminars *before* the campaign, to be prepared and ready.

Grant Writing

Does your professional development plan include the knowledge of grant writing? To be a successful administrator, it should! We discussed in Chapter 3 the importance of aggressively pursuing revenues. Successful grant writing is a key component of this. Your professional development in this arena is vitally important. Most grant applications need the same or similar information in each of the different sections. Since the grant applications are divided into separate sections, don't be afraid to repeat the key points that you think are important to getting the grant. This may seem like overkill, but it works. Just as important, make sure you follow the grant directions. One missed detail can get it declined! Here are some general sections most grant applications include:

Applicant Overview

This overview generally deals with your rationale, showing that you qualify for the grant, and the key personnel involved.

District, or School, Needs?

This is a question in itself. Do you have a better chance to obtain the grant if you apply as a district, a consortium of districts, an individual school, or even an individual classroom or activity? Does this need fit into your goals for teaching and learning? Make sure you spend time emphasizing your need and how you will meet it. Which students will be affected?

Planning Process

What steps are you going to take to get ready to implement the grant? What research component will be in place?

Project Goals and Objectives

This is an overview of the project. It is the substantiation of your proposal. The goals should be measurable and reflect the projected grant's purpose.

Time Line

When will the action phase of the grant take place and who will make sure the guidelines of the grant are followed? Many grant givers will want to know how you are going to carry forth the intent of the grant after the funding period has ended.

Fiscal Agent

Who will oversee the awarded funds? Who is accountable for the audit? How much clerical time will be needed?

Budget

Where are the monies going and to whom? Are there in-kind monies required? Will the district have financial requirements or needs after the grant ends?

Evaluation

What is the project's evaluation procedure? Who will communicate the success or failure of the project and to whom? How will teaching and learning be improved by this grant?

Grant writing requires knowing your district's strengths and using the correct terminology to complete the application properly. That is why professional development is so important in this process. For most districts, a full- or part-time grant writer is no longer a luxury, but rather, a valuable resource that can save administrators many hours of labor.

Another labor saving method is to know where to get grants. Check www.grantshotline.com, the U.S. Department of Education, and your state department of education.

Technology

Administrators must accept that there is more to technology infusion than just buying computers and putting them in a classroom. Once the computer is in the classroom, what software will be available for it? Who is going to unpack, set up, and support the computer? Once the warranty has ended, are there budgeted monies for maintenance and repairs? What about training for the teachers using the computers? Is there money set aside for staff development? Will teachers get a stipend for attending training or is it voluntary?

Consider the staff. How many of them would attend staff development programs if stipends were *not* available? The number would probably be half of those who would attend if stipends *were* available. There is much more to it than just buying boxes and connecting wires!

I'm not a technology expert. But to succeed as a school administrator, there are certain things about technology that I must know. I have to know how to surf the Internet for a variety of educational topics, how to send and receive email, how to attach messages previously saved on a disk, and how to develop list serves so I can send a message to a large number of people at one time. It also helps to know Excel and Power Point.

Computers will never replace teachers in the classroom, but they sure can enhance the learning process and the capability of the school district to turn out effective future citizens. Technology will continue to be the number one issue in education for the 21st century. Technology continually requires upgraded knowledge concerning curriculum, management, and assessment. Training is also needed to develop a variety of methods for the integration of technology into the curriculum.

Administrators, especially at the high school level, are going to need to know and understand technology for career development. More and more state reports must be submitted online. More schools are switching to online resources to replace textbooks.

A good administrator must lead in technology staff development. This is enhanced by a good technology support person. According to Belleville #118 Director of Technology, Chris McMahan, "Staff development provides an excellent opportunity for schools to assist their staff in technology literacy in the classroom. When I refer to technology, I'm not only talking about computers but also TVs, VCRs, calculators, and much more."

The delivery of staff development varies. Both time and money are needed to provide good staff development. Time is needed for teachers to absorb and synthesize what they just learned. Money pays for a knowledgeable instructor who can teach the particular subject. Anyone can call the local computer store and pay someone to come in and teach the basics of word processing or the Internet. This staff development could be more effective if you had someone come in who understood educators. While teaching staff members the basics of word processing, they could show them examples of how this program will allow them to create mini-posters for their classroom, calendars, or a list of links for their students to follow to get on the Internet. Also, show them how they can be creative using shapes, pictures, and clip art to carry the software beyond just being a word processing program.

When giving a workshop on using the Internet, give examples about how looking up maps online could be used in a map unit in the grade school or in a discussion about the location of the field trip the class is taking. Show the teachers where there are sites for displaying lesson plans already proven to work in a classroom.

Teachers don't want to reinvent the wheel, nor do we want them to. Teachers might find that they can expand or enhance the lesson they are already using by seeing what other teachers in other parts of the country, or the world for that matter, are doing. Use what works. What's wrong with taking a lesson plan that a teacher in Arizona has posted about frogs and using it for an upcoming dissecting unit? At some point you will see the excitement when your staff finally "gets it." You will see the light bulbs coming on. The teachers will want to share with everyone what they did and how it helped. It's a great feeling.

College Classes

A professional development activity that I have found to be beneficial is teaching college classes. The benefits are many:

* Being the instructor forces you to stay on top of both current methods of instruction and new curricular techniques.

* The classroom environment allows you to get ideas from other educators outside your district.

* You are generally dealing with a group of people who are motivated learners.

* Being a classroom instructor helps you to not only remember what it was like to be a teacher, but also to empathize with current teachers.

Many times I've gone to class exhausted by the events of the day and left feeling invigorated by what took place in my classroom. Teaching class lets you realize that there are good people everywhere in education.

Other ways of staying current with activities include being a guest speaker for colleges, working with student teachers, becoming a public speaker or workshops presenter, and developing an expertise in some area you love, like finance or curriculum. You may want to contact your state professional administrators' organization to offer your service as a mentor, speaker, advisor....

Professional development has reached a new level in some states where laws now exist on teacher and administrator recertification. Legislators have told me that this is necessary because of the low test scores and that some educators stop pursuing professional development activities during the course of their career. We are judged by our weakest links. If your state has not required recertification rules, be proactive and work to create a collaborative professional development plan that effectively helps teaching and learning.

What we are finding in our district is that our professional development activities are being weakened by the new Illinois recertification law. Before, we were able to concentrate on district-wide initiatives like math solving. Now we are seeing many more individual teachers focusing on achieving state requirements. In addition:

* There is no financial support backing the initiative.
* Individual teacher recertification costs have become topics of collective bargaining. In the past, this was the professional responsibility of the individual teacher.
* As with many state initiatives, the individual and district paperwork component of this process is huge. Districts have had to hire more clerical workers just to deal with the recertification process.
* The process will more than likely become a legalistic nightmare when the certificates come up for renewal.

One can't fault legislatures for their good intentions. In fact, I applaud their efforts to increase professional development for administrators and teachers. But I hope the day comes when legislators and State Boards handle those districts not using sound educational practices individually rather than establishing restrictive rules for all districts that "water down" the professional development plans of many excellent schools and districts. In many ways, we have created this scenario by not having collaborative individual and group professional development plans. Formulate a plan for yourself, your school, and your district.

Summary

Professional development should be tied to teaching and learning. Staff development is best for students when activities are delivered to the entire staff and related to the school's improvement plan. Whether the professional program is about character education, guided reading, technology applications, or structured routines, professional development is best when teachers and administrators work together as a team. Together, they incorporate these newly learned ideas into their instruction. The administrator has even more responsibility when it comes to professional development. There are topics like referenda, grant writing, and legal issues that go beyond the classroom. In addition, the administrator must research ideas to make sure those ideas have a sound, researched basis as they enter the instructional phase.

"No man will make a great leader who wants to do it all himself, or to get all the credit for doing it."

Andrew Carnegie

Chapter Eight

Building Internal Capacity

Max McGee

As the leader of your school, you have many responsibilities. Your top priority is the improvement of teaching and learning. Improving teaching and learning requires leadership, but not in the sense that most educators usually define it. Not in the sense of charisma or a rugged individualism.

According to J.P. Spillane and R. Halverson in *Distributed Leadership: Toward a Theory of School Leadership Practice,*[1] the most effective leadership is shared or distributed in a manner that crafts a common culture where all believe they are responsible and accountable for improving teaching and learning. Real leadership, then, is all about *building the internal capacity* of your staff to improve instruction and student achievement.

The phrase "building capacity" is one you have likely heard before. We fear that it may be headed to the graveyard for educational jargon, with a final resting spot somewhere between the "paradigm shift" memorial and the tomb of "transformational leadership." As with its battlefield companions, Bill Ding Capacity had enormous potential but was woefully misunderstood—if even comprehended—by most school leaders. They are hardly to blame for they were told that they needed to build capacity for improvement, to build capacity for implementing standards-based reform, and to build capacity for literacy. They are hardly to blame because, as idealistic educational leaders, they soon found that their job requirements weren't really driving improvement in teaching and learning but rather protecting teachers and managing central office and state mandates. They discovered that they spent more

---

[1] Annual Meeting of the American Educational Research Association, Montreal, 1999.

time stopping to take care of those pesky little "stones-in-the-shoe" problems than they did moving forward on real improvement. The research about instructional leadership is telling:

> "Insofar as there is any empirical evidence on the frequency of actual instructional leadership in the work of school administrators, it points to a consistent pattern: direct involvement in instruction is among the least frequent activities performed by administrators of any kind at any level, and those who do engage in instructional leadership activities on a consistent basis are a relatively small proportion of the total administrative force.[2]

> "School leaders are hired and retained based largely on their capacity to buffer teachers from outside interference and their capacity to support the logic of confidence between a school system and its constituencies... Principals who develop the skills and knowledge required to actually do instructional leadership in a serious way do so because of their personal preferences and values, often at some personal cost to their own careers, not because they are expected to do so as a condition of their work... The institutional structure does not promote, or select for, knowledge and skill related to instructional leadership; at best, it tolerates some proportion of the population who indulge in it out of personal commitment and taste."[3]

The district leaders aren't to blame. Managing the Board; keeping peace with the teachers unions; and buffering principals, staff, and the Board from irate parents has become their job—with improvement in teaching and learning little more than a fading hope or dashed dream. Moreover, most schools have cultures that strive to sustain status quo, so new research or innovative reform efforts—no matter how compelling—won't lead to change or improvement behind closed classroom doors.

---

[2] Murphy, Joseph, "Principal Instructional Leadership." *Advances in Educational Administration I* (Part B), 1990, pp. 163-200.
[3] Cuban, Larry, *The Managerial Imperative and the Practice of Leadership in Schools*. Albany, NY: State University of New York Press, 1988.

Although Richard Elmore presents a strong case for why public schools must improve in the era of standards based reform, he is skeptical:

> "It is possible that the practice of public schooling will respond to standards-based reform in the same way it has responded to virtually every other large scale reform in the twentieth century. It may, in other words, try to bend the logic of the policy to the logic of how the existing institutions function, making the policy unrecognizable upon its arrival in the classroom. If this is the case, the consequences for public education will be severe."[4]

Elmore contends—and we can attest—that because most school leaders have spent years being inducted and co-opted into the status quo (in other words, preserving business as usual) their chances of building their schools' capacity, much less their own, is nearly impossible. As evidence, just listen to how many administrators talk about how their schools are aligned with standards. Then spend a few minutes walking through their classrooms and we doubt that you will see one shred of evidence that instructional practices or materials have changed. If you find changes in one room, we doubt you will find them in too many others in the same school. Though educators give lip service to standards-based reform, in actuality little evidence of it exists. This is not surprising because leadership as practiced by many, if not most, school administrators is about self-preservation first, followed closely by defense of the status quo as they "buffer the instructional core from disruptions and improvements."[5]

Spending energy on keeping their job, on keeping parents and public reformers out, and on keeping defenses strong, the school administrator has little time to develop and implement collaborative improvement initiatives. As a result, the only improvements that *do* happen are those initiated by a handful of innovative teachers or "as a consequence of purely voluntary acts."[6] In addition to preservation of self and the status quo, the administrator is often quite literally "lonely at the top," isolated from both staff and

---

[4] Elmore. Richard F., "Building a New Structure for a School Leadership." Washington, DC: Albert Shanker Institute, Winter 2000, p. 7.
[5] Ibid., p. 7.
[6] Ibid., pp. 6-7.

colleagues. Since "isolation is the enemy of improvement,"[7] the administrator's chances of becoming a leader are slim.

Ready to leap from your window? Don't! Let me share several practical ideas and proven practices for building internal capacity for real improvement. The many asterisked examples of distributed leadership to follow have worked for others and should work for you.

First, though, some definitions:

Improvement is the change in direction, sustained over time, that moves entire systems (not just individual teachers, departments, or grade levels), raising the average level of quality and performance while at the same time decreasing the variation among groups, and engaging people in analysis and understanding of why some actions seem to work and others don't.

Leadership is guiding instructional improvement and thus improving student achievement.

Distributed leadership is distributing the responsibility for leadership among roles in the organization.

Building capacity is "enhancing the skills and knowledge of people in the organization, creating a common culture of expectations around the use of those skills and knowledge, holding the various pieces of the organization together in a productive relationship with each other, and holding individuals accountable for their contributions to collective results."[8]

We believe that real leaders can and do build capacity. We can't emphasize how important it is to learn how to do this. In fact, much of the advice in this book will, at best, lead to incremental improvements, unless you build the capacity of your staff to improve teaching and learning. This book's goal is to move you from survival to success. Building capacity is critical to effective leadership and that success.

Very few individuals, including the most visionary leaders, succeed at building capacity for sustained improvement. Fortu-

---

[7] Ibid., p. 20.
[8] Ibid., p. 15.

nately, there are a handful of exemplary leaders who can show us how it is done.

In Illinois, there are more than 900 schools with enrollments where over 50% of the students come from families with low income. Of these 900+ schools, 50% of the students meet state standards in less than half of them. Only 40 have been able to have 67% of their children meet state standards over a three-year period. These 40 leaders, however, are special, for they have actually created the capacity for internal accountability, for improving teaching and learning, and for making a "community of learners" a reality.

What follows, then, is what building internal capacity actually looks like. We first describe what the theory of "distributed leadership" looks like (in these successful schools) by examining its four components: focusing the school, fostering productive relationships, establishing reciprocal accountability, and enhancing the knowledge and skills of the staff and developing leaders. We then turn to one of the greatest leadership challenges we face—special education. The chapter closes on how you can hire and fire to assure that the capacity you created continues.

Build Internal Capacity by Focusing the School Purpose

Throughout this book you have read many references to collaboration. Perhaps the most critical time for collaboration is when you are developing the school improvement plan or the district "Big Plan." This is when you have the opportunity to focus the purpose of the school on exactly what you hope to accomplish. The purpose of the plan must be attentive to real, immediate problems or issues, and the common culture must support this purpose. Improvement of instruction must be the common concern for the whole organization as well as for each individual in it. Without involvement and engagement, improvement will not happen. It is important to recall Newman and Rutter's contention that principal leadership and teacher participation in decision making have no effect on a teacher's sense of efficacy unless they are connected to tangible and immediate problems.[9]

To focus on a school purpose or to create a collective vision around an immediate need, you must lay the groundwork in two ways. The first way is to craft a brief and specific message that encapsulates your vision about the purpose of the school, then convey this to the staff.

First, develop your specific, main message to the staff about the purpose of the school. We recommend that one of your points be that everyone is responsible for the quality of education and is expected to make a contribution beyond his or her classroom walls. A second point should be that you will not let children fail, and you will expect every team member to contribute to the success of every child. The final point should specifically describe the purpose and the immediacy of the improvement effort. For example, in one of our districts we found that the language arts scores of middle school boys had significantly lagged behind that of girls. Our school purpose became "to significantly improve the reading and writing achievement of our middle school boys each year for the next three years."

The second way to create a collective vision around an immediate need is to share data and teach your staff what it means. They need to know what the criteria for success are and how the staff impacts it. In one district, it may mean having half the students meet state standards; in another, having all of the students show a year's growth in all subject areas; and in a third, having two-thirds of all children exceed state standards. Whatever the criteria are, teachers must specifically understand them; more importantly, why they matter to them and to their students.

Distributed leadership means that you communicate a sense of purpose and explain the data; further, you give your staff the leadership in developing strategies for addressing the collective goal and for identifying measures of improvement.

Here are some ways that we have successfully created a common culture around school and district improvement:

---

[9] Newman, F.M., R. Rutter, et al, "Organizational Factors that Affect School Sense of Efficacy, Community and Expectations." *Sociology of Education*, vol. 62, no. 4, 1989.

* Wrote a new mission statement or created a new, crisp, concise mission or vision statement from one that is rambling and jargon-laced.

* Held a "data retreat" for all stakeholder groups to analyze the numbers—all numbers. There, staff and Board members looked at historical data on test scores, fund balances, enrollment patterns, attendance, mobility, and the like.

* Designed, administered, compiled, and analyzed community and climate surveys. These surveys enable leaders to have hard data on perceptions rather than just random opinions. They are also a valuable accountability measure, in addition to test scores.

* Conducted benchmark comparative studies with other school districts. (You've read about this in Chapter 3. Compare your results with other districts that are similar to yours. Use census data on median family income, home values, and/or parent education combined with state assessment data to determine if your taxpayers are getting a good "bang for their buck" compared to neighboring districts.)

* After learning how to understand, display, and communicate assessment data to staff, principals, and superintendents, we empowered faculty members with analyzing what the data implied for curriculum instruction and entrusted the staff with communicating those findings to parents and the School Board.

* Used project teams to identify and develop plans for addressing critical issues such as internal communication, improving reading instruction, and differentiating curriculum and instruction to meet individual needs.

* Selected staff to lead key curriculum committees. In addition to selecting staff leaders, the superintendent individually met with each staff committee chair for progress updates and dialog.

* Created a committee to respond to state mandates and assessment issues. For example, project teams, local task forces, SWAT teams, commissions, blue ribbon groups, etc., give staff a way to lead important initiatives that might otherwise be resisted as being too top down.

Build Internal Capacity by Fostering Productive Relationships

Without relationships, improvement simply will not happen. As a leader, you are responsible for forging productive relationships between you and your staff, among your staff members, and between the entire school staff and your children's families. Fostering relationships requires far more than creating a collegial environment. As a leader, you must *model* what you expect. You must demonstrate compassion and concern for your staff, learn all of their names, spend time with parent and family groups, and attend school events. As a leader, you have to create conditions for communication among staff members and remind them constantly about the importance of relationships and communication.

Distributed leadership means that you as a leader encourage staff to develop relationships among grades, departments, and schools. It means that you communicate that you expect them to use their bonds to contribute ideas and innovative practices to improve teaching and learning.

Here are some specific ideas that have worked for us:

* Used staff teams to assist in recruitment and employment of new staff. We believe that staff should be meaningfully involved in the interview process and also have the opportunity to recruit good teachers and administrators from other districts.

* Obtained release time for free discussion for teams of teachers by grade levels and/or by departments. When given time and respect, teachers will tackle tough problems and big issues. Test scores do matter to them and they want to get better. They need time to work together, to learn from one another, to try new practices, and to report back to the group.

* Obtained release time for teachers from consecutive grade levels to discuss expectations surrounding curriculum and instruction. Third-grade teachers know better than anyone what the second-grade curriculum should be, yet most leaders—especially at the district level—don't provide for this articulation. Our third-grade writing is improving because the second-grade teachers are teaching what the third-grade teachers need—how to write a fully developed paragraph with appropriate, ample support.

* Learned the first names of all staff members. As Chapter 5 about building trust notes, *nothing* is more important. Work at it.

* Held brown bag lunches or "second cup of coffee" meetings with staff and/or parents. The school leader does not just visit classrooms, he or she meets with staff and parents when they can have a real dialog about school improvement.

* Attended special events at schools and made a concerted effort to read to most classes. Visibility is of critical importance to building capacity. Not only do simple visits inspire, but they keep you in touch with the success of your leadership and the real messengers—your teachers.

* Attended PTA/O fundraisers and special events. Again, visibility creates capacity.

* Conducted community forums and panels with staff on topics of interest to the community. Rather than preparing speeches on what the leaders want to discuss, we suggest surveying your community and parents to find out what they want to hear. When we did this recently, we found far more broad-based concern about the social/emotional aspects of the middle grades than about the academics. Our staff actually ran a series of parenting panels that ended up creating far more positive parental involvement in children's education than any forum on standards, curriculum, or instruction could have.

* Provided several means for interacting with parents and community members: visits to service clubs, participation in community events and celebrations, feedback cards in newsletters, an Internet forum, and the production of local cable television shows.

Build Internal Capacity through Reciprocal Accountability

Elmore writes that "performance-based accountability in schools requires that certain people be held responsible for the performance of the organization."[10] To build internal capacity, your staff needs to be accountable to you for improving student performance. You, in turn, need to reciprocate by being accountable to them. If they are accountable for the outcomes, as they must be since

---

[10] Ibid., p. 15.

school leaders do not teach the students (except on rare occasions), the leader has to assure that they have the resources necessary to do the job. If, for example, teachers are accountable for improving the reading and writing ability of boys, they need several resources: a repertoire of interesting books and literature, an understanding of how boys and girls differ in their perceptions and capacities to learn at particular ages, training on proven practices, time for planning and peer observation, technology or materials for boys who learn by "getting their hands dirty," and access to male role models in the community who can spend some time with boys in the school setting.

Distributed leadership, then, builds capacity by making expectations and performance criteria for the staff clear and then is accountable for creating the opportunities to succeed. Staff becomes the leaders in delivering instruction while the administrator becomes the leader in delivering the resources necessary to the teachers.

Here are some actions that we have used successfully:

* Written specific, measurable performance-based goals and published them for all staff and community members.

* Required principals/supervisors to observe and comment on each staff member's evaluation form about the impact of professional development. For example, in my district, principals must comment on the extent to which teachers exhibited "differentiated instruction" (a district initiative) during formal observations.

* Presented school improvement plans to the Board in September and reviewed the results in May.

* Presented historical data to staff and asked them to identify problems and potential solutions. As noted above, school leaders make these presentations—or have staff share in the presentations—at data retreats. In our experience, teachers are quick to grasp problems, identify root causes, and plan more effective solutions because they are the closest to the problem.

* Created collective incentives for schools or departments tied to performance goals. In Illinois, one superintendent made headlines by working with the Board to put a significant amount of money in escrow to be distributed to staff as cash bonuses if the school made gains in achievement over a one-year period.

* Written performance-based job descriptions tied to student achievement. In other words, the district rewrote the job descrip-

tion of the principal to hold him or her accountable for improving teaching and learning.

* Included accountability measures for staff and administrators in school improvement goals.

* Required all teachers at the same grade level to submit a common weekly lesson plan. To ensure that all first-grade students learn, one of Illinois' finest principals makes time for her first-grade teachers to plan together and to find ways to support struggling leaders. Because achievement is a team effort, the entire team develops the lesson plan for the week.

* Had one or two staff members present a summary of current research or related reading at staff meetings.

Build Internal Capacity by Enhancing the Knowledge and Skills of Staff

One of the most important components of building capacity is that for improvement to happen, professional learning must be ongoing, continuous, and collective. Letting individuals create isolated staff development plans is not leadership; it is abrogating leadership. "Collective learning demands an environment that guides and directs the acquisition of new knowledge about instruction. The existing institutional structure of public education does one thing very well ... it creates an environment that values idiosyncratic, isolated, and individualistic learning at the expense of collective learning."[11] The best professional development is centered on the school improvement plan. As a leader, your job is to assure that all staff members have similar professional development experiences centered on the school improvement plan.

Distributing the leadership for professional development means that teachers lead in designing, conducting, and participating in professional development. They must also evaluate it and demonstrate its use in the classroom. Your leadership and reciprocal accountability requires that you hold supervisors accountable for observing and documenting instructional improvement as well as practicing what you learn in a highly visible manner.

Yes, you as the leader *must practice* collective staff development and not just pursue your own plan. Unless you model learn-

---

[11] Ibid., p. 20.

ing, you cannot expect others to participate in collective professional development. The well-worn but highly valuable concept of a community of learners means the entire community, including the leader. "Leaders should be doing, and should be seen to be doing, that which they expect or require others to do."[12] This modeling will not only teach you something, but it will also strengthen the collective will to accomplish a collective purpose, foster strong relationships, and exemplify reciprocal accountability.

Without a heavy investment in professional development for instructional improvement, the best plans in our educational world will simply not work. We have heard the phrase "Sell the sizzle, not the steak," but without the steak, everybody goes hungry. Though the school improvement plans are the sizzle, the actual training is the steak. Without both, your customers—your students and their families—will look elsewhere for a quality education.

Examples of building internal capacity through professional development abound. Here are a few that have worked well in our state:

* Used teacher committees to plan professional development. The most successful superintendents and principals then spend time meeting with these committees to discuss the policy implications and to ensure that plans will be implemented and executed.

* Enlisted a committee of stakeholders to evaluate professional development and make recommendations for improvement. In my districts, for example, I have worked with a team of teachers and parents to write reports that review the literature and best practices on a particular topic, conduct staff and student surveys, and make important policy recommendations.

* Created grade level or school-wide book or study groups. Several school principals have found that book groups are a way to get all teachers thinking about collective reform. Again, "Isolation is the enemy of improvement."[13] Book groups pull teachers out of isolation. One of our favorite books is Diamond and Hopson's *Magic Trees of the Mind*,[14] a very readable piece about the practical applications of brain research.

---

[12] Ibid., p. 21.

[13] Ibid., p. 20.

[14] *Magic Trees of the Mind: How to Nurture Your Child's Intelligence, Creativity and Healthy Emotions from Birth through Adolescence*. New York: Dutton, 1998.

* Used a comprehensive school reform model such as Success for All, a model that has enabled some of our districts with enormous numbers of low-income students to succeed.

* Partnered with a nearby university for a long-term professional development initiative.

* Provided significant incentives for staff development tied to school improvement plans. These school leaders give a larger weighting to each teacher's hours, workshops, or conferences that were directly related to the school improvement goals.

* Taught all teachers how to teach reading. One of our poorest schools in Illinois—in terms of both wealth and achievement—made measurable progress once the principal ensured that all teachers learned how to really teach reading.

* Paid for teachers to create curricular materials tied to school improvement plans.

* Modified the school calendar to add significant time for professional development activities.

Build Internal Capacity by Developing Leaders

One of our greatest challenges is finding outstanding leaders for our schools. Have consulted on superintendent searches and conducted more than two hundred interviews for principals, I am frequently dismayed by the inadequate preparation of candidates. Although we authors would like to think that reading this book could make anyone a great leader, we also realize that there is no substitute for experience and "on the job" training.

Unfortunately, all too often the only "on the job" training is through the assistant principalship. Although this role can be invaluable, all too often we have found that assistant principals are delegated to specific responsibilities or tasks that do not let them develop fully as leaders. More often than not, they are the disciplinarians or responsible for special education. As leaders, our job is to insist that assistant principals have a full array of leadership opportunities. They should lead project teams or curriculum committees, evaluate tenured and pre-tenured teachers, conduct program evaluations, make presentations and speeches in the community, lead school improvement activities, participate in and/or actively lead professional development activities, and the like.

A good leader will find other ways than the traditional assistant principal to develop future leaders. We have recently read about "administrators in residence," i.e. an extended internship, interdistrict cooperatives, and university partnerships for developing leaders. The "First Ring Leadership Academy is an outstanding example (www.ecs.org/clearinghouse/65/66/6566.pdf.). School districts surrounding Cleveland (hence, the name) have collaborated to create a process for growing their own leaders in partnership with Cleveland State University. The thirteen superintendents have decided that instead of working on district-by-district basis to produce leaders with the leadership capabilities to meet the common challenges that their districts share (poverty, high mobility, achievement gaps, etc.), they can provide better leaders if they work together: The mission of the First Ring Leadership Academy is to recruit, train and retain school leaders capable of meeting challenges unique to First Ring school districts to increase the region's capacity for educational leadership and school reform. To achieve these goals, the thirteen district superintendents committed to some unique agreements: to openly share program graduates across the districts, to be personally and actively involved in the program, to lend senior staff as faculty, and to provide release time and financial and administrative support to program participants." (Katy Anthes and Arika Long, "The First Ring Leadership Academy: A Multidistrict Model for Developing, Sharing and Supporting Leadership Talent," Education Commission of the States, October 2005, page 3).

In Wilmette School District 39, we have had terrific success by tapping teachers to lead the Project Teams to implement specific components of the Strategic Plan. We select the teacher based on her interest, passion, drive, expertise and leadership development and free her up half time from her teaching duties to lead the project. We also pay her a $3,000 stipend. As a result, our Elementary Foreign Language initiative, which involves twenty minutes daily of classroom instruction in grades 1-4 (and somewhat less in kindergarten) has become Wilmette's greatest success stories, despite the fact that a similar initiative had failed miserably eight years earlier. As the Superintendent, I wholly attribute the success to our project leader, Kelly, whose leadership ability, collaborative skills, credibility, and personable demeanor established almost unanimous buy-in and staff support, not to mention ample funding and support from the Board of Education and greater community. Had a traditional administrative model been used to lead this initiative, we would not have made nearly the progress we have seen and in fact, it may not have succeeded at all. Though still a half-time teacher and project director, Kelly will be one of the top school administrators in Illinois as she has had the time and support to develop and to practice leading for meaningful change and improvement. We are tapping other talented teachers with leadership potential to spearhead curriculum mapping as well as the revamping of our progress reporting system.

Please do not forget that principals need mentoring. Being a principal is the toughest and also the most important job in the school system, yet too often they begin their career floundering and are soon overwhelmed by day-to-day demands thus losing sight of, and the ability to, effect meaningful change. They need direction, face time with the superintendent, and support and advice from other colleagues. We are highly encouraged that Illinois is poised to pass legislation that requires mentoring of all first-year principals and that many districts have already developed their own programs. If your school district does not have a mentoring program for principals, we urge you to establish one that will provide the new principal safe supports, answers to questions, alternative solutions to difficult problems, and the like at his or her own building. That last phrase is important. Mentoring activities must take place in the building, not the central office. Principals need to be visible and their teachers must sense their presence. They will also respect that you as superintendent understand their needs and are taking the time to ensure that their principal succeeds.

Special Education

Not a week goes by without my son, the gearhead, complaining about the catalytic converter on his '89 Mustang. For those of you who are as mechanically challenged as I am, I have learned that a catalytic converter is a piece of equipment that is required by law. It reduces automobile emissions, thus reducing the Greenhouse Effect. Reducing global warming seems like a fine idea to me, but according to number one son, the catalytic converter also reduces horsepower and engine performance. In my mind, that exchange is almost positive, but in his mind, it is a crime because when he steps on the gas he only burns 30 feet of rubber instead of 40.

Though that may have evoked a chuckle, it is similar to how administrators perceive special education. Not a week goes by without a complaint to me about special education. "It costs too much." "It's not fair to the average kids." "Gifted kids should receive the same attention." "Those special ed kids are disrupting the regular ed kids." "Inclusion is killing us." "Fifty percent of my time is spent on 12% of my students." The list goes on and on. The fact is that federal law requires special education, and, yes, special education students are a protected group of students. If we do a good job of educating them now and preparing them for life after they leave school—even just to perform basic functions like toileting and personal hygiene—we are saving society a lot of money down the line. That is, every dollar we spend on special education students now saves taxpayers significant dollars in the future. Though this concept is not new to school leaders—we use the same argument when talking about the importance of providing a high quality education and small primary grade class sizes—special education is too often perceived as a necessary burden somehow apart from the rest of the smooth running engine of the school, a burden that "slows down" the progress of the other students.

If you are waiting for the special education to swing back from the current "inclusionary practices," you have a long wait. In Illinois, a federal judge recently struck down the categorical certificates for special education. Instead of having seven separate certificates for varying disabilities—learning disabled, behavior disordered, educable mentally handicapped, visually impaired, hearing impaired, physically handicapped, and trainable mentally handicapped—there are now two certificates: the Learning Behavior Specialist I and II, in addition to Visually Impaired and Hearing Impaired. LBS II is merely an extension of LBS I, so basically every special education teacher is now a "cross-categorical" teacher.

In other words, almost overnight all special education teachers became cross-categorical teachers. The Illinois legislature passed a law saying that the State Teacher Certification Board could and should still issue categorical certificates. The governor signed the law. The governor's exercise in futility was pointless. Federal law prevailed.

Special education is here to stay, and whether you call it mainstreaming, inclusion, or something less printable, more and more special education students will be educated in regular classroom settings.

What do effective and successful leaders do about special education? They develop an internal capacity for delivering the service and collective support for special education. The internal capacity begins with sharing leadership by including special education staff in all key committees and collaborative decisions.

Here are some specific ideas that we have found worked well in building the capacity to handle special education students, to control some of the costs, and, most importantly, to help all teachers succeed in educating all children:

* Create a long-term plan to reduce the number of students with IEPs through effective early literacy programs and services. We have some evidence in Illinois that the districts that ensure that five-, six-, and seven-year-olds are readers have substantially fewer students in special education and spend substantially less money per pupil. *As the leader, the most important initiative you can implement is one to ensure that all students will read at grade level before they leave third grade.*

* Make your special education administrator part of your core educational team.

* Create in-house, on-site professional development workshops, and classes on "differentiated instruction" to meet the needs of special education teachers in regular classrooms.

* Have your special education and classroom teachers work as partners in teaching the entire class.

* Resist the urge to have all your special education students take the state test. Make sure that there is some type of local assessment or accountability for attainment of the IEP goals.

* Either create or support a special education parents advisory group. Develop monthly meetings around an educational agenda— that is, a topic that educates the parents. Invite the staff and the entire parent community. Use this group to generate ideas for and to assist you with educating the parents of regular education students about special education.

* Involve your special education teachers in aligning the regular education curriculum to state standards.

* Have your special education teachers help your regular classroom teachers with non-special education students who are struggling.

* When you hire administrators, look for special education training in their background. The single best junior high school principal I have known worked as a BD (behavior disordered) teacher before she became a principal. Likewise, many of the Golden Spike principals (we will meet in the next chapter) had special education in their background, often as reading teachers.

* Create time for regular teachers to read and review IEPs, even if it means hiring a substitute teacher for a day.

* Analyze your budget to see how much you actually spend on special education—after you receive your state and federal money. A careful analysis will show how special education funding impacts and interacts with regular education funding. The findings may well enable you to convince the public of the need for for a referendum to support and/or to get involved in advocating increased funding at the state and federal levels.

* Devote a portion of one Board meeting and your annual report to illustrate the progress your special needs students have made.

* Enlist your teachers in aggressively advocating for Congress to fund its commitment to IDEA (plus NCLB and other federal categorical grants). Congresspersons listen to teachers more often than to administrators, so your teachers must carry the message calling for funding of the federal commitment.

Continuing the Capacity

The astute reader certainly has noticed that very little was said about building capacity from the ground up. That is because school leaders haven't the time nor the legal authority to start from scratch. They can't "divest" unproductive divisions or throw out uncooperative and unproductive staff—they can seldom even find all the staff they need.

Once school leaders have built capacity, however, they need to continue to nurture it. Here are two key suggestions and seven helpful tips for ensuring that your staff will continue their collective commitment to school improvement:

* First, aggressively seek to move or remove those individuals who refuse to participate in the improvement process. We prefer "moving" them—that is, moving them to "see the light" or become a "team player." At some point, however, if that doesn't happen, they need to be transferred, have their contract bought out, or fired. In our experience, if you have developed trusting relationships with your staff unions, if you have exhibited and demonstrated in actions—not just words—how you have tried to work with a teacher, and if you have shown how you put your students' needs first, you can get an obstreperous or obstructionist staff member out the door in a matter of months. In many cases, you will find it harder to convince your Board to buy out a staff member than to convince the union to assist you in removing one. Too often, however, it is a single staff member standing in the way of a positive cultural change. Showing your Board how many children that single individual is actually impacting is a successful strategy in shaking money loose for an amicable parting.

* A second, and more positive, means of both building capacity and maintaining it is to hire top staff members. Earlier, we suggested that successful leaders use their current staff to recruit and interview prospective teachers. Though this is important, you cannot leave recruitment solely up to your staff. It is a leader's responsibility to select the best person for the job.

Here are seven tips:

1. We are believers in working closely with universities to identify the top candidates each year.

2. We believe in keeping our teachers at or near the top of the salary range of the districts near us so we will attract good, new teachers and good, experienced teachers from other districts.

3. We use positive press as a way to showcase our district's successes and to attract teachers from neighboring districts.

4. When good candidates come to us, we do not delay. We find a way to hire them immediately.

5. We do not over-rely on interviews. I have personally made far too many mistakes by hiring good interviewers instead of good teachers or principals. I now feel that the answers to interview questions generally count far less than the poise, presence, general

intelligence, and thinking of the candidate. Though there are a few red flags—I don't hire teachers who believe gifted children should be used to teach other students, I don't hire administrators who are not readers, and I don't hire weird people just because they are "unique." (I rejected one candidate, despite a principal's recommendation, whose primary qualification seemed to be that he had a skull collection.) I find the interview is better suited to laying out the expectations I have for the staff than for finding out how well they teach reading or math.

6. To find out what new teachers can do, we rely primarily on extensive reference checks. When resumes are sent with the standard "references available on request," we send them back asking for a list of references. We contact all of them, asking each some very specific, pointed questions. Then we insist that the principals find four additional references to be asked the same questions.

7. Some of our schools insist on demonstration lessons. We actually have the teacher teach a class of students in our own school! We learn more from twenty minutes of a demonstration lesson than from four hours of interview questions.

Hiring and firing staff is an important function of leadership, one that can and should be shared. Remember, though, that the successful leader must first create the internal capacity for improvement with existing staff. Strategic hiring and firing can enhance but will not create that capacity.

Summary

Building internal capacity sounds complicated and perhaps profound, but it all boils down to the two key points made in this chapter. First, leadership is about improving teaching and learning. Second, a good leader can build capacity for improving teaching and learning for all students, including those with special needs, by actively engaging in the components of "distributed leadership." That is done by having a focused purpose, creating a clear message of vision, fostering productive relationships, holding individuals accountable, and being accountable for improved student performance and educating the school community.

Chapter Nine

Visionary Leadership

Max McGee

Every great leader has a grand vision that both engages and inspires legions of followers. The leader's vision is their vision and they will make incredible sacrifices for it. You may be the best communicator, remarkably trustworthy, and embody every other characteristic we explore in this book, but we contend that without vision you will not be a leader.

The term "visionary leader" quite literally means seeing beyond the present and transcending time. According to anthropologist Jennifer James,[1] the early leaders were literally visionaries because they were the tallest. Thus they could see the herds first for food, and they were the first to see impending danger, and then literally led the way to safer grounds.

Many great visionaries and leaders, including Leonardo Da Vinci and George Washington, were not only exceptionally tall for their day, but they were exceptionally strong physically and highly skilled horseman. In 1776, David McCulloch cites diary entries and letters attesting to Washington's strength and endurance:

Thomas Jefferson considered him "the best horseman of his age." That Washington was known to hunt up to seven hours straight ... "leaping fences and going extremely quick" ... was considered not only a measure of his love of the chase and his exceptional physical stamina, but also his uncommon, unrelenting determination.

Stories were told of extraordinary feats of strength. How, for example, Washington had thrown a stone from the bed of a stream to the top of Virginia's famous Natural Bridge, a height of 215

---

[1] McCullough, David, *1776*. New York: Simon and Schuster, 2005, pp. 47-8.

feet [that is 20 stories and slightly higher than the ceiling of the Houston Astrodome].

Size, however, is no longer the defining characteristic for with vision comes power. Two of the greatest leaders of the modern day, Martin Luther King and Mahatma Gandhi, were more powerful than they were mighty.

On a lesser but arguably as important scale, think of the great school leaders you know. Chances are they aren't confined by "normal" boundaries. They are great because they expand and surpass them. In this chapter, we will share examples of the actions of leaders who have made a monumental difference in the lives of their children and their communities. They stretched boundaries not just by "out of the box" thinking, but by "out of the box" action. Though they will never achieve the stature of da Vinci, Washington, King, or Gandhi, their vision for their schools, their districts, their students, and their communities may well create the fertile ground for tomorrow's leaders who may be the ones who change the world. Their vision has and will continue to make a lasting difference.

We will read of public school leaders who realize that schooling does not begin in kindergarten and that the school day does not end at 3 p.m. We'll meet public school principals who teach basic skills to parents and children. And we will share success stories of leaders who hire teachers before they are certified, who combine public education and public health, who graduate high school students with more than a diploma, who use the whole village— including faith-based institutions—to educate a child.

Who Are These People?

The most visionary leaders in American schools are the leaders of high-poverty, high-performing schools who have succeeded in closing the Achievement Gap. We call their schools the "Golden Spike" schools because these schools have faced incredibly daunting obstacles yet managed to close the Achievement Gap, just as American and immigrant laborers faced enormous challenges in the late 1860s yet managed to close the gap between East and West with a Golden Spike connecting the transcontinental railroad at Promontory, Utah.

In many ways the accomplishments of the Golden Spike school leaders are not unlike another great leader, albeit on a smaller scale.

Abraham Lincoln is best known for freeing the slaves and pre-serving the Union, but his third, and far less noted, accomplishment was arguably as important. His vision and hard work not only united the North and South, but it linked the East and the West through the planning, financing, and construction of the transcontinental railroad. The linkage was Lincoln's vision long before his election, and because of that vision, his legal skills, and his ability to persevere and surmount enormous obstacles, the Golden Spike was driven in Utah (a few years after his assassination). In a remarkable book, *Nothing Like it in the World*,[2] Stephen Ambrose describes this accomplishment in detail, concluding that "Next to winning the Civil War and abolishing slavery, building the first trans-Continental railroad… was the greatest achievement of the American People in the 19th century…"

"The railroad took brains, muscles and sweat in quantities and scope never before put into a single project… Most of all, it could not have been done without teamwork."[3]

There are schools and school districts with leaders who, like Lincoln, have closed the achievement gap between rich and poor and black and white. These leaders are not only visionary, but they are heroic. They are leaders who should be accorded the kind of praise, admiration, and adulation that our firefighters currently receive, for they too have quite literally saved countless lives. These leaders have not only used "brains, muscles and sweat" to get the job done in schools, but they have also have gone beyond district boundaries to forge teams with a shared commitment to educate all children.

These are the individuals who work in the "Golden Spike" schools in Illinois. These are schools which enroll more than half of their students from low-income families yet have at least two out of every three students meeting Illinois' rigorous state standards in all subjects and all grades for the past three years. From interviewing the principals and superintendents who ran these schools, we learned that they were successful in closing the

---

[2] New York: Simon and Schuster, 2000.
[3] Ibid, p. 17.

achievement gap because they had been successful in working be-yond boundaries.

To put their success in perspective, Illinois has approximately 900 elementary schools with enrollment comprised of more than 50% of the children from low-income families (as determined by eligibility for free and reduced lunch). Of these 900 schools, only 40 have been able to attain the goal of having at least two-thirds of the students meet state standards for the past three years. Another 19 have improved by 5% a year to reach that level. Merely 59 of 900 schools, less than 5%, are the Golden Spike (GS) schools.

As we talked to their principals and teachers, visited schools, and read countless documents (including school improvement plans, media accounts, meeting minutes, professional development initiatives, district standards, and the like), some common factors emerged. The single most important commonality among all schools was leadership—exhibited by a focused commitment, ex-traordinary work ethic, shared vision of high expectations, and solution-seeking well beyond school boundaries. Their leadership style was not about being transformational or transactional; the leaders were not all charismatic or colorful. They had different personality types, whether they were an ENTJ, ISFP, or NUTS was unimportant. What distinguished them was commitment. The leaders had unwavering commitment to each child, every family, and the entire school. This commitment was evident in how they went outside the school and outside the system—how they built extended teams—to assure that all children, especially those of poverty, learned and excelled in school.

I suspect that America's schools are full of other leaders equally deserving of this attention and applause. But the examples I cite I know first-hand, and I want you to know about them too. The leaders in these schools and these districts are examples for all of us.

Here is what they do.

Beyond K-12

First and foremost, visionary leaders create a culture of high ex-pectations. In their schools all teachers can believe that every child can excel and that they, as teachers, have the responsibility for assuring that each child in the school succeeds. Their schools are like revival meetings. One can "feel the spirit" the moment the door opens, and after thirty minutes you will truly believe that every child, no matter how poor, no matter how shattered a family life he or she has, no matter how poorly his or parents were educated, will learn in that school. They use many different methods to instill this belief throughout the school. Some hold daily assemblies to celebrate successes to get the day off to a great start, others use quantitative and qualitative data to make their point, a few leaders are charismatic story tellers whose narrative power creates a passionate commitment in staff, and all are able to build a community of learners through teamwork, informal networks, common professional development sessions, and school spirit. The evidence of their success in creating this culture transcends test scores. As one teacher from Whittier School in Peoria, Illinois, states about all her colleagues at her Golden Spike School, "We are responsible for student achievement. When a child fails, it is our responsibility. Children come to us with a great deal of baggage. We set that aside and teach them. If a child does not do well in our classroom, we reevaluate our teaching rather than make excuses and *we never give up!"*

Next to creating this culture, the second most critical commonality among the Golden Spike schools is the primary importance of reading. A minimum of grade level literacy is expected in GS schools, and struggling students are supported in kindergarten, first, and second grade at school, home, and at summer activities. The leaders understand, however, that if they wait until kindergarten, they have waited too long. Consequently, leaders in the GS schools reach out to the preschool community or, in some instances, even bring the preschool children into their schools. The leaders strive to create classroom spaces and find financial support for three- and four-year-olds. They make them and their parents part of the school family.

Why is it so important for K-8 or K-12 school leaders to work with the children before they enter the system? The short answer is that both the educational and financial returns on this early investment are monumental: educationally, because the children enter school with the background they need to learn, and financially, because the districts save thousands of dollars on remedial and special education programming in later years.

Nearly every week, we read remarkable accounts of how the brain works. We now know that learning begins at birth and that the development of a child's brain is greater in the first five years of life than at any other time. Grover Whitehurst,[4] Craig Ramey,[5] and Dorothy Strickland[6] have written about the impact of the early years (birth through five) on success in school. From birth, children need to be nurtured. The physical contact of a parent enhances learning. Preschoolers need to build a working vocabulary from having parents talk *with* them instead of *at* them; they also need to learn their sounds.

Sounds not acquired at this age are lost. Toddlers deposited in front of television, constantly told to shush, and talked *to* instead of *with* do not learn to make the sounds they will need in order to read.

A significant body of research exists[7] supporting early childhood education as the most effective intervention in closing the achievement gap. Jencks and Phillips[8] contend, "If we want equal outcomes among twelfth-graders, we will also have to narrow the skill gap between black and white children before they enter school."[9]

This is a critical point. Much has been written about the impact of poverty on family structure—drug and alcohol use, violence, and the like—but one of the most deleterious impacts is on how parenting affects children's linguistic development.

---

[4] Remarks at the White House Summit on Early Childhood Cognitive Development, 2001.

[5] Craig T. and Sharon L. Ramey, "Early Intervention and Early Experience," *American Psychologist*, vol. 53, no. 2, 1998, pp. 109-20.

[6] Neuman, S. and D. Dickinson, "Early Intervention for African American Children Considered to be at Risk," in **Handbook of Early Literacy Research**. New York: Guilford Press, 2001.

[7] Ramey and Ramey, 1998, loc. cit.; Thomas, M.D., and W. Bainbridge, "All Children Can Learn: Facts and Fallacies," *Education Research Service Spectrum*, Winter 2001; L.A. Karoly et. al., **Investing in Our Children: What We Know and Don't Know about the Costs and Benefits of Early Childhood Interventions**. Santa Monica, CA: Rand, 1998, and C. Jencks and M. Phillips, eds., **The Black-White Test Score Gap**. Washington, D.C.: Brookings Institution Press, 1998.

[8] Christopher Jencks and Meredith Phillips, *The Black-White Test Score Gap*, Washington, D.C.: The Brookings Institution Press, 1998, p. 46.

[9] Meredith Phillips, Jeanne Brooks-Gunn, Gred Duncan, Pamela Klebanov, and Jonathan Crane, "Family Background, Parenting Practices and the Black-White Test Score Gap," in Jencks and Phillips, Ibid., pp. 103-148.

Impoverished students are far more likely than their class-mates to enter school "linguistically disadvantaged" because they do not have experiences that will promote literacy and reading readiness: "Children from low-income families are substantially behind their more affluent peers in both ... components of pre-reading. For instance, the typical child in some urban public schools enters kindergarten at the fifth percentile in vocabulary knowledge, and does not know words such as chicken, leaf and triangle."[10]

Citing Hart and Risley,[11] Grover Whitehurst continues, "The professional families' children at age three actually had a larger recorded vocabulary than the welfare families' parents. I must re-peat that: at three, children from affluent families had a larger spo-ken vocabulary than the parents from welfare families."[12]

Given the importance of education well before school and to help reduce this vocabulary gap, we have found successful school leaders who extended their K-8 or K-12 schools to pre-kinder-garten.

Principals and superintendents have created parent-infant cen-ters out of empty classrooms. These centers are for parents to learn about parenting by playing with their children. They are shown how to read to young children, how to let them handle books, how to manage crying toddlers, and how to appropriately correct mis-behavior. The school leaders stock these centers with resources such as toys, picture books, and audiotapes they can use and even check out. Though few, if any, of these resources come from the K-12 budget, the leaders use both their civic connections and par-ents to obtain donations for these centers.

In some schools, the leaders make room in their building for preschool classrooms for at-risk students. Vacant classroom space serves these children first. In Illinois, this practice is becoming more and more common, from the poorest districts to the most affluent. The leaders have learned that by teaching the preschool-ers, they not only ensure success, but they will also most likely save the district significant dollars in the long run because these children will be less likely to need special education services.

---

[10] Grover Whitehurst, Remarks to the White House Conference on Preschool Cognitive Development, Georgetown University, July 26, 2001, p. 7.
[11] Betty Hart and Todd Risley, *Meaningful Differences in the Everyday Experi-ence of Young American Children*. Baltimore: P.H. Brookes, 1995.
[12] Ibid., p. 8.

Visionary leaders fight to the last round to maintain these spaces. They resist pressures to replace pre-K spaces with other programs and services.

Exceptional leaders also make a concerted effort to communicate kindergarten expectations to preschool providers and parents. They list books to read, sounds and words to know, and letters, shapes, and numbers to recognize. They meet with the directors and hold get-togethers for parents before children ever enter school. Put simply, these leaders see all children in the community as their students from birth! Though kindergarten is the beginning of formal schooling, leaders who realize that learning begins at birth do not ignore the most important years in a child's education—the years before kindergarten.

High school leaders have also discovered the power of extending the boundaries beyond kindergarten through twelfth grade by attending to the preschool babies of their high school students! Yes, you read that correctly. In Illinois, Morton Grove East High School has a Hispanic/Latino enrollment of 90%, with 84% of the students from low-income families, yet their graduation rate is 95%! One key to their success is welcoming high school parents and teaching them how to care for their babies. They have a partnership with a medical facility that has set up a clinic in the school. On a recent visit, I watched sixteen-year-old parents learn how to diaper their newborn and how to comfort a crying baby with soothing singing or by gently reading a book.

Great leaders work beyond boundaries.

Beyond Children

School is not just for kids anymore. The Golden Spike principals realize that parent education and a child's education are inexorably intertwined. Knowing that many parents of low-income children have had less-than-positive past experience with schools when they were students, the leaders find ways to make school both a welcoming and a learning experience. Ziebell School in Posen-Robins, Illinois—annually ranked as one of the least desirable places in America to live—has the strongest three-year record of improvement in Illinois, due, in large part, to parent education.

Ziebell's principal realized that many of her students' parents hated school when they were children and that a high percentage of parents were English language learners or had minimal literacy skills. She determined to make her school a special place for both parents and children. To do this, the principal began with family nights during which parents learned about school and their role in supporting their children. Because she served food and had donated clothing to give away, attendance improved with each session. She also began holding classes to help parents become better readers. With hard work, she was able to obtain a grant for two parent coordinators. These individuals ran parent workshops throughout the year at the school. The workshops all had a "make and take" activity combined with plenty of socializing and fun, along with a message about helping their children learn. The coordinators made school a parent-friendly place and actually taught parents, grandparents, and other caregivers how to interact with teachers: what questions to ask, how and when to make contact, how to obtain extra help with difficult assignments, and the like. In addition, the coordinators conducted a formal parent survey at the beginning and end of every year. The information from the survey was shared with the school improvement team and used to measure success and to set the agenda for the forthcoming year's activities.

Parents are welcomed to school for several assemblies. On the required report card day, they leave the school with the report card and a bag of treats. The homework policy programs ensure daily home-school communication. Parents get a Home Link folder every day. At the beginning of the year, they also sign a parent compact stating what they will do for their kids.

To support parent literacy, the principal developed a parent lending library that is open every Friday. Parents can check out books and tapes. With the assistance of a Follet grant, she obtained books for adult learners, complete with comprehension and vocabulary exercises. As a recipient of a significant Case Foundation grant plus the financial support of the Illinois State Board of Education, they have Power UP Computer labs that are open for students and parents to work on reading activities for three hours after school each day. Parent involvement certainly played a role in making Ziebell the "most improved" school of all high-poverty schools, gaining nearly 36 percentage points over the last three years!

Getting more books in parents' hands is a challenge. Susan Neumann, Undersecretary at the USDE, has published research showing that parents in low-income neighborhoods simply do not have access to print.[13] Counting every possible source of literacy, including the magazine racks at Walgreen's, she studied four neighborhoods in Philadelphia to determine access to print. In one middle-income neighborhood there were 1,200 children. The families had 11 places to buy books and over 16,000 titles were available—approximately 12 titles for every child. In contrast, in one of the low-income neighborhoods there were approximately 10,000 children yet only four places to buy books and only 33 different titles. This was one book for every 353 children! Principals and superintendents in the GS schools may not have read Susan Neuman's research, but they clearly knew that parents needed books. The leaders found a way to get books home to families on a weekly basis. Some had school library hours for parents; others used a "book in a bag" program where every weekend they sent home a book in a sealed bag with every child. Some even had after-school or evening parent-child reading clubs.

Beyond Diplomas

Successful, visionary high school leaders in low-income schools are working with business and high-tech companies like Cisco and Intel to help students graduate with certificates as well as diplomas.

These leaders understand that technology is the future and that many students, especially those from low-income families, need more than a diploma or admission to community college. They find ways to bring training programs into schools. Students learn to be computer technicians, receive credit for mechanics requirements, and gain admission to extended job training programs.

School leaders see business partnerships as something entirely different than the standard financial support or occasional volunteer tutoring. Though we certainly don't discredit those types of partnerships, we are more encouraged seeing business partnerships that provide real-life training and work experiences for children. Jobs for America's Graduates is one such example, funding for which is available in many state budgets. We have heard testi-

---

[13] Susan B. Neuman, "Access to Print: Problems, Consequences, and Instructional Solutions," Remarks at the White House Summit on Early Childhood Cognitive Development, Georgetown University, July 26-27, 2001.

mony of how high school students' lives have changed by working next to a veterinarian, helping OB-GYNs deliver babies, and even tutoring in classrooms. Cisco and Intel offer high-tech training and certification so students graduating from high school can immediately begin earning money solving network problems. At a lower-tech level, high school leaders are developing partnerships with local auto shops to help students acquire hours of experience necessary for certification. In fact, at one school the "final exam" for work-study involves putting in a full forty-hour week at a used car dealership.

"Beyond Diplomas" also means that the successful school leaders strive to recruit the very best teachers—even before they are certified. One local district has developed a partnership with a university to place promising teacher candidates in schools before they graduate or are certified. These teachers are actually paid interns until they graduate; if they succeed, they get hired as teachers immediately upon graduation. These school leaders don't wait for applicants to come to them nor do they worry about competing with more affluent schools. They go to where the best teachers are learning their trade and get those teachers in their schools.

Beyond Academics

In many of our chapters you read about the importance of attending to the basic needs of children, like health and safety. A commonality of the Golden Spike leaders is assuring that each and every child is fed and healthy. They may not have read the research by Snow, Burns and Griffin (1998), but they knew their critical contention through experience: "Families that lack sufficient resources to provide adequate housing, health care, and nutrition for their children are less likely to focus on their children's educational needs."[14]

Many Golden Spike leaders make sure that everyone gets a healthy breakfast. They do more than offer a breakfast program, they deliver it! They make it fun for kids. At lunchtime, junk food

---

[14] C.E. Snow, S. Burns, and P. Griffin, eds. *Preventing Reading Difficulties in Young Children*. Washington, D.C.: National Academy Press, 1998, from Strickland, Dorothy, "Early Intervention for African American Children Considered to be at Risk," in S. Neuman and D. Dickinson's *Handbook of Early Literary Research*, New York: Guilford Press, 2001.

is junked. One of my more vivid memories from a day in a Golden Spike school was a principal who was walking through the lunch-room and found a second grader struggling to open a *huge* bag of corn chips and 16-ounce jar of salsa. She took these from him and bought him a healthy hot lunch.

In addition to watching what children ingest, Golden Spike principals make sure that nutrition is put to good use! Exercise and activity count. The brain functions better with exercise. Low-income children from minority families tend toward obesity, so principals assure that they get their exercise. Many sponsor special events such as walks or "feet meets."

Savage Inequalities: Children in America's Schools by Jona-thon Kozol[15] includes vivid descriptions of the poverty of East St. Louis, Illinois. Even though East St. Louis schools have made in-cremental progress since that time, the neighboring community of Belleville, with an 80% low-income population, has a record of both achievement and improvement that is the envy of every school in Illinois. With the ISAT (Illinois state test) scores com-petitive with wealthy Chicago suburbs, two of the district's schools achieved Golden Spike recognition. Those schools are quick to acknowledge unwavering district leadership in looking after the welfare of students. "Health for Kids" consists of two district vans that ferry students to physicals, immunizations, and other dental, doctor, and eye appointments. At Franklin School in Belleville, the principal conducts a health fair through Southern Illinois University at Edwardsville, to immunize preschoolers. The "Bright Smiles" dental program ensures that *every* child sees a dentist at least once a year. It is a district philosophy and a clear commitment to take care of the child's basic needs first—food, clothing, and shelter—so learning can then flourish. And flourish it does, as evidenced by Franklin and Jefferson schools where 88% of the students met state standards in 2001!

In Golden Spike schools that have upper-grade students, suc-cessful leaders provide support for students struggling with eating disorders. They set up counseling and weekly monitoring to help students resolve anxieties about their body types and to ensure that they are taking care of basic health needs.

---

[15] 2nd ed., New York: Perennial, 1992.

Beyond Schools

From reading Chapter 1, you know that the successful school leader is a civic leader as well. He or she understands the importance of engaging the community in the success of the schools. We all know the value of this strategy in terms of quality education and community economics. Good schools make good communities, and good communities make good schools. Though many assume the quality of schools is directly linked to the home values, Golden Spikes schools illustrate how great leaders and great schools can shatter this assumption. With proper support, poor children are fully capable of high-level learning and schools in poor communities can excel!

The best leaders are not only civic leaders, they build close relationships with other community leaders to enlist their help in promoting the value of school, getting children to school and keeping them there, and providing programs and services after school and during the summer. It takes more than an open-door policy. The good school leaders go out the open door of their offices, open the door of their schools, and from there go out into the community.

For example, at one Golden Spike school, the principal and teachers do not wait for parents to come to Open House, they go to the parents—during the summer! Well before the first day of school, each teacher walks the neighborhood and hand delivers an invitation to a parent orientation and Open House. Unlike most districts, where these events are held after school begins, these parent meetings are held before the semester starts! The teachers make very clear their expectation that all children can and will succeed. They also directly tell the parents what they expect from them and what the children need from them in order to achieve that success. Parent contact continues throughout the school year and culminates in a celebration picnic when that year ends. One teacher fondly recalls those traditions, describing how she attended the school picnic as a student many, many years ago and that this year she was attending her last before she retired from a career spanning more than three decades.

In addition, this school relies on the neighborhood association to run summer school. Because the students do so well, they are, ironically, ineligible for state summer school funding. Working with various community grants and an avid director, who is a retired phone company executive, the administration has ensured that all students have an active summer of learning and exploration. Struggling students are tutored every morning. The afternoon is filled with a host of activities ranging from art projects to athletics. The one or two trips each week are the students' favorite activity. They return to school each fall ready to learn.

Learning doesn't take place solely in a classroom or only during the regular school day and school year. The school and district's leaders' community outreach and successful summer school were, in part, responsible for having it be one of the three schools to make the Golden Spike list (in terms of *both* absolute performance and improvement). During the last three years, an average of 82% of the students met state standards, and they improved by more than five percentage points each year on the Illinois state test.

Another profound example of community involvement that makes a difference is a high school on the far edge of suburban Chicago, where the subdivisions abut cornfields. The school brought farmers into biology classes to teach students how to grow corn and use test plots to study growth and yield rates. In chemistry class the following year, a chemist from a nearby town taught students how to convert corn into diesel fuel. The fuel was used to power an old VW beetle that the auto class had converted from gas to diesel with support from a local mechanic. Completing the project, the art students added plenty of "decorative touches" to the salvaged bug. The entire community not only raised a child, it raised a beetle! More importantly, by going beyond school boundaries, the school leaders provided learning that was motivating and meaningful, thus keeping a far higher percentage of students in school than one would ordinarily expect.

Beyond District Boundaries

Real school leaders take their mission so seriously that during some weeks they are out of the district as much as they are in it! Though this observation may seem inconsistent, real leaders realize that many policies impacting their district are made miles away from the Board room. They get themselves key committee appointments with their state agencies. In fact, two of the authors of this book have covered the state assessment ground thoroughly, with one on the tech committee and the other on the task force charged with deciding what the annual state assessment required by NCLB will be! Our third author performs an even more valuable function. A gifted speaker, he carries the message of the need for policy reform into every area of the state.

Other leaders have realized that every nickel of appropriation is from the legislature, and they work hard to help the system help their students. Too often school leaders think that a donation to the PAC is all the political involvement they need. Even worse, we hear that politics and education do not mix. Mix they must! Good school leaders know how to work the legislature and they know how to work a room. They understand the importance of a handwritten note to a legislator. They get to know politicians on a first-name basis. They even attend a modest fund-raiser or two.

They spend time in the halls of the Capitol. They have a lunch or a breakfast with legislators and invite them into their Board rooms and classrooms.

Is the effort worth it? In Illinois, hundreds of thousands of "member initiative" or "pork" dollars have been directed to schools by individual legislators. More importantly, visionary school and district leaders have succeeded in influencing funding decisions involving millions of dollars. With the support of her superintendent, one of Illinois' top early childhood teachers convinced the state's Senate Education Committee to increase funding for early childhood education. Likewise, by meeting frequently with local state representatives and senators, by including them in school events, by persistently contacting other legislative leaders, school leaders in Illinois have preserved funding for critical programs such as the state's Reading Block Grant and for Alternative Education. A shining moment in Illinois was when school leaders worked hand in hand with local legislators to reverse a state education budget "deal" made by the governor and four legislative leaders (behind closed doors) that would have sent nearly $70 million to private schools. Cultivating relationships with your state and federal legislators may take you out of the office, but spending time with them may be one of the most beneficial things that you can do for your students.

Lessons in Leadership

Though I do not work in a high poverty school district, and my principals do not deal with the challenge of impoverished schools, what we have learned from the visionary "Golden Spike" leaders has changed our schools and made them even better places for "tomorrow's leaders" to learn and grow. In fact, I learned long ago that high achieving and high functioning are not one and the same. When I began working with the leadership team in a high performing district that had been on "cruise control" for sometime, I sought advice from leaders in the profession. A good friend, who could have made a very lucrative consulting arrangement to work with my administrative team, advised me to use the proven expertise of the Golden Spike leaders rather than bring him in to run some workshops or send them off to various conferences and professional development events. He was right, and during the next few years, we strengthened our administrative team, built extensive leadership capacity among staff, and created a collaborative leadership model with our teachers' association. In fact, our shared vision has become so powerful that the administrative and union leadership teams have issued joint memos and letters articulating the vision and supporting initiatives, we have developed and administered a common staff climate survey and used the results to make a difference in the lives of staff, and we have solved innumerable "stone in the shoe" problems quickly and effectively. There has not been a grievance filed in five years. Specifically, what have we done? Here are a few examples:

We developed a collective vision to move not just from "Good to Great," but from "Great to Greater" as we pursued our mission of "Teaching Tomorrow's Leaders." Using data, "branding" methods outlined in Chapter Three, and a regular presence in the schools, the administrative team developed trusting, respectful relationships focused on moving the district forward rather than maintaining the status quo.

We completely transformed the professional development model from one of pursuing individual goals to a community of learners. The Board of Education agreed to substitute two student instructional days for two staff development days, and the new union contract set aside significant reimbursements for teachers taking workshops or classes or for teaching internal workshops if and when these were directly tied to District goals and the School Improvement Plans. The professional development days were focused on one topic, so everyone developed a common vocabulary and shared a common learning experience. In addition to the formal professional development days, the staff led workshops after school and on Saturdays, and even the superintendent conducted a book club for staff, who in turn shared the books in their schools. In short, we determined that the only effective professional development was like that found in the Golden Spike Schools, that is, professional development linked to a common mission for the collective good. As Richard Elmore wrote, "Professional development is effective only to the degree that it engages teachers and administrators in *large-scale improvement...*"

Professional development must support a *collective good* and its value must be judged by what it contributes to building individual capacity to improve the quality of instruction *in the school and school system."* [16]

Additionally, as we learned from the Golden Spike leaders, literacy needed to come first. As a result, we revamped our intervention program for struggling readers, we made it a requirement that all newly hired primary grade teachers must have a teaching certificate with a Reading Endorsement or similar Reading credential, and we identified ways in which we could assure that our male students learned to read and write as well as their female classmates.

Finally, knowing full well that moving from "Great to Greater" requires a highly skilled, energized, and passionate teaching staff, we involved them in every aspect of decision making. We asked their opinions on joint union/administration surveys, followed through with their ideas and suggestions, and addressed their concerns. We replaced some more traditional principals with individuals who had enormous vision and understanding of how to reach beyond the walls of the school. We devoted a minimum of one afternoon a month to developing visionary leaders through common readings, video analyses, and discussions of current research.

---

[16] Elmore, Richard, "Bridging the Gap Between Standards and Achievement: The Imperative for Professional Development in Education." Albert Shanker Institute, 2002, p. 14.

Aligned with the principles of "distributed leadership," we also identified teachers with exceptional leadership potential and selected them to run project teams necessary to execute initiatives in our Strategic Plan. Each teacher's workload was reduced, and all received a $3,000 stipend. Due to their passion, energy, vision, and commitment, their projects all succeeded beyond even my high expectations. Projects is capitalized because these were not small assignments, but rather transforming initiatives. Kelly spearheaded our successful Elementary Foreign Language initiative so now every child in the primary grades receives 20 minutes of Spanish language instruction and immersion daily, Christy and Cathy drove our district-wide Curriculum Mapping project, and Penny led the team that developed an innovative, effective progress reporting system.

Finally, we directly borrowed the Golden Spike principals' expertise in helping all of their teachers become competent consumers of data. We began with Board members and administrators, demonstrating how to find the gold nuggets in the endless riverbeds of numbers. We taught them and our staff which results are worth attending to and which are white noise. Every principal learned how to conduct an analysis of variance to identify whether gains or declines were statistically significant. Graphs were used to tell stories and we tracked improvement over time. Presentations were held for staff and parents, so that we could all develop a common vocabulary and focus on that information which was most useful in improving teaching and in reaching individual children.

These are a few of the "leadership lessons" from the visionary Golden Spike principals that can make a difference in your school, be it rich or poor, homogeneous or diverse, elementary or high school. Insularity and isolation are the enemies of improvement. If you are willing to look beyond your own boundaries, to peer into the horizon to identify what great leaders do, and if you have the courage to share that knowledge and vision, there is no limit on what your district and/or your school can accomplish.

Summary

The most successful leaders in the most challenging schools go well outside what most of us see as normal boundaries to ensure the success of their students. They work very closely with pre-schools, childcare providers, and parents of pre-kindergarten students to assure that children zero to five years of age are getting care, nutrition, nurturing, and the experiences they need to have a productive kindergarten year. Some of the most successful leaders even find space in their buildings for preschool classrooms or parent-infant centers.

They teach parents how to parent; they also help parents learn to read and compute.

They establish health clinics in their buildings, provide breakfasts, keep junk food out of the lunchroom, and get children and families to the doctor, dentist, and optometrist.

They have different kinds of corporate partners who provide students with work-study experiences from which they graduate with skills, computer technician certificates, and credits toward apprenticeships or trade certifications.

The churches and other community groups carry the same message as the schools. They are places for tutoring, they promote attendance, they reward achievement, and they support parents. The school leaders initiate, develop, nurture, and cherish these relationships with the churches and other community groups.

The leaders lobby for their schools. Whether seeking a few extra state dollars from the local legislator or actively spearheading funding reform, they are on a first-name basis with their local legislators and are a presence in the state capitols.

They are ordinary people facing exceptional challenges in extraordinary ways. For these visionary leaders, thinking out of the box is a cliché. Acting out of the box is what they do. It is a lesson for us and should be our "gold standard" of leadership. Leading beyond boundaries not only closes gaps, it enables *all* children to achieve beyond what was thought to be their "potential."

"Again and again, the impossible problem is solved when we see that the problem is only a tough decision waiting to be made."

Robert Schuller

Chapter Ten

Successful Teaching and Learning

Jim Rosborg

Let's set the record straight right away. As an administrator, you must realize that teachers are the single most important component to not only a student's success, but also the school's success. Teachers are the first line of defense against problems that arise. And the *total* success of the teaching staff is important because too often a school is judged by its weakest teacher.

This chapter talks about how to make teachers successful and how that leads to greater learning. Many times it is the intangibles that make teaching succeed. In Chapter 7, we have dealt with professional development, a huge factor for administrative and teaching success. In this chapter, we will deal with the administrative involvement in successful teaching, including collaboration, collective bargaining, labor problems, and setting the proper environment. (Proper environment here means good salaries, enforced discipline, ample supplies and instructional tools, planned curricula, and updated buildings and grounds.) The final portion of the chapter will discuss the creation of a foundation.

I recently retired after having the honor and privilege of serving as Superintendent of Schools for Belleville District #118 in Belleville, Illinois.

Let me explain a few things about the district since I will draw heavily from it on these pages. I was long blessed with a knowledgeable and supportive Board of Education. In addition, my administrative team and teaching staff continue to be, in my opinion, second to none. That's not all luck. We chose them because we felt that good people make good leaders. If the people around us are successful, then we as leaders will be successful too.

My Board and its administration also enjoy a strong partnership with the teachers' union (AFT/IFT Local 673). This relationship is based on trust, open communication, and shared decision making. It is a collaborative model that has fostered a sense of pride and ownership in staff members. As a result of working together, the district and the Teachers' Union was recognized with the national United Auto Workers/Saturn Partnership Award in 1999 and the Bill Weir Labor Management Award in 2001. The district also was recognized by the Illinois State Board of Education as a model district for local accountability and was selected by the State Board to be a member of a select group of schools called Leadership in Accountability and Quality Assurance Program (LAQA). This group looked at ways to improve reading and mathematics techniques to go along with instructional and test score improvement.

I am bragging, of course, but I want to establish a base from which to explain the following methods that the District #118 partners used to collaboratively find and implement educational excellence:

New Teachers. Collaboration has to take place at the beginning of one's career. At our new-teacher orientation, one of the sessions is a joint appearance by the superintendent and the union president to encourage new teachers to join the union and become active in educational issues. In our district, the union enjoys 100% membership. One might ask why an administration would want this to happen. For us it is easy. By having the teachers in agreement about unionism, a great deal of divisiveness within the staff is prevented. A natural conflict occurs if some members of the staff are union members and some are not. Our attitude is that we would rather the teachers have issues with the Board and administration than representational issues with each other. The reality? Less conflict occurs with the Board and administration because of the lack of conflict among the teachers.

Also included in this initial meeting of new teachers is the creation of a mentoring program that offers not only mentor partners but also mini-workshops and peer-support groups. How do you set up a mentoring program? First of all, you set up times for new teachers to meet with their mentors and in-service leaders. You must also set the topics for in-services. District #118 established the following topics:

* Discipline
* School/home/family relationships
* Special Education
* Peer relationships
* Assessment and its impact on curriculum
* Dealing with a diverse population
* Sharing

In addition, mentor teachers are assigned to the newly hired individuals. In conjunction with a local university, the new teachers are offered the opportunity to get four graduate credit hours by attending a support program specifically designed for first-year teachers. You, as a school leader, must set up this formula to ensure the success of your teaching newcomers.

Union Advisory. This is the hallmark of the collaboration in the partnership between the union and district administration. For District #118, it is the most important forum to deal with policies, building issues, and contractual questions. The Union Advisory meeting between union building representatives, officers, and the superintendent is held monthly. Information, questions, and concerns are shared with candor. The key for the superintendent is two-fold. First, the superintendent must allow open communication and not consider any question unimportant. Second, the superintendent must let this group evolve so that beyond identifying problems, it also helps to solve them. This step can take place by involving the group in some positive activities.

This advisory group has been active in working with the administration on such things as Veterans' Day activities, the district's holiday party, the retirement reception, and various community-wide events associated with the district. A good statement would be as follows to make the problem-solving transition, "We have done a great job identifying the problem, now what can we do to solve it?"

While these meetings can be somewhat challenging for the superintendent, they are essential for the positive collaboration to take place in the district.

How do you set these meetings up? First of all, you must go into these meetings with a positive attitude. I began each meeting by reviewing the good things that were happening in the district. Next, I went over issues that I knew were pending. I encouraged all building issues to be solved in that building. The meeting was then turned over to the union president to present questions that individual building representatives felt uncomfortable asking. Finally, I asked each building rep for individual questions.

Initially, this may seem a little threatening. After a while though, it all starts to come together as you see improvements in morale and communications. The key is to allow time for your union representatives to meet before you come into the meeting. Then get the issues on the table and solve them.

Board of Education Involvement with the Union and Staff. It is harder for people to be inconsiderate to each other if they know each other and are not surprised by the decisions made. Besides social activities in the district, there are other ways to create non-threatening communication between the Board and the staff members. Two examples: (1) District #118 has a faculty curriculum committee that has representation from each building and each grade level. This committee meets periodically with the Board Curriculum Committee to go over curricular issues in the district and to collectively celebrate district education successes. This has proven to be a wonderfully collaborative activity. (2) The union has initiated another activity with the Board that has been very productive. Every other summer, representatives of the Board and administration accompany the local union officers to the American Federation of Teachers Quest Conference that the A.F.T. sponsors in Washington, D.C. This conference provides the forum to collectively tackle educational issues.

Collaborative Decision Making. While collaboration is needed with all stakeholders, this chapter's focus is on teacher-district leadership partnerships. Teachers must be involved to feel ownership in the educational process. In our district, teachers and administrators work together on district-wide committees to discuss a variety of topics. In addition to the previously mentioned curriculum and advisory committees, these include committees for character education, crisis prevention, math problem solving, creative writing, young authors, field days, textbook selection, the spelling bee, the science fair, reading improvement, and various other curriculum committees formed on an as-needed basis meet to discuss ways to improve the student learning process. Administration needs to have a plan of action for each of these committees, but it also needs to respect committee decisions. This attitude fosters that needed sense of ownership for district initiatives among staff members. As stated in Chapter 1, every effort should be made to help teachers receive reimbursement for their participation in these committees. A district that not only allows teachers to share the district's vision but also to help define the vision will get a broader view of education which will translate into educational excellence.

Developing Good Teachers. As administrators we must work hard to develop good teachers, and also help them believe that all students can learn. Close relationships, mutual respect and admiration, and genuine fondness for children must characterize the classroom. Administrators can set the tone by making sure that positive messages are given either through personal interactions or displays on the walls. The good administrator helps teachers incorporate a significant range of strategies and a vast array of resources to help each individual child. The administrator helps develop a team spirit among the teachers. The goal is to create an attitude where the entire school exudes a zealous commitment to reach each and every child. This team spirit, along with a solid work ethic, develops a school family that takes the necessary risks to help students be successful.

You develop a team spirit by setting the proper environment for the team to grow and by addressing specific details that could become major problems if not dealt with. Remember, if a teacher contacts you, the issue is important to him/her, however insignificant it may appear to you.

Here are some additional things that can directly and indirectly help lead to academic excellence:

* Learn the names of your staff members.
* Have a day to wear school colors or staff shirts.
* Recognize important events in people's lives: births, deaths, marriages, awards, etc.
* Have a staff picnic.
* Participate in a food drive and Secret Santa gift giving at Christmas.
* Let staff members leave early on occasion.
* Work with staff members in emergency situations, including appointments with doctors or dentists.

* Laugh with your staff; cry with your staff; let them know you are human.
* Make every effort to recognize staff members.
* Work hard. Play hard. Stick together. Support each other.

Collective Bargaining—Negotiations

A district that is happily rolling along with collaborative peace and positive relationships can have all of it wiped out by the emotions of a work stoppage or, as most would call it, a labor strike. Generally, the Board negotiates with the teachers' union. The success of the negotiations starts with one major objective—to reach an agreement. The superintendent's goal has to be to keep the emotions down on both sides and to present a clear picture of the financial status for both the Board and the union. As an administrator, you must research the collective bargaining issue. A good source for me was *Collective Bargaining and the School Board* by Ronald R. Booth (Illinois Association of School Boards).

I personally feel that negotiations go better for both the Board and the union without outside representation (that is, lawyers or paid negotiators). Face-to-face negotiations are tough, but trust is easier to achieve without parties from the outside. Often outside representation puts both sides on the defensive.

What is the superintendent's role? Much of the answer to this question depends upon the parameters established by the Board. In Belleville #118, the Board has given the superintendent the ability to meet with union officers to discuss funding sources, lay out the budget and revenue projections, establish priorities, consider potential problem issues, and attempt to make joint administrative/union recommendations to the Board concerning non-monetary language issues in the contract. These meetings are based upon open communication and trust, and they are far less threatening than the actual negotiation session with the Board.

The superintendent can perform a variety of other positive behind-the-scenes activities. For example, the superintendent can attempt to get both groups to bring an equal number of people to the negotiations session. This prevents intimidation by numbers. Next, the superintendent can offer budget figures and projected revenues before the union asks for them. The union will ask for them anyway, so take the initiative. Other common mistakes that school districts make are trying to hide money or making fund transfers during the negotiation process, which gives the perception that money is being hidden. The superintendent should be as open as possible with information. The unions have access to the financial information and are sophisticated enough in negotiations to see trickery. So why do it? Financial cover-ups just lead to mistrust, which inhibits the success of reaching that main objective, settlement. The superintendent's leadership success is often determined by his/her ability to handle labor relations.

Other issues may lead to unnecessary strikes.

I've seen teachers go on strike when they and the Board are only 1% apart. Then when the strike starts, the settlement is reached for an amount equal to or higher than that initial percent! That strike was avoidable; it should have been settled. It shows poor leadership from both the district administration and the union. The negative feelings that are caused by a labor stoppage are deep and long lasting.

Strikes become even more complicated when the school has a sports team vying for a state championship or just after a local, state, or national tragedy. Emotions are extraordinarily high or low at these moments. The strike further exacerbates the tension. In the case of the sports event, it is a once-in-a-lifetime occurrence for players and long-residing community members. The strike detracts from or prevents this singular event. In those situations, both the school district and the teachers lose community support for years to come. Mediation could have saved that extreme discomfort for everyone. It is the superintendent's role to make sure that neither party makes this mistake.

The superintendent is the key instrument for reaching a settlement. Many times the superintendent becomes a mediator between the two parties. If asked to do so, how do you mediate? Here are some useful guidelines:

* You tell the Board that the union negotiators are good people.

* You constantly remind the Board of the successes of the staff.

* You establish an attitude that a raise is needed and that these raises help keep the employees happy which, in turn, can lead to higher student achievement.

* You remind the teachers that Board members are not professional negotiators and may make mistakes. You also remind the teachers that the Board has always supported them and given them raises.

* You work hard with staff members so they propose a reasonable request.

* When it comes close to settlement, you may have to convince the Board to accept an offer they do not think they can afford. Show them possibilities of additional revenue. Have this information ready before this eleventh-hour moment.

* You help the Board avoid trivialities.

* You get both parties to drop their concerns about a particularly meaningless clause or section in the contract.

* You know your staff so well that you recognize union requests that are only satisfying the needs of a district's vocal minority.

The superintendent must make sure that the contract doesn't get in the way of successfully running the district. The superintendent must also be cognizant of the ramifications of a long-term contract, while acknowledging that it can save the emotionalism that goes with contract negotiations on a year-to-year basis. The superintendent must be prepared to inform the Board what the total costs to the district would be for every monetary request by the union. Some of the costs are difficult to know. An example of this would be requests for increases in health coverage. With the recent and rapid rise of health-care costs, inattention or a wrong guesstimate could be devastating to district finances. Keep these in mind at contract time:

* The superintendent should want the staff to have good salaries and benefits as long as the district remains financially solvent. If the district is not competitive in compensation, staff members will leave, which will impact continuity of instruction and the ultimate success of students.

* If you see that a settlement is possible late at night, continue until you get it done. Otherwise, set a date for the next meeting.

* Expect that all members on both sides will be treated with respect.

* Understand that even though there will be emotionalism and adversity in negotiations, successful settlements prevent negative union issues throughout the year.

* Shake hands and smile once the settlement is reached.

* Once an agreement is reached and ratification takes place, set up a "settlement celebration night" with the entire Board. Consider inviting the union negotiating teams (to build relationships for the next negotiation). The latter should only be done if the negotiations went smoothly.

Handling Labor Problems

If you are going to go into administration, expect conflict. If you think you won't experience problems in a 30-year career, you should consider another occupation. In fact, one of the major reasons administrators have jobs is to solve personnel and labor problems. I have seen superintendents and principals switch districts to escape their problems. This generally doesn't work. Only if you are just so sick of dealing with the specific problems in your present district that you can't take it another day, does it make any sense. Accept that each district, no matter its size or location, is going to have its own set of problems. We are in the people business. People can bring great rewards, but they can also bring huge problems.

Dealing with labor problems requires you to look beyond the face and the words. What are the side issues that influence the conflict? Are things happening in a person's life outside of work that is compounding the problems? Are political or power struggles impacting behavior? Are personality conflicts involved? Are the individuals operating under some negative influence? There is always something beyond the words. Find out what that is. Never take conflicts personally. Keep them issue-related.

Many times in my career, some of my best employees raised issues that were completely goofy. But I had to deal with the issue at hand, not the person or their emotions. Ultimately, the employee appreciated my taking the time to listen to the problem.

The best way to handle labor problems is to rely upon labor law. Make sure your district has a uniform grievance policy that provides an avenue for conflict resolution. In today's litigious society, the uniform grievance policy must cover a variety of topics. Think about including these in your policy:

* Title 2 with the Americans With Disabilities Act
* Title 9 of the Education Amendments of 1972
* Section 504 of the Rehabilitation Act of 1973, Individuals with Disabilities Education Act
* Title 6 of the Civil Rights Act, Equal Employment Opportunities Act
* Title 7 of the Civil Rights Act
* Claims of sexual harassment
* Human rights violations
* Misuse of funds received for services to improve educational opportunities for educationally deprived children
* Unfair labor practices as established by law and contract

After a labor complaint is filed, a fair and impartial investigation must take place before the decision is made to resolve the issue. The complainant should be made aware of all of the steps in the grievance procedure, including the entire appeal process.

What can the administrator do to help settle a problem early in the grievance process?

* Know Board policy and procedure.
* Memorize the specifics of the contract.
* Know the steps of the grievance procedure.
* Directly tackle the issue at hand. For example, make sure that either you, as the superintendent, or your administrative designee try to solve the complaint before it becomes an official grievance.
* Know labor law.
* Use the policies, procedures, and contract to solve the problem.
* Set up procedures to solve problems before they reach the official grievance stage.
* Have as much open communication with union leadership as possible so that problems can be solved at the leadership level.
* Have a reason for your decision. There will always be some conflict between labor and management. These can be minimized by explaining the rationale for your decisions. People will generally respect you if you give them a reason. As stated many times before, your criteria for formulating the decision should be based on what is best for the kids.

One key to successful labor relations is getting people to reason before responding. This type of situation also promotes growth in education.

Despite all of this, you are going to have labor issues. Our district has over 500 employees, and we pride ourselves on open communication and problem solving with all of them. We still have to deal with issues like gender conflict, sexual harassment, staff dismissals, contract interpretation, and policy interpretation. It's simply part of the educational environment today. Deal with the problems. Don't think they will just go away. As a matter of fact, procrastination generally leads to an escalation of the problem. Be forthright. Be honest. Communicate your rationale. Abide by the policies, procedures, and contract. Using those tools, labor problems generally become manageable.

Setting the Proper Environment

Administrators must make sure that the proper resources get to their service providers (staff members) and that the proper framework is established for effective instruction to take place. To set the optimal environment, four major areas should be addressed: curriculum, instructional resources, facilities, and a safe atmosphere that has fair and consistent discipline.

Curriculum. The development of a sound curriculum is the single most important element for instructional and student success, yet often times it is put on the back burner by school districts. When you build your house, you need an architectural plan for it to be built properly. Likewise, a school district needs a curricular blueprint to have substance and for learning to take place. Belleville #118 has a philosophy that unless mandated by law to change a specific part of the curriculum during the present year, the earliest implementation change is the next school year. This four-year cycle is followed:

Year 1. Research and planning
Year 2. Piloting of the program with feedback
Year 3. Implementation
Year 4. Evaluation and fine tuning

Sometimes in education we don't properly research the changes. What looks good on paper isn't always good in the classroom. The actual practice doesn't back up the theory.

Curriculum development has to be ongoing to meet the students' needs. There are many ways that curriculum develops. A good administrator is in tune with all of them.

Here are some of those ways:

* A general mapping of course sequencing and individual course content happens with key stakeholders researching the best possible scenario for the students. This mapping must include an alignment to the standards of corresponding local assessments.

* Recent estimates tell us that the amount of factual information doubles every five years. Because of this, it has become just as important to decide what *not* to teach as what to teach. For example, instead of memorizing facts, we must teach research skills for finding and understanding information.

* Curriculum development is driven by assessment. This has been further accentuated by the adequate yearly progress portion of the No Child Left Behind Act of 2002 (see Chapter 13).

* There are many outside factors that impact curriculum development: politics, the local community, club meetings, and co-curricular activities. This especially holds true for athletic, band, choral, and drama programs. Many times a school district is judged by how successful each school is in these co-curricular activities.

* The best individuals to develop curriculum are teachers. In a school system, they are the closest to what is going on in a child's world. They know the student's degree of progress and the points of his/her learning difficulties. Good teachers are continuous learners who review proposals, gather data, conduct research, make contact with parents, write curriculum, try new ideas, obtain feedback, and evaluate programs.

What are some basic assumptions regarding curriculum?

* Every student deserves the best program of studies and the best instructional strategies we can apply to help facilitate learning. Our goal has to be that each student has the opportunity to become a productive citizen.

* Kids aren't widgets. They have things in their own environment that impede their ability to fully learn. Administrators and teachers must work together to find out what those impediments are so that an educational program can include the content, skills, and strategies to help overcome them.

* We must instill in students the ability to deal with change. In this process, the teaching must instill also in students the desire to become life-long learners.

* Because curriculum is the pillar of student success, it deserves ongoing and comprehensive monitoring.

* Legislation has to be continually and carefully monitored by all staff members. It can dramatically impact the curriculum.

Administratively, there are specific items in the framework of the curriculum that teachers require for success. They include:

* Report cards. This is how the district and its staff communicate student success to parents. Developing a report card is a difficult task for administrators because teachers have divided opinions about this issue. Setting the standards for the corresponding honor roll is also vitally important, but equally difficult.

* Alignment to the standards, corresponding benchmarks, instructional guidelines, and evaluation techniques (See "Best Practices" in Chapter 11.)

* Ideas that take make technology a useful tool to support and enhance basic instruction

* Professional development that discusses learning styles, assessment, core subject area improvement, portfolios, and other topics identified by the staff

* A district-wide needs assessments to get input from the stakeholders

* A public relations program that helps to disseminate curricular information

* The understanding that teachers are expected to be pro-student and positive in the classroom

* A plan for textbook adoption. This plan should include:
    1. A pre-survey of teacher attitudes
    2. The selection of a committee
    3. Awareness of state standards
    4. Research of the present top adoptions
    5. Study timelines
    6. Evaluation criteria

7. Committee work that includes screening, discussions, and establishing what the reading level is
8. Book selection (We feel that should be narrowed to three textbooks before salespeople make their presentations. Each salesperson should be limited to a 45-minute presentation, with 15 minutes allowed for discussion. A 30-minute time slot should be allotted between each presentation for committee discussion.)
9. Once the selection is made, discussion should be held with the Board before adoption.
10. Once adoption takes place, a comprehensive professional development cycle has to take place.

One of the key components in curriculum development is evaluation of weak areas in the curriculum. Many times schools just talk about the problems but do nothing about them. There is a systematic process to fixing a problem:

* Identify the problem.
* Check to make sure the textbook and instructional methods are aligned to the standards.
* Evaluate the assessment. Look at old tests. Become knowledgeable of the rubrics.
* Have a brainstorming session that includes a self-assessment. What is right? What is wrong?
* Research the topic.
* Find an expert who can in-service the staff. This person might already be in your district.
* Set up peer coaching.
* Map your curricular and assessment strategy.
* Consider assessments at every grade level. Get cross-grade-level ownership into the improvement strategies.
* Implement your plan.
* Celebrate successes.

Instructional Resources. A great tragedy in the learning process takes place when teachers do not have the needed supplies to carry out instruction. Old textbooks hurt student learning. A lack of a curricular plan is just as bad. I observed a school district that was in a high economic area but had poor test scores. I couldn't understand why until I saw that the district had no curricular plan and had granted each teacher autonomy to plan his/her school day, select textbooks, and so on. In the same grade level of the same school, teachers had different textbooks and different emphases of instruction. I believe strongly in teacher autonomy, but not at the expense of children. This school district did a great disservice to its students.

Administratively, we cannot allow this to happen. Your district should have a plan of what instructional materials are needed in each classroom. This is especially important for new teachers. Many times the new teachers, the ones who need curriculum supplies the most, are the teachers who get the least. Sometimes, because of budget constraints, new teachers do not even get necessary items for basic instruction. Adequate supplies need to be provided to all teachers. Even in tough financial times, you can get them. Ask experienced teachers if they have extra supplies. Go to your retired teachers to see if they want to pass on some of their materials.

One of the funniest events I ever observed as a principal was when a retiring teacher put her old bulletin board materials and excess classroom resource items on the stage in the gym. She filled the stage. (Her old room practically yelped with relief over the extra space!) I made an announcement to other staff members at 8 a.m. saying that the materials were available. By noon, every bit of the material was off the stage. Even the staff laughed at itself about how fast the supplies were devoured.

What else can you do? Get support from local businesses and industry. What about your foundation, PTAs, Booster Clubs, community organizations? You simply must supply every classroom adequately.

Ask yourself questions regarding supplies. Are there enough maps to teach geography and history? Are your science labs fully equipped? Does each classroom have computers hooked up to the Internet? Is there enough paper for creative writing assignments? Is enough effort being made to get band instruments for indigent children? Is the budget sufficient for successful art and industrial arts programs? Develop a checklist to make sure these types of questions are answered so that classrooms are well equipped.

Also, look at your school's instructional tools.

How can you get more instructional tools in the classroom? Be creative and work hard. Look for grants. In our district, we were able to air-condition the entire district using funds saved from our construction project because the director of buildings and grounds, the assistant superintendent for finance, and I served as construction managers on the project. We were able to get computers in every classroom because the Assistant Superintendent for Curriculum and the Director of Technology wrote and received technology grants for over one million dollars. In our old buildings, we lowered ceilings and retrofitted lights for sound and eye comfort. We are continually looking for ways to get curricular support materials for the teachers. Our libraries are funded by grants, PTAs, and donations from the community. We have a truly wonderful volunteer support system of parents and senior citizens for our libraries and computer labs. These same groups work with us in our after-school programs and our mentoring programs. Our teachers also write grants both locally and statewide to get supplies in the classroom. Our recently established foundation is providing band instruments, choir gowns, literature series, library books, gifted competition monies, and more for our students. Just keeping your schools properly maintained with supplies and tools requires a lot of work, but how do the kids learn without them?

A Foundation. I would be remiss not to discuss a foundation for your schools or district. A foundation is a wonderful tool to support instructional resources and programs.

If you don't have one, get one started! It involves a great deal of work, but it is worthwhile. Your foundation should be nonprofit, independent, and a tax-exempt corporation (501-C-3).

The purpose of a foundation is to raise money, strategically invest it, and use the money generated by the investment (without using the principal). With this money you can pay for supplies, programs, and services for kids by providing unique opportunities and experiences the school could not otherwise afford. We have used our foundation funds for technology enhancements, student scholarships for community and school programs, band instruments, gifted education competitions, the library, and further support of fine and practical arts programs. A nearby community is using their foundation monies to build an all-weather track for both the students and the community.

The side benefit of the foundation is the interest it brings from community leaders. By being tax-exempt, it offers a way for people to do something good for the children and still save personal tax dollars. And it provides those involved with greater insight into the educational activities of the district.

Belleville #118's foundation is administered by an independent volunteer Board of Directors which operates under its own charter. Gifts can be accepted many ways:

* Cash, check, securities, or personal property
* Bequest in a will or estate plan
* Land, real estate, or life insurance
* A tribute to a friend or a memorial to a loved one
* A gift in a special area of interest
* Payroll deduction
* Bank draft or credit card withdrawal

Once the gifts are received, it's important to acknowledge them. We use the school newsletter, notes, thanks, media coverage, or we display plaques in our schools—or all of them!

Foundations are an excellent way to expand your educational program while also building allegiance to your schools.

Facilities. The classroom environment is very important to student success. If the classroom looks good, students will not only achieve more, but they will take better care of the building.

Are the rooms:

* Well lighted?
* Free of marks on the walls?
* Recently painted?
* Comfortable throughout the year. Do they have heating and air-conditioning?
* Sound controlled?
* Generally pleasing to the eye?
* Complete with sufficient white boards, bulletin boards, and instructional support materials?

If the answer to any of these questions is no, then you have a project to look into at your next Buildings and Grounds Meeting with the Board. Each and every one of the above questions, when answered no, can inhibit the learning process.

A Safe Environment. Maintaining a safe environment is directly affected by discipline. The ability to maintain discipline is a cornerstone of academic success. More and more school districts' hands are tied over the ability to discipline students. I think this has been a great mistake. There are many ways to keep discipline in check. In order to do this, more human resources are needed. Another compounding factor is the dwindling support from some parents concerning discipline.

What can you do as an administrator? First, you have to back your staff members when they discipline a child. Without this backing, staff members will back off on discipline. You as the administrator must assure your staff that they have total building responsibility when it comes to discipline.

Often staff members want to limit discipline to the children in their own classroom. More is needed. All adults have to take the responsibility for discipline. The students have to know that this is a team approach. The same goes for parents.

One of the greatest compliments I got from parents is when they said, sarcastically, to me, "My friend told me not to waste my time coming in to talk to you because you, as the superintendent, are just going to back your principals and teachers on discipline issues." Of course they are using the comment to control my attitude on the situation—but how right they are. I trust the professionalism of our staff members. Superintendents simply can't cave in regarding discipline. Children want discipline and good parents want a strong disciplinary environment in the school. Parents want the school to be a safe haven for students. We must make that so, then share that with students, parents, and the community.

What are the specifics? First of all, a district-wide code of conduct needs to be developed. This disciplinary code should include input from all stakeholders. In fact, I suggest that the code of conduct be recommended by a committee of stakeholders for adoption at a regular Board meeting. That way, the district starts off with general support from inside and outside the school.

The code of conduct should have a stair-step method of discipline, depending upon the offense and the number of times students have to be disciplined. You hear so much about kids being bad these days. My findings don't reflect that. Even though 50% of our students came from homes with income below the poverty level, a few years back we found that 85% of our students had never been referred to the office, and 8% rarely sent. That left 7% who made frequent visits to the principal. We must celebrate the

85% and keep our focus on them, not the 7% who administratively wear us out.

The code of conduct should include as many alternatives as possible to keep the children in school. This includes detentions before, during, and after school, plus Saturday morning detentions, and in-school suspensions. The Saturday morning detentions are particularly effective because they generally disrupt the parents' weekend. Consequently, you get a better chance for parent follow-up regarding the behavior. When these parents angrily blame the administrator, your response is, "If your child had not displayed inappropriate behavior, would we be having this conversation?"

The only problem we had with in-school suspension is that some students will do almost anything to get out of class. What we have done to alleviate this is to extend the day for in-schoolers. This does involve some transportation inconvenience, but we felt it has been worth it as it has cut down on the number of in-school suspensions.

Another good discipline method is the "ecology" unit. This method has students picking up trash on the playground, sweeping rocks and other debris off the asphalt and sidewalk area, picking up sticks, etc. A word of caution here: the students must still be monitored, and you can never have them do any school service work that involves toxic chemicals.

Of course, your code of conduct has to include out-of-school suspensions and expulsions. One hopes that these are last resorts in the disciplinary process. There are more out-of-school suspensions than ever before. These are the same kids who need to stay in school. The bottom line here is this: Your discipline program has to be fair, consistent, and articulated to staff, students, and parents. Good discipline does indeed remain a cornerstone for academic success.

While we are discussing discipline, I must mention "zero tolerance," which is included in many schools' Codes of Conduct. These policies usually refer to areas where weapons, drugs, alcohol, and felonies are involved. While we're not totally against these policies, we urge you to use caution when implementing them. For example, our district does have a zero tolerance policy regarding drug sales, but we also have a very effective first-offender program for alcohol and drug use. The latter program requires the parents to take their student offender to six sessions of drug and alcohol counseling. We've had great success with this program, mainly because the parents get directly involved with their child's behavior.

Zero tolerance, we feel, should be divided into two categories.

The first category covers activities that lead to a consequence. For example, in our district we have a total hands-off policy. Any altercation leads to a consequence. But flexibility is given to our administrators about the degree of the consequence based upon the intensity of the confrontation.

The second category of zero tolerance leads to suspension, followed often by expulsion. Situations such as bringing a gun to school, selling drugs, and committing felonies fit into this category. Even here, we feel that a degree of flexibility must be permitted.

A recent example concerning a district near us explains why. Their policy was inflexible. Unfortunately, it boxed the Board into expelling a second-grade student who brought a fingernail clipper/file to school. Hearings took place until the decision was overturned by the State Board. It cost the district dearly in dollars and negative public relations. Reasonable flexibility could have sidestepped the dilemma. The bottom line is that we have to inform the students that we will not tolerate certain behaviors. But we must also create a policy that is not so narrow that it gets in the way of effectively managing the school.

Some final thoughts before the summary: If you are going to be a successful administrator, you are going to have to work harder than you would imagine. I see so many administrators fail because they simply do not have a strong work ethic. You have taken the responsibility to be a leader of teachers. Lead by example and be pro-teacher. They are the foundation of your success.

Summary

The classroom is the basis for all learning. Do everything in your power to maximize learning opportunities for kids. This chapter has mostly dealt with teachers. Collaborate with them. Pay them well. Be fair with them. Be strong for them. Secure great facilities for them. Make sure they have adequate classroom supplies and instructional tools. Their success will lead to student success and, ultimately, to your success as an administrator.

Chapter Eleven

Adventures in Innovation

Jim Rosborg

Have we worn you down with ten chapters about the multitude of problems that educators now face? Had enough alternative solutions? You get a break in Chapter 11. Here we will change the pace and direction. The goal of this chapter is to explain some "best practices" and build support for special projects.

Even though we know that the accountability movement drives many of our decisions in education today, we can't forget to build innovative and entertaining activities into our daily instructional schedule. Success with students demands that there be some fun in the school day! (Just so long as learning takes place.) In the past fifteen years, the pendulum has swung dramatically to accountability. It's now time for it to swing back to enrichment and entertaining activities. Students are up to here with accountability.

Have you spoken with students lately? Asked them about their memories of fun things they did at school? Many will struggle to find even one fun memory! No surprise there. We have let entities like business, media, and government dominate our recent educational thought.

I attended my 35th high school class reunion in the summer of 2003. The weekend was spent sharing and exaggerating the great memories of our K-12 school experiences. Of those conversations I do not recall a single person mentioning a specific reading or math lesson. We spent the entire weekend talking about fun school activities. I am not so sure that many of today's graduates will have that same attitude or opportunity 35 years from now. So it's time to reevaluate the fun component of our curriculum. An eye-opener: Japan is a world leader in math test scores, and is also near the top in youth suicide. There must be a happy medium.

You will see the educational component of the activities recommended in this chapter. The administrator must not forget that the school environment still competes with other diversions such as television, video games, and the computer. Why not incorporate some of these stimulating media into the educational system? Why fight the trend? Use it to make school more fun rather then blaming the visual media for students' academic failure.

For example, television can be used to reinforce lessons. In science, photosynthesis is very difficult to explain. So why not use a video or DVD to explain it and bring the lesson alive? Videos about character building are needed in today's curriculum. PBS produced just such videos in *The Book of Virtues* from the book of the same title by former Secretary of Education, William J. Bennett.[1] There are other excellent videos that explain the differences among ethnic groups, valuable for studying diversity of today's society. Videos can provide virtual field trips to places outside your geographical area and bring historical figures to life. As long as the video or DVD aren't overused, both can bring excitement and reinforcement to instruction

Look at computers. There are computer programs that reinforce the flash card concept of learning basic addition, subtraction, multiplication, and division. Digital cameras can be used for Power Point presentations and for the development of web pages. What better way to teach editing skills in creative writing than with the computer? The Internet, used properly, provides students with communication tools and direct interactivity with the world.

While it's harder to think up effective ways to use video games in the educational environment, they might be used as reward activities or to productively fill time while waiting for a bus or having to stay inside for recess because of bad weather. I'll bet students and teachers brainstorming together could find a dozen innovative educational uses for video games!

Likewise, a mentally stimulated student has a better chance of success in the classroom. Let's look at some creative ways that we can incorporate activities to both enhance the curriculum during the regular school day and expand the student's learning potential beyond the regular instruction hours.

---

[1] William J. Bennett, ed., *The Book of Virtues*. New York: Simon and Schuster, 1993.

The last portion of this chapter will discuss future innovations at the state and national level. From there, we will discuss how we can incorporate "best practices" into the curriculum. There is still much room for the exploration process in the curriculum. What is exciting about this process is that these activities can also engage parents, thus bringing the family unit into the educational program.

Combining Education and Fun

Let's first look at some educational activities that combine educational standards with entertainment. With small adjustments, most of these activities can be used at both the elementary and secondary levels.

Book Fairs

Book fairs are a wonderful way of increasing literacy with children. To engage parents as well, have an ice cream social as part of the Book Fair. This brings parents into the school and increases the opportunities for students to purchase books suitable to their individual interests, as well as to expand their personal libraries. It also gives you a chance to interact with the parents and students in another positive way.

Family Math Nights

Family Math Nights are evenings where parents are invited to the school to do math problem-solving activities along with their child. The problems should be set up so that both the parent and child can be successful. In fact, I would suggest that the teachers work with students to make sure they know how to solve the problems before their parents come in. This greatly helps student math skills. By teaching their parents, students learn subject matter and communication skills. Family Math Nights also give the school the opportunity to show parents that there is often more than one correct way to solve math problems. In addition, it is a positive way to demonstrate to parents how we are using higher order thinking skills in the learning process. Having a poster of Bloom's *Taxonomy* and corresponding questions for each of the six categories (knowledge, comprehension, application, analysis, synthesis, and evaluation)[2] can take a fun night farther by giving parents functional knowledge of higher order thinking skills.

Technology Nights

In today's society, Technology Nights can greatly enhance the growth of overall student knowledge. Ironically, the student often has a greater comfort level and more knowledge about working with the computer than his/her parents. Like Family Math Nights, the activities should be doable by both student and parent. Activities should be done during the regular school day to set the stage for success on Technology Night. See the wide variety of things that might be done that night:

* Invite companies like Microsoft to provide a speaker to talk to parents, students, and teachers about new software products and how they can be used in the classroom and at home.
* Help students and parents make cards for holidays such as Christmas, Mother's Day, Father's Day, or Birthdays.

These nights are especially effective in school districts with students from low socio-economic households. Need more ideas? Ask your students. Technology Nights can be set up as a family social time. They are great for a home-school collaboration that can bring long-lasting, positive effects.

Fine Arts Festival

The fine arts programs in many districts have taken a major hit in school curricula because of the nationwide accountability movement. One way that school districts can make up for the loss of instruction time during the school day is to provide activities beyond the regular hours. (Let's talk later in this chapter about after-school programs.) A Fine Arts Festival can help keep fine and practical arts alive. What takes place? Student work is displayed, students perform in both art and choral activities, and community members (including parents) display their talents in art, drama, instrumental music, vocal music, and crafts. The festival is also an opportunity to recognize and reward their talents and achievements, bringing them the visibility more often given to athletics.

---

[2] Benjamin S. Bloom, ed., ***Taxonomy of Educational Objectives***. New York: David McKay Co. Inc., 1956.

During the day, a typical Fine Arts Festival would be focused on children only. Activities provided would be artist demonstrations, student instrumental and vocal performances, student art exhibits, student hands-on projects, student drama recitations, special craft displays, and musical guests. In the evening, a typical Fine Arts Festival might include all of the daytime activities plus artwork, crafts, and other items developed by professionals or students for sale to parents and the community.

Reading for Fun Week

The ability to read is one of the greatest gifts a person can have. It can also fill one's life with instant, portable entertainment. As school leaders, we must help keep reading dynamic. It's a true challenge. With the heavy emphasis on teaching, I feel we tend to over-teach some books. After finishing their school reading, kids often have too little time to read for enjoyment. Many school districts use summer reading programs to encourage students to read in a non-stressful environment.

A good school administrator knows that the success a child has in reading leads to success in all of the other core subjects. One way the school can help keep reading exciting is to have, during the academic year, a week of specific fun reading activities. Reading for Fun Week is great for collaboration and bringing out the creativity of your faculty and staff. Listed below are some things you might consider. Students can also suggest super ideas appropriate to your district and its specific educational environment.

* Have students bring their favorite book. Set aside half an hour each day during that week to either read the book or share it with the rest of the class.

* Have reading classes perform a choral reading contest that is judged by their peers to see who does the best job.

* Have a Community Leader Day when community leaders come to the school and read a portion (or all) of their favorite books or childhood stories.

* Have a Patriotic Reading Day when students wear red, white, and blue clothing and read about their favorite historical personalities.

* Pick a well-known series of books (like those by Dr. Suess) and provide themes surrounding the series for school-wide activities.

* Read a book about your favorite sport, team, or sports personality. Build the day around the local professional sports team active at the time of the activity, like the St. Louis Rams, the Chicago Cubs, or the Detroit Red Wings.

* Buddy Reading is a great way for students to show their reading talent to other students in their own grade level or to students at other grade levels. For example, having a fifth-grade student read to a first-grade student many times enhances the self-confidence of the fifth-grade student while showing the younger student the additional excitement of being able to read. This activity many times has the carryover advantage of helping to stop bullying in the school as the older child develops a protective feeling toward the younger buddy.

* Students enjoy dressing up as their favorite character from a book. This allows the students an opportunity to "act out" their characters. The teacher along with the school must take special precautions here to help those who want to do this activity. For example, some students cannot afford to purchase costumes for the character. Another example would be a costume that is too scanty or infers some kind of devil worship. These problems can be avoided relatively easily with some planning before the actual event and with some class exchanges of materials. Just make sure you know the costumes the students will wear.

* The reading enhancement can be extended by inviting a local author to school. These professionals bring alive the excitement of reading and provide a rich source for answering student questions about writing as a career.

There are many more activities that can be developed locally to make this a great learning week. Reading is important. Students must also learn that it can be fun.

Veterans' Day Activities

Of all the public relations activities the school does, it is hard to beat the good will and education associated with Veterans' Day. Invite the veterans in your community to the school. Ask some of them if they would feel comfortable talking about their experiences in the military. Also invite active duty military personnel as a symbol of the school's gratitude for what each soldier does. It is good to start off Veterans' Day with a Flag Ceremony, followed by an assembly that includes patriotic songs, recognition of veterans and active military personnel, and speeches from dignitaries. Veterans' Day provides a setting to get legislators into the school, which generally enhances their perception of its good learning environment. Veterans' Day is a win-win situation for everyone. The day is good for the students, school, district, veterans, and other community members. Student contests can also be woven into the day: poster, speech, essay, etc. Veterans can be invited to eat lunch with the students. Students can in turn read their winning essays at the Veterans' Day Celebration, display their posters, and be active with the veterans. What a great day to involve the community in the learning process!

Sports Field Day

Much has been written about our youth not getting enough exercise. Sports Field Day should be a day that involves *all* students in physical activities. In fact, the day can start out with a fun exercise drill with the entire student body. This can be followed by a variety of activities such as tug of war, egg toss, sprint races, low hurdle races using cones, softball throwing for distance and accuracy, soccer kicking for distance and accuracy, football throwing for distance and accuracy, an obstacle course for time, relay races, standing long jump, running long jump, and high jump.

Young Authors' Conference

A Young Authors' Conference is one of the best means to sustain a writing program. It exhibits the best of student writing throughout the year. The conference helps teachers emphasize writing in the classroom, which in turn improves the writing standard of excellence for the students. The conference itself provides another opportunity to get parents into the school for a positive reason. The best part of a Young Authors' Conference is that it provides yet another way that more students can be successful. As previously mentioned (regarding classroom reading activities), the conference is enhanced if funds are available to invite a published author to speak at the conference.

Science Fair

To continue a well-rounded curriculum that maximizes the effort to meet or exceed set standards, a Science Fair fills the bill. Science fairs provide students the opportunity to create and display their special interest in science. Also, they are ideal for a hands-on science curriculum. Science fairs should not be mandatory, but should be encouraged by teachers through extra credit, classroom allocation, and project ideas. Set guidelines must be established for the Science Fair, including the size of the projects, their physical or chemical designations, and the allowed degree of parental involvement.

Learning Fairs

Another way to enhance your curriculum and even to deal, outside the regular school day, with identified instructional weaknesses is to conduct a Learning Fair. Consider having a different topic every year. Some topics might be careers, your state, the environment, American history, and many more. This also allows new forms of creativity to be added to the school learning environment.

Positive Mental Attitude Programs

Zig Ziglar, the famous speaker about positive thinking, states, "It is your attitude, not your aptitude, that determines your success!"[3] As school administrators, we must facilitate getting our students to reach their potential and find that "special skill" each student has. Some of the best skilled tradesmen in America had difficulty with reading, writing, and arithmetic. Despite this, they had very successful, sometimes spectacular, careers. This was achieved because, for the most part, these individuals focused on something that they did well, and through it they believed in themselves. Some of this success came from their attitude. In the schoolhouse, assessment is important, but we must also help students believe in themselves so that they can reach achievable goals. Using authors such as Dale Carnegie,[4] Norman Vincent Peale,[5] and Zig Ziglar can help you change student attitudes in your school, which, in

---

[3] *See You At The Top*. 3rd ed. Gretna, LA: Pelican Publishing Company, 1978, p.128.
[4] *How to Win Friends and Influence People*. New York: Simon and Schuster, 1936.
[5] *The Power of Positive Thinking*. New York: Simon and Schuster, 1952.

turn, often helps change negative parents' and community attitudes.

Teacher Switch Day

In this era of accountability, the blame game has become endemic, like upper grade level teachers blaming lower level teachers for not getting the job done academically. The reality is that most teachers are good teachers who are only in a student's life about 10% of any given year. Parenting, environment, and poverty are still the best predictors of success, as we saw in Chapter 9. One way to minimize the internal bickering of staff is to have a Teacher Switch Day, when each staff member teaches in three different grade levels during the course of the day. This gives teachers a better understanding of what their colleagues are facing. Students enjoy the activity because it breaks the everyday routine. Learning still takes place and communication is generally enhanced between staff members.

Career Days

Studies show that today's students are woefully inept at knowing where to head in the work force. In fact, many students do not even know where to begin to build their strengths so they can be productive at a specific job. Career Days are wonderful to get the student to think about a future career. They also give those in the community an opportunity to discuss and demonstrate what they do on a day-to-day basis. A hidden virtue of this day is that community members are able to directly observe the school in action. Often the direct observation changes that person's attitude about the school. The results are more community support in the future.

Field Trips

In many communities, field trips are the only way students leave their local neighborhood. Even in affluent communities, exploring the local, state, and national arena is important to educational growth. As administrators, you can help ensure that these trips are educational by developing Field Trip Application forms to identify the state learning standard that applies to the learning experience. The school administrator should also develop a grade level plan so that field trips are not duplicated from year to year.

These are just a few ideas to help stimulate creative thought in your district. We can't forget creativity and fun in the school setting.

State and National Innovations

State and national innovations often require tough political decisions. We think these issues are worthy of research and debate.

As part of this adventure in innovation, let's stop the onslaught of more and more tests. Let's just make better tests. We don't need more tests to tell us how to help students improve their learning. The tests we do need would tell the school and parents what skills the student needs to improve to succeed. (See more about this in Chapter 13.)

The nine questions that follow will help you define the steps needed for student improvement. They raise tough, important issues central to future educational growth. Administrators should start the dialog on these issues nationwide.

1. **Should the school day be extended?** We think it should. A longer school day would restore such presently neglected parts of the curriculum such as fine/practical arts, career exploration, physical education, field trips, positive mental attitude programs, foreign languages, and violence prevention. The extended day would allow time for more remedial work in reading and math. It would also greatly help working parents trying to fit their child's school day into their schedule.

2. **Should the school year be extended?** As with the school day, we feel the school year should be extended for many of the reasons just cited. The extended school year brings additional benefits. It would help keep kids off the streets. In high-poverty areas, kids would eat more nutritional meals. The loss of knowledge over the summer months would be minimized with the extended year. Of course, extending the school day and school year would cost more money. Staff members would have to be fairly compensated. Air-conditioning may have to be installed. Yet we feel that students are worth it.

3. **Should school funding be re-evaluated?** Another yes. If government is going to be involved in the day-to-day operations of a school district, then it must provide the funding. At the federal

level, school districts are funded at approximately one-half of the original percentage, which is 40%, allocated for special education (IDEA). In Illinois, we are tops in bureaucracy and next to last in funding. We consistently rank 49th in per capita funding yet each year we receive fewer dollars but more paperwork and accountability laws. Students must be a national priority in action, not political rhetoric. The nationwide funding inequity must be addressed.

4. **Should more local control be given to successful districts?** That's a strong yes! A successful district's flexibility in professional development, teacher recertification, special education, and curriculum should be more in its own control. Financially reward districts for doing a good job. As it is now, school districts with high test scores are financially punished by limiting their summer school programs and their opportunities to apply for grants—solely because of their academic success!

5. **Should tenure laws be loosened?** In most states, we think the answer is yes. We believe in tenure because it protects the right of professional exchange of ideas, even those we disagree with! But we also believe that, over time, if a teacher is unsuccessful, that teacher should be dismissed. We should no longer tolerate poor teachers in the classroom. That said, teachers should also be financially rewarded for being successful. We think there should be financial incentives for National Board Certified teachers. And we feel that, in general, teachers should be better paid. We also suggest that good teachers' job evaluations in poverty environments should not be solely based on test scores.

6. **Should the accountability movement continue?** Yes, we think it should. Schools need to be accountable for the success of their students, a success, in part, driven by that accountability. In order to establish accurate accountability standards, though, baseline data should be secured from all schools (including private, parochial, and home schools) about how students are doing before testing result standards are set. We support a parent's right to home school as long as home school parents are held accountable for educational growth. As part of the accountability movement, we feel that all parents should be held responsible for getting their children to school and providing them with the basic needs of food, shelter, clothing, and safety.

7. **Should curriculum change?** It should evolve and change with time. We recommend the redevelopment of vocational educa-

tion with the respective students held accountable in their vocational field. We recommend the reemergence of career development activities that include job shadowing, simulation of real-world activities, and team development. Also, since most workers in America must speak in front of colleagues or clients, we strongly recommend more oral communication/speech training in the curriculum.

8. **Should tort immunity be extended in schools?** We think so. America has become such a litigious society that administrators and Boards are getting buried in legal issues. What can we do? First, make the loser in the case pay for court costs. This would limit the number of trivial suits and ultimately save the taxpayers millions of dollars. Then, limit the amount of the awards. Both liability and medical insurance premiums are unduly draining school districts' budgets. We must tackle this problem.

9. **Should there be an evaluation of current educational laws on the book?** Yes—nine for nine! Currently, we have so many laws that administrators almost need law degrees to keep out of a legal quagmire. Let's look at emotional-based legislation in the past and limit it in the future. Let's make sure that legislation isn't destroyed by bureaucrats. For example, the 2001 No Child Left Behind Act is full of good intentions but has become the most negative law that I've seen in my career because of bureaucratic interpretations. As it now stands, no district can achieve 100% of the state's requirements, especially with special education and transfer students included in that requirement. The law implies increased flexibility and local control, but early results point to the opposite. This goes back to respecting the professionalism of the local educator. Our society is eventually going to have to learn that the teacher is the most important component to the child's academic success outside of the home.

Rules in education established in general seem easy until they are implemented locally. We must be cognizant of this. As we evaluate educators, let's also look at society's problems. While educators must continually strive for improvement, they shouldn't shoulder the major blame for society's ills. We must address the historical problems of families living in poverty and/or struggling with drugs or alcohol. Professional educators know more about child development than the general public. They should be judged by how they implement that knowledge.

These are some of the major innovations that need to be debated and discussed for student improvement. We must look beyond testing to seek other innovations for educational change. Tackling the tough issues that will move education and our society forward should be a collaborative effort between education leaders, business, industry, government, parents, and the community.

Best Practices

When I ask my graduate classes what "best practices" are, I am continually surprised at the lack of a response. Best practices are ideas that withstand the test of time and different educational trends. Best practices are recognized as being effective both in your district and in other districts, no matter the district's size, location, or grade levels of governance. They're not well known because educators don't take the time to record what works well in the learning process. Best practices are vital for a school system to be successful.

Education has been going through different philosophical cycles for years. As a matter of fact, since the late 1950s with the educational scare of Sputnik, educators have often been told to prepare for different philosophical ideas.

Sputnik was the Russian spaceship that was the world's first to be rocketed into space. It was feared that the Russians were going to pass the Americans academically. Thus came a cry for educational accountability in mathematics and science. This lasted until the late 1960s when the Vietnam War led to a more humanistic approach in education. Then came *A Nation at Risk*, a report in 1983, in which schools were blamed for the poor economy. The present accountability movement that came from that has stayed with us ever since even though the United States had an unprecedented economic growth in the 1990s.

Yet best practices survive the elements of time, political change, and educational philosophies. They are good for kids any time, any place.

The cycling of educational philosophies is also seen in academic careers, with the same cycle often repeating three times. The first time is when the career begins. The administrator starts with the cycle then in vogue. When the cycle occurs again, they must live with it and adjust to it. The third time it comes around, it is generally time to retire!

Let's discuss some best practices that can be implemented in your school. Since we can't list all of the best practices available, we suggest that the best way to see other excellent examples is to visit successful schools in your own state. Your goal is to assimilate best practices that are functional and practical for your school.

We have previously discussed the importance of having fun activities outside the normal school curriculum. These activities in themselves fit into the category of best practices. The learning process can be further enhanced by an enthusiastic staff that presents lessons in a positive way. I have heard it said "if students do not learn the way we teach, then we need to teach the way they learn." I believe this. The students have to know and believe that the staff feels that each student can be successful. They must know that the entire staff expects every one of them to put forth their best efforts.

It can be done. I taught at the junior high level for 13 years. Some of my students were very challenging, yet, honestly, there wasn't one in whom I couldn't find something uniquely valuable. We have to search for that special strength in each child, then reinforce that child so he or she can be successful. How can that happen every time? We must:

* Use different methods to reward students for achievements.
* Keep up-to-date on learning styles.
* Keep current on the events surrounding a student's life that may impact his/her learning, like a parent's divorce, a death in the family, or a parent laid off at work.
* Make certain that we constantly reassess our own leadership and instructional styles so they continually and positively impact student learning.

Let's look at some specific best practices within the guidelines of general categories.

Alignment to Standards

It is important in establishing best practices in curriculum to align your curriculum to state standards. In Table 11-1 below, you can see how to take a state goal and the learning standard behind it to establish benchmarks for success and the curriculum alignment.

This simple method was developed by staff under the leadership of Bill Porzukowiak, Assistant Superintendent for Curriculum, in Belleville District #118, Belleville, Illinois. This table provides a guide to teachers regarding instruction.

Table 11-1

STATE GOAL: Write to communicate for a variety of purposes.

Why this goal is important: The ability to write clearly is essential to any person's ability to effectively communicate. High-level writing skills can produce documents that show planning and organization and effectively convey intended message and meaning. Clear writing is critical to employment and production in today's world. Individuals can be capable of writing for a variety of audiences in differing styles, including standard rhetoric themes, business reports, financial proposals, and technical and professional communications. Students should also be able to use computers to enhance their writing proficiency and improve their career opportunities.

Learning Standard: A.	Use correct grammar, spelling, punctuation, capitalization, and structure.

Benchmarks:

Early Elementary (K-3)

3.A.1 Construct complete sentences which demonstrate subject/verb agreement; appropriate capitalization and punctuation; correct spelling of appropriate, high-frequency words; and appropriate use of the eight parts of speech.

Late Elementary (4-5)

3.A.2 Write paragraphs that include a variety of sentence types; appropriate use of the eight parts of speech; and accurate spelling, capitalization and punctuation.

Middle Junior High (6-8)

3.A.3 Write compositions that contain complete sentences and effective paragraphs using English conventions.

Curriculum Alignment:

	K	1	2	3	4	5	6	7	8
Sentence Structure A. Recognizing Sentences	*	X	X	X	X	-	-	-	-
B. Sentence Types 1. Telling (Declarative)	*	X	X	X	X	X	X	X	X

Stars (*) indicate periods of readiness, cross marks (X) indicate instruction and development, and dashes (-) indicate levels of reinforcement.

This is not the only concept needed to align the curriculum. General administrative support of the standards also needs to occur. Other support activities:

* Have each classroom develop a large, inclusive poster of the learning standards. This is a constant reminder to teachers to instruct to the standards.

* Develop a resource book of sample test questions that are aligned with learning standards and their corresponding benchmarks.

* Design a Field Trip Plan that prevents duplication of trips. The field trip form itself should require teachers to identify the learning standard that applies to the field trip experience.

* Establish the Classroom Observation Form so it includes information regarding the learning standard that will be addressed in the lesson.

* Allow time to have teachers articulate with each other how the different standards are being addressed from one grade level to the next. For example, have grade 5-6 and then grade 6-7 teachers have time to meet to discuss instructional strategies and the sequence of instruction.

* Make sure writing occurs across the curriculum with corresponding assessments. This keeps in focus this important learning domain in conjunction with reading, math, English, science, and social studies.

Parent Involvement

No matter how effective the administration and staff are, parents must be involved for a district to be successful. Some of this involvement needs to be on a volunteer basis, but some components of a successful parent involvement program also need to be of quiet persuasion. Let's discuss those components.

  * **Parent orientation nights** provide a great source of communication along with a rapid increase in trust between the home and school. We recommend getting the parents into the school for an orientation on a night just prior to the beginning of school. In elementary schools, don't release whom the child has for a teacher until the parent orientation night. At the middle school and high school level, do not release the student's schedule of classes until the orientation meeting. Parents will come to find out. Their child will put pressure on them to attend so he or she will know what their schedule is when they walk into school the first day. Once you have the captive audience, use it to your benefit to communicate your goals and expectations for the academic year. Tell your staff how the school is going to communicate with the parent. Provide them with an outline of topics to be covered.

  * **Establish a school/parent/community council** to discuss school issues throughout the year. This group represents parents and the community; it increases communication on these topics. This group is also an efficient way to meet many of the parental input requirements of state and federal grants.

  * **Parent conferences** are another way to use quiet persuasion to ensure that direct communication takes place between the home and school. How do you do this? Hold report cards until the parent comes in for the conference. Then at the conference, set up half-hour sessions to go over the report cards, academic progress, learning standards, and assessment results.

  * **Summer home visits** are a great way to show the parents that the school district is willing to make the special effort to communicate. This technique is especially effective in low economic areas. These visits should never be done alone. Every effort should be made to inform the parent ahead of time that the visit will take place. The agenda should be positive in nature. These are some suggestions:

1. Ask questions like "How can we help you to better educate your child?" and "How can we get in contact with you in case of an emergency?"

2. Let the parent know the best time to contact the school.

3. Make the parent aware of community opportunities to get the child involved in sports, band, art, gifted programs, etc.

4. Let the parent know that there are no dumb questions and that they are welcome any time as guests.

5. Encourage them to become parent volunteers and ask them if they have any special skills.

How do you make this happen? First of all, you try to use grant or district money to pay the teachers an hourly wage. They should be compensated for using vacation time. If money is not available, the program has to be voluntary and based upon long-term successes. By letter, inform parents that two staff members will be visiting their home. Give a specific time and date. Inform the parents of some of the topics you will be discussing while also letting the parents know that you will discuss any issue they wish to bring up. There are some homes you may not be able to send staff to because of past criminal conduct either by the owner or in a complex. Find a neutral area determined by the school to meet. Make sure that teams have a cell phone to use in emergency situations. When planned correctly, this program alleviates many conflict situations during the school year, and it remarkably expands the channels of communications.

* Involve your parents in school-wide activities such as a school picnic, Sports Field Day, Young Authors' Conference, etc. Another way to involve parents is to help establish community centers in low economic areas. In the Belleville school district, the Franklin Neighborhood Community Association is a community center that provides open gyms; activities at Halloween, Thanksgiving, and Christmas; health support systems; computer support for student and parents; and, most important of all, a summer program for kids. The program consists of tutoring throughout the day and a camp from noon to five every afternoon in the summer. The students have access to the computer room, library, and the gym in the school. Field trips take place throughout the summer. City facilities such as the local swimming pool are also used. Americorp workers and college students generally staff the program. A teacher coordinates the academic activities. In this area, 75% of

our students are on the free lunch program. The summer program helps the kids academically, provides good summer meals, keeps them off the streets, and helps them gain self-confidence for future success.

Big Picture Items

Any organized school district that is effectively communicating with all of its stakeholders has the following components:

* A mission statement that explains the district's and school's major goals.

* A strategic plan that includes five-year goals and objectives in all of the major Board areas, i.e. personnel, finance, buildings and grounds, curriculum, special education, technology, etc. The plan should also include the major beliefs of the district and the assumptions that helped formulate those beliefs.

* A written "code of conduct" that is up-front with students and parents about the rewards/consequences of both exemplary and bad behavior. These discipline standards must be set and maintained so that effective learning can take place. Staff members need to implement the philosophy that discipline is a total school activity, not just one's individual classroom duty.

* With an ever-increasing number of parents working during the day, after-school programs are becoming more and more necessary. Many times these programs can be funded by grants such as Urban Education, 21st Century Learning, and Project Success. In addition, business groups love this type of program and will even fund them under the right circumstances. Businesses have been very supportive of our after-school programs both financially and by supplying individuals to teach the classes. These programs provide learning enrichment plus lots of fun.

* Give your parents the opportunity to use their special skills in these programs. Staff members, along with other community members, can be also invited to take part. Tutoring and enrichment activities can take place. For example, we refer to our tutoring programs as the Bug Club (Bringing Up Grades). We also teach sewing, embroidery, life-skill adventures, soccer, baseball, basketball, cheerleading, first aid, self-esteem, Spanish, and cooking. What a wonderful way to bring parents, staff, and community together to benefit kids!

Recognition Programs to Save Your Sanity

Our opinion is that many administrators get so bogged down in the everyday routine of discipline that they never take time to "smell the roses." I was a principal of a school with nearly 600 students. On the days that I had to deal with 15 or more students with disciplinary needs, I left the school exhausted. But one thing I did do as I left school that day was to give thanks for the other 585 students who had been good citizens. Most kids in today's society are still good despite all of the negative media that surrounds them. You, as the administrator, have to figure out ways to communicate with the good students. There are many ways you can do this at any grade level. Here are some of them:

1. Honor "students of the month" at every grade level. Call them to the office. Talk to these award winners.

2. Send positive letters home to parents when a student does something good. Focus on these good things in articles incorporated in the school's monthly newsletter.

3. Have monthly honor assemblies to recognize awards and efforts.

4. Try to get many of the students' accomplishments in the local newspaper. Most newspapers gain a greater respect for you as the administrator if you help them fill the pages of the local newspaper with positive "news."

5. Work with the student council, service groups, and like organizations so that the good students see you in a positive light.

6. Read one of your favorite stories to classes.

7. Call students to the office on their birthday and give them a card, a pencil, or candy.

8. Let the students see you in a happy mood. That lets them know that you are proud of them and their school.

Promoting Community Ownership

A best practice for the school district is to share the facilities with community and corresponding agencies. Why not make the school grounds part of the recreational areas of the city? A wonderful offering is to provide walk paths for seniors and others on the school grounds (when the weather is good) and hallways and/or the gym for walking outside of school hours (when the weather is bad). Senior citizens gain ownership with the school when they can use the facilities. Another great thing for seniors is to periodically invite them to lunch with the children. We have found that the senior group is more than willing to pay the adult lunch price since it's still a savings, compared to going to a fast food restaurant. We can't forget that, in many local elections, senior citizens compose over 50% of the voting public. Many are on fixed incomes and fight higher taxes. Schools must give them a reason for supporting tax initiatives. Being part of the schools in action is a way to do this.

We also feel that school districts should share their facilities with community groups such as the local parks and recreation department, the YMCA, Little League, soccer leagues, and other agencies that provide positive activities for children. The school district usually gets back much more from these agencies than it gives. It is not uncommon for these groups to provide additional activities and money for the children in the school, which helps to enhance the school's total program along with provide more community support in elections and during times of negative publicity.

Best Practices In Instruction

Good school districts know that good instruction is still the key component to the school's success. Best practices in instruction include early literacy programs along with corresponding support programs. We have found the Reading Recovery program to be an outstanding way to help overcome early literacy problems. The program *is* costly because of the one-on-one format, but it provides students the opportunity to be successful academically when otherwise they would not. We have found other outstanding programs to help support our basal reading program. Building Blocks at the early childhood level provides reading development skills. Develop kindergarten programs that emphasize phonemic awareness. At the primary level, we use the Four Block program for growth in reading, vocabulary, writing, and grammar. The Kentucky Reads program provides tutoring designed for second-grade students. The Reading Counts and Accelerated Reader computer programs provide reading opportunities that emphasize reading comprehension. Another outstanding computerized reading program is the Waterford Early Reading Program. For grades K-2, this program develops phonemic awareness, decoding skills, and letter recognition. The program also tracks children's development with printed reports for teachers and parents. The students are also able to keep books for their own home library. The program is expensive and requires a computer that is specific to the Waterford program, but many feel it is a great tool for early literacy. All of these programs must be supported by sound instruction.

The curriculum is student-focused with the goal of high student achievement. There is open communication between the Board, administration, and staff to create a collaborative environment so ownership takes place in the instructional process.

Networking plays a role by making sure that there is an assimilation of best practices. A systemic, research-based change module needs to be in place with parent, teacher, and community committees. Pilot programs should take effect, whenever possible, before implementation. Stay focused on the things that are good for students and schools. As we have stated many times before, ask the question "What is best for kids?" Finally, believe that good instruction can take place and that your school and district can have a positive impact on kids.

Summary

While assessment has to be a major focus in the school district's day-to-day experiences, it should not be the only focus. There are many activities that the school can do to make learning entertaining while still focusing on the standards. This chapter provided some examples of how those activities can be brought into the yearly educational plan. This was followed by some examples of how the school district can implement "best practices" to maximize student performance. That is important because most educators have a tough time sitting back and analyzing things that they do well, especially if they have to express their feelings in words. Every district has activities and procedures of which they can be justly proud. We share those successes and that pride so that instructional improvement and student progress can continue to take place.

Chapter Twelve

Taking Care of YOU!

or

How to Stay Alive Long Enough to Draw Retirement

Jim Burgett

Did you ever hear the saying, "If mama ain't happy, ain't nobody happy"? Well, I think the same can be said for the school administrator. If he or she is having a bad day, a bad life, is feeling poorly or is excessively preoccupied with negative thoughts away from work, there is a good chance that others will feel the repercussions.

Contrary to what some may think, even administrators are human! Thus this chapter on wellness. We've got to keep our own clocks in order.

It's odd that this chapter is near the back of the book since it may be the most important chapter of all. Yet that may also be oddly appropriate because many of us put ourselves last rather than first.

This chapter talks about what works, what doesn't, and the life priorities we need to survive and make a difference. It talks about your lifestyle and changes that might be necessary. And that the life you save may be your own!

You might be asking yourself what makes the three of us experts on wellness? One is a marathon runner, and all three of us are in decent physical, mental, and emotional health. Personally, we like to think that we have collectively jumped through many of the hoops that we list in this chapter and that we have done enough research to know that the information is both valid and important.

We also feel qualified to write this chapter because we are all survivors. One of us survived seven bond issues and a school consolidation—enough battles to qualify for combat pay. Another survived a stay as State Superintendent in the world of cutthroat politics, and the other has survived running a very large district in an extremely challenging climate. We all did these things with success and satisfaction. We also have been long married, and all of us have families that still claim us as their fathers. We have all taught all of our children to drive, survived their teens, and in many cases, their weddings. One of us has five grandchildren. That's me; I even watch *Telletubbies* and *Sponge Bob* with them.

Yet however I try to avoid or deny it, I'm still getting older. In fact, I am so old that I have begun to enjoy accordion music. I look both ways before crossing a room, and my favorite movies are now being re-released in color. I'm so old that insurance companies have started to send me their free calendars one month at a time, and I *enjoy* watching the weather channel. I've even stopped hoping for a BMW and will happily settle for a BM.

Enough bad jokes. Although if you laughed at anything in the preceding paragraph, you exercised the right muscles, tuned-up your attitude, and probably reduced some stress. Almost any list of health tips will include "maintain a sense of humor." It never says that the jokes have to be good.

So for the rest of this chapter, I am going to lead you through five categories of health (five areas that interact with each other and with each of us) and set the stage for success or failure.

First, a disclaimer. I'm not a doctor or psychiatrist nor a social worker or a prophet. But I am a relatively healthy and happy school administrator, as are my author partners. We think we got to where we are because along the way we learned how to balance our priorities. So as you read on, think about what I'm saying from a base of common sense. If the shoe doesn't fit your foot, don't cram it on. If what I say does strike a nerve, at least think about it. I can honestly tell you that since I speak widely, and often, I've been able to share this material with many administrators. Many put some of these ideas to work; some have told me that it literally did save their life! See if any of these shoes fit you.

Learn what you Control

I credit my good physical, mental, social, spiritual, and professional health to the fact that I am a content human being and a productive educator. I have learned along the way that the *most important thing of all is to know and respond to the things over which we have control.* For instance, we can control what we eat, and we can control how we respond to stressful situations. We can control our aerobic and strength-building options, our daily habits, our half of most relationships, what we believe in, and our own value systems. When you think about it, we can control quite a bit of our lives!

School administrators aren't idiots. (Okay, there are always exceptions to everything.) We know that we might die before the day ends and that there is no guarantee that we won't get cancer or have a heart attack or "lose our marbles." On the other hand, we also know that we can adjust the odds in our favor by believing proven research, following reasonable rules, and living responsibly.

Have you ever wondered, as a school leader who stands in front of multitudes of coworkers, community members, students, and fellow educators, what they think of you? Do they see a healthy, energetic, positive role model? Do they see someone who exemplifies self-control? Do they see a person who is well dressed, professional looking, and attractive? Do they see someone they can respect on the job and off? If so, they will more than likely follow your lead. Your wellness affects more than just you and your family; it models your beliefs and sets the stage for others. Remember: you lead, they follow.

And remember too that *you* are the last stop, the bottom line, the one who makes the key decisions that determine your own fate. Did you ever see a person have a cigarette stuffed down his throat? Or see anybody force fed that extra taco with hot sauce and a third beer or administrators velcroed to their desks so they couldn't walk? *You* have the control, so let's talk about taking charge of that control and making a difference.

What you Control is the Key Element

For the next few pages, let me share some short, quick, easy tips to change the way you act, think, and behave. I will dip into all five human realms: physical, mental, social, spiritual, and professional. While each tip is shared individually, they are really but one important *part* of the whole. That whole is *you*. Change any of these five elements and you change them all. Drop ten pounds and I almost guarantee that you will improve all five of these areas of your life. Strengthen your faith and you will also improve your total life. And so on.... Most important is the fact that you control much of your own life and that you have the power to make the right decisions.

While this is but one chapter of one book, perhaps one tip may hit home so deeply that it could keep you with us longer, happier, and much healthier.

Physical Health

The first, and most obvious, area is your physical health. Here is a simple plan to make a significant difference physically.

Do a self assessment
Get an unbiased, true picture of yourself. Weigh yourself. Measure yourself. Stand naked in front of a mirror. See yourself as you are right now. Then think about what you can and can't do. Can you run around the block without getting dizzy or dropping into the neighbor's bushes? Can you walk up four flights of stairs without stopping? Can you touch your toes without tumbling over? What can't you do now that you once could? When did you have your last physical?

Develop a vision
See yourself as you want others to see you. Don't plan on going from Oliver Hardy (for the old timers) or Drew Carey (for the young studs) to Matthew McConaughey or from Rosanne to Julia Roberts before your next paycheck. It won't happen. Just be honest and realistic. If you have bad teeth, get them fixed. If you need a new "do," then do it. If you need to update your wardrobe, go to

J.C. Penney's. If you need to build muscles and strength, make a plan.

Set realistic goals

If you need to lose 40 pounds, shoot for 10. When you reach that goal, set another. To help you reach your goal of being a non-smoker, picture your lungs pink and soft instead of black and crusty. If you want to regain lost strength and to be able to press 200 pounds again, set a goal of 75. You can always up it later. If you can't curl 25 pounds, start with five. Don't fret about where you begin, just look forward to where you want to go.

Implement your plan

Making a plan is easy. Not following it is easier still. The result is obvious: you not only remain in the same rotten shape as before, but now you also have a load of guilt to add to your excess tonnage! You can avoid all this by simply following your plan. If you find it too aggressive, modify it. Remember, *some* progress is *better* than no progress. That must be repeated because it is the key to improvement: *Some progress is better than no progress.* If you set a goal to walk two miles every day and at the end of the first week you have only walked a total of five, that is five miles better than the week before! Just restate your goals and stick to them. Once you see results, you will want to do more. Let me repeat that as well: *Once you see results, you will want to do more.*

Evaluate your plan

Give yourself one month of stick-to-itiveness before you evaluate. If after a month of real dedication you don't see any improvement, then either (1) kick the plan up a notch, (2) rewrite the plan from scratch, or (3) give it another month. Just don't quit!

Don't make it difficult

To lose weight, eat less and exercise more. There, I just saved you $39.95 for that weight loss program you were thinking about buying. Or $1,500 for the home gym you don't need. Buy $25 worth of dumbbells and find a space on the floor in front of a TV. Exercise and watch the tube. A treadmill is also simple to use the same way. You can buy them used and cheap from someone, unlike you, who didn't follow their plan!

A Free Physical Wellness Plan!

I bet when you bought this book you didn't think you were going to get a free Physical Wellness Plan! What a bonus! And, if you use it, you might actually improve not just how you feel but how effective you are as an administrator. If, however, you are in great shape, the right weight, and don't feel you need to improve physically, just skip to the mental wellness section. (Nobody is ever 100% mentally fit, certainly no school leader!) If you are like the rest of us, in need of some fine-tuning or a complete overhaul, read on.

Has it been a while since you exercised? Do you pant after a flight of stairs? Have you added 10, 20, 50, 80 or more pounds since you were at your best fighting or modeling weight? Do you find yourself nodding off during the day? Are you a tad less friendly and more short-tempered than you used to be? If the answer is "yes" to any of these questions, please get a routine physical before you start an enthusiastic plan of renovation. (Of course, you should do this anyway, at least once every other year.) Don't forget those prostate tests and breast and gynecological exams on a regular basis too. Do you have a family history of heart disease, diabetes, lung cancer, or other serious conditions? If so, doctors suggest an annual exam. Catch 'em early and you can beat almost anything these days. Okay, stop reading and go make an appointment. Go ahead, I'll wait. And one more thing, have those moles and other skin oddities looked at too, even if they aren't bothering you. (They're bothering us.)

Let's start with the fundamentals of weight. You don't need a book for this; it really is basic. Fat and muscle add weight to your body. To lose weight you have to lose fat or muscle. You lose weight by burning calories. You gain weight by consuming more calories than you burn. The math is simple. If you use more calories than you consume, you lose weight. You are burning calories as you read this book, when you sit at the computer, when you sleep, when you watch a movie, or when you sit on a bench and look at the sunset—as long as you are not eating at the same time. You can even drink a nice cold glass of water when you do all of these things and still burn calories because water doesn't have any calories to start with. If you don't consume any food in a day and just sit around and watch TV, read the paper, and play Solitaire, you'll lose weight. Duh. But you'll pack it back on the next day when your appetite kicks in.

So here is my theory after years of deep research and endless study. I call it the Two-A-Month Plan: two pounds off every month until your goal is reached. That's 24 pounds in a year. Kick it up a notch and it is a Three-A-Month Plan. It takes very little change in your life, and once it begins to work you get into it big time. You only need one thing before you start: a steady weight level. If your weight has not fluctuated more than two to three pounds in the last three months, you have a steady weight level. If you have picked up 10 or more pounds, you will have to modify this plan. If you are already purposefully losing weight (thus the instability), this plan will help the process.

Ready? Here it is: lose 200 calories a day. That's it. You can do it lots of ways. I recommend a combination of burning calories (action) and reducing intake (less food). Why do I think this plan is so cool? It takes almost no effort to do either. If you drink one can of regular soda each day, switch to diet and you save about 150 calories. Do you eat a candy bar every day? Eat half a bar and you save 100 calories. Devour a doughnut every morning? Eat half, or cut it out altogether. Do you drink a big glass of orange juice? Drink eight ounces and save about 100 calories. One pat of butter is 84 calories. Order a medium-sized bag of fries instead of the jumbo one at McDonalds and you save over 300 calories—300 more if you eat a regular hamburger instead of a Big Mac.

You want to know the easiest way to cut 200 calories a day? Sit down at any meal and eat only 3/4 of what is put in front of you. If you usually pour on a healthy dose of salad dressing, pour on 3/4 as much. (Of course, if you replace regular salad dressing with no-fat dressing, or no dressing at all, you eliminate calories and fat!) If you eat pizza, put a paper towel on top of your pizza for ten seconds, and you will reduce the calories by an average of 17% just from the fat absorbed off the top! (Just don't wring the towel and drink the drippings.) Put salsa or barbecue sauce on your baked potato instead of butter or sour cream and you not only saved a humongous amount of calories, but the end product might just taste better! Isn't that easy? Eat less, but do it reasonably. Sidestep one treat a day and you will easily meet your goal. But remember two things: you must do this every day, and your diet must remain stable.

Now the exercise part. You might want to start walking 30 minutes every night. A nice, easy half-hour walk burns about 150 calories. You can also burn 50 calories if you walk ten minutes more during the day than you are used to. You can even do this on company time and get paid for it! The next time you have a message to deliver, walk across the office, go to the next building, climb the stairs, move. If you move ten minutes more than usual each day, chalk up 50 calories burned on your road to better health. Wash a normal load of dishes rather than use the dishwasher: 94 calories burned. Ride your bike slowly and on flat land for only 15 minutes and you chop off 110 calories. Drink water and you burn no calories, but you don't add any either. Drink a large glass (16 ounces) of ice water and you will lose 15 calories as your system heats up the cold water to normal body temperature. I told you this was easy.

In summary: Drink one less beer or one less Pepsi or eat one less handful of snacks each day, do about 15 minutes of easy (no-sweat) exercise, and you will lose 10 pounds or more in the next three months (as long as everything else in your diet or activity is stable). Best yet, you will most likely keep it off since you have developed both an awareness of healthy habits and the ability to put them into action.

That's it. Want to learn lots more and find links to tons of websites about good health? Go to http://www.nutrition.gov. You can also get good information from the website of your favorite fast food place about what foods are best to eat and hence what to avoid.

Mental Wellness
or How to Avoid a Lobotomy

Okay, you're tweaking your diet and kicking up your exercise. Great. Now it is time to check your mental wellness.

If you are a typical school administrator, you can spell stress at least 30 different ways. If you experience aches or pains only when you are under stress, see a doctor. Do it now. Don't die thinking it over. Stress *does* cause physical problems; sometimes delay is fatal. But one thing is absolutely sure, *no administrator is an effective leader when he/she is dead!* Avoid this situation as fast as possible!

If your stress is occasional and doesn't cause you to turn blue, sing the Muppet Song during Board meetings, or to fall on your head, then try to control your stress yourself. Here are two starter ideas:

* Set some time aside each day for yourself, like 15 minutes in the morning. Do things you enjoy: reading, writing, surfing the Internet, playing the piano, walking.

* Schedule regular family time, like a weekly date with your spouse or a commitment to watch your kids' activities. (Research tells us that if you kiss your spouse hello and good-bye each day, you'll live 5½ years longer. That's a trick you may want to start today! It burns calories too.)

You can reduce stress by reducing time wasters. Begin by organizing your day better, then learn to control the phone, email, and other distractions. Delegate more and learn the magic words "please" and "thank you." When you lead with politeness and kindness, you establish that kind of environment. It will reduce your stress dramatically.

Take a nap when you need one. I'm serious. When you can't keep your eyes open, or just need to escape the pressure, close your door, turn off the lights, and nap. If you are afraid you'll still be zzzing hours later, set a kitchen timer for 15 minutes. If you feel guilty about this, get over it. You will be more productive, do a better job, and give the school higher quality work after a short nap. If you are worried about what your boss will think, remember—*you are the boss!*

I'll bet you don't take coffee breaks, get a full "duty-free lunch," have a prep hour, or go home at 3:30. Get the picture? Take a nap or a walk if you need one. Depressurize yourself by getting away for 10 minutes. (Don't forget to come back.) Or just call a friend, your spouse, or the operator when you need to talk to someone. Remember that all it takes for some people to get over a problem is to have someone listen to them. The same with you. So be a talker when necessary.

Here's another idea: keep your office and your desk orderly. That helps you keep your mind in order. And don't whine, moan, or gripe about your stressful job. Spend that energy making changes. You don't like to hear whiners, so don't be one. (If people start sending cheese to your office, it's probably to complement your whine. Strive to be a cheeseless leader.)

Mental wellness is sometimes hard to address. Here are some indicators that you might need to find someone professional to talk to now:

* You experience longer than normal bouts of confusion or depression.

* You find yourself angry for no reason (or what later seems like a minor incident).

* You discover suddenly that lots of things really bother you.

* You have a serious urge to do something harmful to yourself or others.

* You think of leaving your job or home to escape your present situation.

* You don't care about your family or work and don't know why.

Employee Assistance Programs help. So can ministers, priests, rabbis, or other clerics. Your medical doctor can help or direct you to the best specialist. The key word here is *help*. Get some if you think you need it. If you're not sure, get some anyway. It's kind of like accidentally changing your oil before 3,000 miles; it isn't necessary but it does no damage. You are a talented, educated, proven leader. You are also a human being and you work in a tough profession. All of us are challenged to keep things in order, to balance our responsibilities, and to make life work. Getting help is not a sign of weakness, it is a sign of strength.

Social Wellness, The Art of Good Relationships

Your social wellness is very important. We are told that the six most frequent problems in this area are in-laws, money, housework, sex, stress, and parenthood. No surprise to anyone with half a brain, even less to the full-brained. So how do we come up with a quick solution for maintaining social wellness? Experts say we improve our social wellness through better communication, sharing the workload, trusting each other, getting outside help, accepting relationships, and adapting to change. Many good books exist about this topic.[1] Why not read one and learn how to improve your relationship skills? Learn the importance of treating your spouse better than you treat the copy machine repairman. Learn that it is more important to watch your kids play ball than to go to every school meeting. Learn the need to have something to do away from work, like gardening, singing, seeing movies or plays, pumping gas (or iron), golfing, playing cards, or doing yard work for your in-laws. (Who said that all my ideas would be good ones?)

What should you consider when it comes to social wellness? First, get your priorities in line. Ask questions like: What is most important to you? Is it the job or your spouse? Is it family or income? Is it your spiritual beliefs or your social life? Is it a beer with the guys, volleyball with the girls, cards on Friday night, watching the kids play baseball, spending Sundays with the family, never missing church, or being at school for every athletic event? It is your list, no one else's. But the choices you make do affect the social wellness you develop.

This may seem too basic, but I feel that it is indeed high-level decision making. Pledge to "date" your spouse one night a week. You may save a marriage—your own! Talk about sexual needs openly, and you may improve that relationship by one letter grade or more. Work on your half of the relationship and you will see the immediate benefits. Set your priorities so they fit with those of your family, friends, support systems, and employer and you are one step closer to solid social health and wellness.

And if you are single, regularly make a date or plan an activity with friends outside of work. Include other singles too, and strive to expand your circle of new friends.

Is all of this easy? Hardly. It takes planning, trial and error, and a firm commitment.

Spiritual Wellness

You needn't tell me: tread lightly here. This is a personal zone and we are all well programmed to tiptoe around religion when related to school issues.

---

[1] Those I particularly commend are by Charles Clayman, Lee G. Bolman, Eric Harvey, Ken Blanchard, and Thomas Sergiovanni. See the bibliography at the end of this book.

If you don't think spiritual wellness is important, skip this section. No one will know except you (and perhaps that all-knowing spiritual being in whom you may or may not believe). Go ahead, move on if you want. It's your choice.

Some of you are still here. Good. Personally, I don't see how any administrator could feel that they have done anything important without the minute-by-minute help of some higher power. If you have a religious faith, don't be afraid to share it. Wellness comes from honest communication. Don't impose your faith on others, but never feel you need to hide or avoid it. God is not a dirty word, nor is Jesus, Buddha, Islam, synagogue, or the Pope. Spirituality is a personal thing. It is who you are. If you are comfortable with who you are, then you are on the way to real, personal wellness.

Staying spiritually connected promotes fewer health problems, longevity, and greater satisfaction with life. It also boosts immunity levels, promotes better health habits, improves mental stability, and slows memory loss. The choice is yours. To me, spiritual health is the umbrella of success for everything else.

Let's not beat this issue to death. (A dead horse is no more effective than a dead administrator.) But I do worry about educational leaders who are dead spiritually. I know they exist, but I thankfully don't know many. If you are dead or dying in this arena, open your heart to renewed faith. It helps to have someone with you always and in all ways.

Professional Health

Often forgotten and seldom discussed is the administrator's "professional health." I define professional health simply as how you behave, look, and grow in your profession.

Don't you feel better when you are comfortable about how you look? Dress is a very important part of your professional image and health. Pay attention to style and trends. Improvements in dress and grooming are easy. Look at others whom you respect, then compare yourself to them. If it is time for an overhaul, do it. If in doubt, go to a store that has a suit or dress department with people that cater to professionals and ask for their advice.

Want a few tips in this area? Pick up a copy of any popular "style" magazine or hit the Internet. (Start with a search engine if you're clueless, like http://www.google.com, and type in groom-ing+male [or female], then follow the two million links!).

Did you know that your tie should extend to about one inch below the top of your belt when you are standing, not six inches above or so long that you can zip most of it into your fly? Sit in the mall and look at what people are wearing. If 90% of the women wear shoes that show their toes, maybe it is time to box up your "dress" combat boots. Are you still wearing a size 34 waist pant but the length has gone from 34 to 30? That's because you are wearing it below your tire rather than around your waist. (Hurry back and reread the part about physical wellness!) Had the same hairstyle for 15 years? How might a new one look?

We were on a family trip a few years ago and my two daugh-ters, both teenagers then, decided that I needed a new "do." So somewhere between Illinois and Florida, they unpacked their combs, brushes, hairspray, and do stuff and went to it. Yikes! My hair was combed back rather than over, and they raved about my "new look." It took a few more days, a few more compliments from others, one haircut, and I changed the way I look. I kind of liked the old way, but I also liked the new compliments. Simple things that keep us professionally contemporary.

One more thought. Find friends whom you trust and admire. Tell them you want a professional makeover. Tell them you ad-mire how they look professionally. Ask for their advice. They will be complimented and helpful. Make no promises that you will im-plement their suggestions, and do tell them you are asking others too, to help gather opinions and suggestions. That way if you don't like something they say, they will not be offended if you show up a month later still looking like the "before" picture in a "make-over" article.

Are you professionally bored? It happens to all of us. The so-lution is simple, but not always easy: *change*. Change your rou-tine. Change your job description (give yourself some different responsibilities). Change your employer (move). Or maybe all you need to do is *change your attitude*!

I could go on and on about professional wellness: ethics, mo-rality, motivating others, knowledge of your job, leadership style, ability to manage—the list is long.

You know your strengths. Build on them. You probably know your weaknesses. Improve. If you aren't sure, sit down with some-one who will honestly help you evaluate your professional well-

wellness. It's far more important than just your looks and attitude. It defines you. It's how others describe you. Are you classy, sophisticated, down-to-earth, snobbish, hard to know, conceited, special, always on top of things, dowdy, out-of-touch, boring, exciting, knowledgeable, willing to help? How do others define you? How do you want them to?

Ten Basic Rules You Already Know

Are you a list person? Someone who likes things in neat packages, boxes to check off, executive summaries? If so, then the following list of ten top ideas of healthful suggestions (in part stolen from dozens of others' lists) might just make your day. If you follow this "executive summary," you should enjoy a more healthful, happy, less stressful life.

1. Exercise for 30 minutes a day. Don't panic and uncork the usual excuses like no time, no equipment, too tired, too weak, or claim "I'm active enough already." This is probably the easiest of the rules to follow. Save the excuses for the other nine.

2. Don't use any type of tobacco product. Can you read? If you can, then read *carefully* the side of the package that contains the cigar, cigarettes, or chew. Tobacco kills, and it doesn't take a rocket scientist to know that it complicates and compromises your body, your systems, your mind, and your presentation to others. It makes you cough, stink, get sick, and it contributes to an earlier death. Sure, there are smokers who live to a hundred. There are also survivors who have jumped out of airplanes using parachutes that didn't open. Get the point? And, by the way, tobacco kills those around you too.

3. Don't drink alcohol (but if you do, do it in considerable and consistent moderation). My dad died from cirrhosis of the liver, as did his father. He stopped drinking the last two years of his life and only began drinking at about 40. Too late and too long. It was a miserable way to lose a good guy. How many people do you know who died too young while driving drunk—or were hit by a "driving drunk"? Is a glass of wine bad for you? Probably not. Will a couple of beers do you in? Who knows? Can alcohol do funny things to people who have high stress jobs *like you*? You bet—alcohol can be the fuse on a stick of dynamite. So why take the chance? Why risk your health, your reputation, and your re-

cord? Ever hear of a community member, professional peer, or coworker who was criticized for *not* drinking?

4. Eat a balanced diet that includes fruits, vegetables, and whole grains each day. I know that you have heard this a thousand times and probably feel this is either a no-brainer to do or absolutely impossible. You want to know just how easy it is? Have a glass of V8, an apple, and two helpings of vegetables (even french fries count) and you meet the "daily minimum requirements." Vary that a little and you are doing fine. Is it important? Virtually every health list gives this recommendation top billing. Almost any culture that boasts good health statistics also has a good diet. So why don't we?

5. Maintain a healthy weight. It's easier than you think. No, you don't have to be a Twiggy-look-alike to be healthy. (Please don't make us feel older by asking who Twiggy is!) A healthy weight for you might be a bit on the "hefty" side. Research is finding that individuals have a unique "prime weight." (Good news for most of us!)

6. Spend time on relationships. Yes, I'm jumping from fruits and exercise to being lovey-dovey. A happy home life is just as important to good health as bananas and bike rides. A healthy family life reduces stress, aids digestion, minimizes some diseases, and gives you a better attitude. Remember what I said earlier; kissing your spouse twice a day adds 5½ years to your life? Since reading that research, I kiss my spouse six times a day, hoping to make it to 130!

7. Be strong spiritually. The relationship between spiritual and physical wellness is proven. No religion has the edge here. Spirituality covers anyone and everyone! It promotes a sense of belonging and a trust in others. A practiced, well-developed faith adds up to a longer life. Research tells us that those who are married live longer than the unmarried, and further, those who married in a church live even longer than those who didn't.

8. Challenge your mind every day. This means reading, tackling crossword puzzles, learning another language, playing board games, engaging in topical discussions, playing cards, or creating something. It means keeping your mind challenged. Mental exercise is as important as physical exercise.

9. Be proactive. Have routine physical exams. Get flu shots. Take a multivitamin pill daily. Plan, and take, vacations. Think

about your diet; plan before you eat. Schedule stress-reducing activities. Ask for help if you need it. Exercise.

10. Wear your seat belt. Yes, this makes the top-ten list most of the time because it *does* save lives. Wear it when you go to the grocery store or to another state. Before you turn the key, click your belt. Also make sure everyone in the car does the same. Even if you don't love them, it's the law.

What a simple yet effective list! If each of us developed a plan that embraced just these items, we would be in prime physical, mental, and emotional shape.

An Executive Summary, Needed or Not

Physical, mental, social, spiritual, and professional wellness are essential components of a healthy school administrator. Each component affects the others. Each fits under the category of things you control.

If you want to take control of your life, the time to start is *now*. Take a personal inventory: your strengths, your weaknesses, and your desires. Consider positive changes you want to make and forge a plan. In doing this remember the following:

* You can control what goes into your body, so start the process today and you will feel better immediately.

* You can control how you respond to stressful situations, so consider what causes those situations and carefully plan how you can prevent them or react to them. Become a problem solver rather than a problem victim. If things get really tough in your heart and your head, seek help immediately.

* You can control your aerobic and strength-building programs. It takes effort and planning every day, but it is as easy as getting out of your chair right now and spending the next ten minutes walking, riding, moving, dancing, lifting this book 20 times over your head, anything, and building on that *until it is part of your life*. The results are simply amazing.

* You can control your half of most relationships, so start today. Who needs to be called, kissed, patted on the back, apologized to, or supported? Who needs your compliment, your steady response to a situation, your guidance, your leadership? Who

needs you to make a difference in his or her life—and thus one in yours?

* You can control your beliefs and your personal value systems. Probably more than anything, this defines not only who you are, but what people think you are. This is personal, but definitive. Don't take shortcuts here. This change may be eternal.

Want to be a leader who makes a difference? Want to be someone that kids, parents, peers, friends, and family will long admire, remember, and love? If so, take care of *yourself.*

"The service we render to others is really the rent we pay for room on this earth. It is obvious that man himself is a traveler; that the purpose of this world is not 'to have and to hold' but 'to give and serve.'

There can be no other meaning."

Sir Wilfred T. Grenfell

Chapter Thirteen

Standards, Assessment, and Accountability

Max McGee and Jim Rosborg

The single most debated issue in education the past fifteen years is student achievement—or at least measurement of it. Student achievement has become synonymous with the test scores printed in the news media. As educators, we know that there are several, better measures of student achievement, but we also know that the public does not have an inkling of what the other measures are or what they mean. Like it or not, in the public's eye school quality is defined by test scores and very little else. A successful school has high scores; a failing school has poor scores. The public gauges improvement by performance on standardized tests, period. They do not care what reading series you use, how much you spend on professional development, how you deal with multiple intelligences, how many kids you have in algebra, how many you have living in poverty, or about any other measure you use internally. The bottom line is test results—and they want good ones.

In our opinion, educators, including most educational leaders, spend too much time decrying this fact and too little time managing it. Though we blame the public, we probably use similar measures in our own lives. I (Max McGee) have a whole lot of shares of Cisco that free-fell from $70 a share to $15 in a matter of weeks. I know Cisco makes routers (not that I would know a router from a Roto-rooter) and I have read they are a good company. But right now, in my estimation, they are a lousy company because the measure most important to me—Cisco's stock price—has fallen fast and hard. My personal wealth has plummeted with the stock—I want Cisco to do something about it *now*!

Sound familiar? When our school test scores go down or when they stay low for a couple of years, we are no longer a good school. If the measure—the state test score—declines, then our quality, and perhaps even our credibility, drops as well. I expect a better performance from Cisco, as taxpayers expect a better performance from us. When scores are low, our common response is to retreat into a defensive mode. Blame the tests, blame the kids, blame the parents, blame the teachers, blame the media, and blame the public for not knowing better. This gets us no further than CEOs blaming "tough times" for their economic woes. I expect results from my companies, and the public expects results from us.

Another response is a full-scale offensive. We may immediately drive to improve the test scores through artificial means— buy more study guides, give more practice tests, have students write five paragraph essays each day. In truth, neither the offensive nor defensive reactions will make a bit of difference. So what is a leader to do? In our profession, we need to do what we do best, teach. We need to teach the public what scores mean and how to interpret them. We need to teach our teachers and administrators what the data tell us and how to mine the results for information to improve teaching and learning. So let's get on with it.

There is not one effective school administrator who doesn't care deeply about the improvement of student achievement, yet many do not take action to improve their district's or school's test scores. Many school administrators feel overwhelmed and undermanned. This chapter is about how to tackle test scores, how to manage accountability, and how to cope with imposed standards. It will provide practical ideas on how the educational leader can improve those scores.

A good school administrator knows the importance of testing and assessment. Not only are assessment results important for the media, realtors, and the general public regarding the perception of your school district, they are even more important to determining the effectiveness of your district's programs and services. Assessment can empower curriculum. "What gets tested gets taught," is as true an adage as "What gets measured gets improved." Most of our colleagues—even our suburban ones who don't know a cow from a sow—frequently comment, "You don't fatten the hog by weighing it." This comment is invariably followed by laughter, mutual agreement, and disdain for assessment. We contend, however, that if said farmer does not weigh the hog, he is not going to know whether he is feeding it enough food or the right food. He is not going to know which food is best for the hog—and his bank account. That's why farmers weigh hogs a lot. They make most, if not all, of their agricultural decisions from that kind of assessment. Cost effectiveness and results matter to farmers as much as they do to us. They feed and weigh the hog and we need to teach and regularly measure progress. In other words, we do need to measure what's important to us, and we do need to use the information to identify what we can do to help students learn.

Your responsibility, as a leader, is to do the following:

* Embrace accountability.
* Insist on quality assessments.
* Understand what the assessments measure.
* Communicate with and teach the public and staff what the results say about curriculum and instruction.
* Use the information (aka data) to improve teaching and learning.
* Maintain high standards for students and staff.

In the following sections, we will explore each of these as a way of improving your students' achievement.

Embrace Accountability

I can hear the groans halfway across America. Embrace accountability? Love being put on the line? Cherish public flogging? Yes, we believe that the most effective leaders welcome accountability. They know for what they are accountable and to whom they are accountable. They know where the buck stops. They realize that if children are not learning, they are not doing their job.

The first step in embracing accountability is to talk about it. You literally have to say (and write) that you welcome accountability and that you are holding yourself accountable. If you're not willing to stand up for improving teaching and learning, what contribution are you making? You may excel at protecting teachers, at buffering your principals, at selling referenda, and at handling parental complaints, but you are not leading if you do not make yourself accountable. When leaders do make themselves accountable, their teachers will emulate their example. Since we do not directly teach children, our teachers—to be successful—need to realize, understand, and accept that they are accountable for what their kids learn. That accountability may be to parents, to the principal, or to you, but each of your teachers should be leading a personal crusade to help all children learn. This is what happens in Illinois' high-poverty, high-performing Golden Spike schools that have closed the Achievement Gap. This is what happens with teachers who win Golden Apple Awards. They do not let children fail; they are accountable.

What measures of accountability do they use? Test scores. Leaders and teachers who are accountable understand how the public and parents measure success. Test scores. They strive to improve test scores by analyzing results and changing instruction to meet the needs of their students.

Several of the Golden Spike schools' leaders excel at presenting data in a manner that interests teachers and motivates them to improve the results. The leaders are very non-directive, but when presenting the information, they point out areas of success and highlight where improvement is needed. They suggest the goals or targets—the level where they think students can and should be. Like a good teacher, they ask questions that involve the staff in analyzing, synthesizing, and evaluating data. In these schools, the teachers then drive the rest of the discussion. They talk among themselves about what they can do to assure that students do better the next year, they generate ideas for professional development, and they engage all teachers in the improvement process. They take responsibility for improving the results. Though the teachers know better than anyone that the students are impacted daily by poverty in their neighborhoods and, in many cases, by serious problems at home, the teachers work as a team to be sure that when the students are in school they are learning and loved. In these schools, everyone has a stake in accountability because they realize that they are the ones responsible for helping all children achieve. Though there is a subtle difference between responsibility and accountability, we have found that when leaders take responsibility for learning, a collective effort for accountability follows. But when leaders try to force accountability first, the staff seldom follows.

Insist on Quality Assessments

As a leader, insist upon quality assessments. Insert and immerse yourself in state policies. You know state testing is here to stay, so insist that they are the best tests. You as a leader need to be a *loud voice* to ensure that state assessments measure what your students are learning and give you usable, meaningful, timely results that will help you develop, implement, and use school improvement plans that will lead to significant changes in student achievement over time. Your staff will admire you for fighting hard for fair assessments. You must become the symbol of strong leadership for quality assessment. Like the proverbial "white knight," an effective school leader should be a champion who battles bad public policies.

For example, *demand* that the tests do not change every few years. Trend data is essential to gauging improvement. One current problem we have in state-level assessment is that there is no consistent trend data because state education agencies frequently change their tests or revise their cut scores, thus making the tests more difficult to evaluate. The sad part of this is that many times these changes occur because of political pressure without a good research foundation. School leaders throughout the nation are frustrated by this testing merry-go-round, where school districts continue to shoot for different stars instead of set standards.

It's been almost twenty years since the accountability movement started with the publishing of *A Nation At Risk*. Nearly all of the same school districts that had low test scores in the mid-eighties still have low test scores today. Despite this fact and the fact that we know poverty is the dominant indicator of academic success, more and more testing-related bureaucratic paperwork is being placed on local school districts. We have taken the basic concept of assessment and have made it a bureaucratic nightmare. John Katzman, editor of the *Princeton Review*, shared an important assessment fact in a phone interview, "Policies surrounding the state test are just as important as the test itself."[1] With all of these frustrations, what can we do?

Our model of sound state assessment is:

---

[1] On August 15, 2002.

* Test reading and math every year for grades 3-11; test science, social studies, and writing once in elementary school, once in middle school, and once in high school; and have the ACT or SAT be the culminating test in grade 11. For the most part, the rules behind the No Child Left Behind Act has embraced this idea.

* Incorporate tests in grades 8, 9, and 10 to help students prepare for the ACT or SAT.

* Have a national testing company develop a research-based, criterion-referenced test that is reliable, valid, and consistent. The test should not be changed for at least five years.

* Thoroughly pilot the test before administering it.

* Concentrate funding and resources on low-scoring districts as long as they comply with research-based programs of improvement.

* Reward districts and schools—especially those performing well over time—with additional funding and substantive recognition.

* Develop a special education alternative test that meets the special needs of each classroom. Move the federal government to accept out of level testing for special education students who clearly do not have the cognitive ability to be successful on the grade level test. Make the test achievable for the student. (While the alternative test is a requirement of federal IDEA mandates, many state agencies do not have the expertise to deal with the alternative tests in such a way that the tests meet the specific assessment needs of the special education student.)

* Make sure the tests are vertically designed so there is consistent scores from one grade to the next.

* Score the tests using a continuous scale such as 0-100 so parents understand the results.

* Do an individual item analysis on student results so strategies for student improvement can take place.

Understanding What Assessments Measure

Tests tend to take on a life of their own. Like the neighborhood bully or the mob boss, their reputation—perhaps well deserved—fuels fear on one hand and disdain on the other. As educators, we treat tests in a compliance/survival mode. They are something to endure. When they are not around, life is easier and we tend to forget about them. When they are in the neighborhood, however, fear and trepidation abound. To help your staff and students stand up to the bully and cuff the hit man, they need strength and resolve. First and foremost, they need a tough, cool leader who fuels himself or herself on information and uses it to build bulging brains by facilitating, guiding, and even requiring changes in curriculum and instruction.

A critical piece of this information is knowing what the tests test. Though state tests differ, typically they all test a limited number of the state standards. Learn which standards they are and communicate them to your staff so they are taught.

The tests are also reading tests. The inter-correlations among tests are amazing. For example, in Illinois the correlation factor between the reading tests and other tests, including mathematics, is generally above .8! Such high inter-correlations tell us that the score on one test is highly related to the score on the second test, and the score of the third-grade reading tests closely predicts the score on any other assessment. This information tells us that students need to read both the directions and the questions carefully. To help your students succeed on state tests, insist and assure that they all know how to read well. Every administrator knows that time spent on reading improvement, at any grade level, is time spent on test score improvement for any subject in any grade. *Reading improvement is the single most important "score booster" we have.*

Knowing and articulating what the state tests *do not* test is also important. For example, if your state has a writing sample, chances are that it measures how well students write a rough draft in a short amount of time. It is far from a measurement of a student's writing ability. To succeed on writing tests, students have to practice this skill and you need to communicate very clearly what the test does test and how it is evaluated.

Communicate to the Public and Staff
What Test Results Really Mean

It is obvious that you need to take these results and report them to the Board of Education, staff, parents, public, media, realtors, businesses, and other interested community members. But more than simply reporting them, you need to *teach* what they mean. If scores are on a continuous scale and tests are vertically equated, you can track student achievement from one year to the next. In other words, if 60% of a group of third-grade students meet state standards, you would expect at least that same percentage to meet state standards in following grades *if and only if* the tests are vertically equated and scored on a continuous scale. If they are not, it is quite possible that at third grade 60% of the students meet state standards, yet when they become fifth graders only 40% meet standards. In this case, students may actually be doing much better as fifth graders if the test is exceptionally difficult or the "cut scores" for the standards have been set much higher than for the third-grade test. Find out if your state tests are vertically equated. The Iowa Test of Basic Skill is; the Illinois Standards Assessment Test is not.

When communicating results, there are four guiding principles to keep in mind:

* KISS (keep it simple, superintendent).
* Use tables *and graphs.*
* Present results with improvement plans.
* Develop and repeat three main message points.

Keeping it simple is a challenge. If your results are like ours, you know that for all the paper you use and copies you make there is a large clearing in a distant forest named for your district. If you get your results electronically instead of on paper, as we do from our beloved State Board, it takes the Son of Cray to run the information—or you need to hire Bill Gates to decode the ASCII (or SHMASCII) into a vaguely understandable format. That said, you can make results understandable and user-friendly for your Board, parents, and staff by following three principles.

1. When you present the results, **use simple tables and clear graphs**. All of the columns and rows need a label. Highlight cells you want to illustrate. Do *not* try to cram too much information into one table. If you want to communicate the results and teach your community what they need to know, you are better off having many tables with just one piece of data on each one rather than one table with lots of data on it.

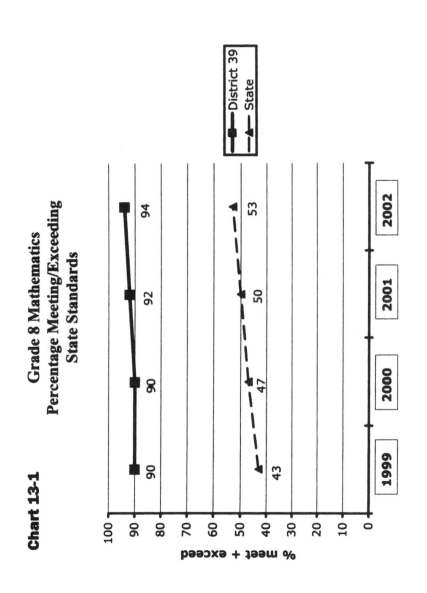

Chart 13-1

**Grade 8 Mathematics
Percentage Meeting/Exceeding
State Standards**

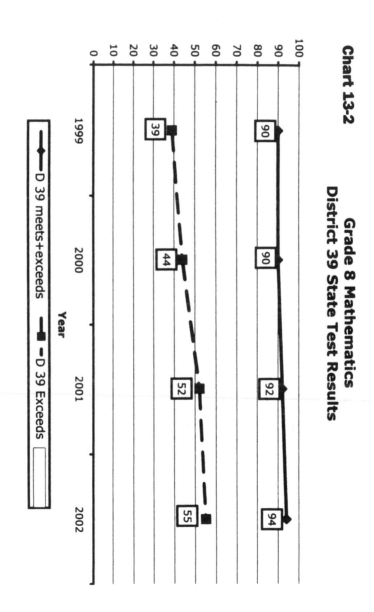

Chart 13-2

Grade 8 Mathematics
District 39 State Test Results

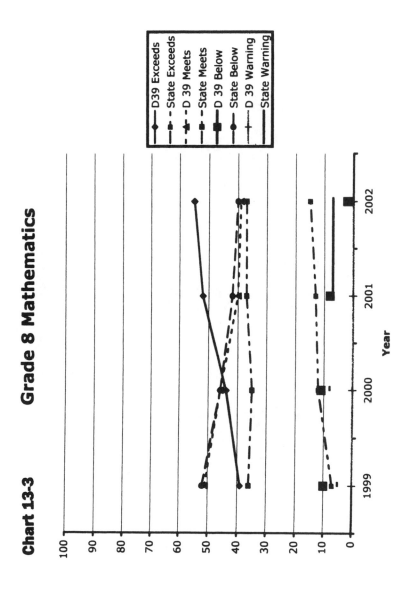

Chart 13-3   Grade 8 Mathematics

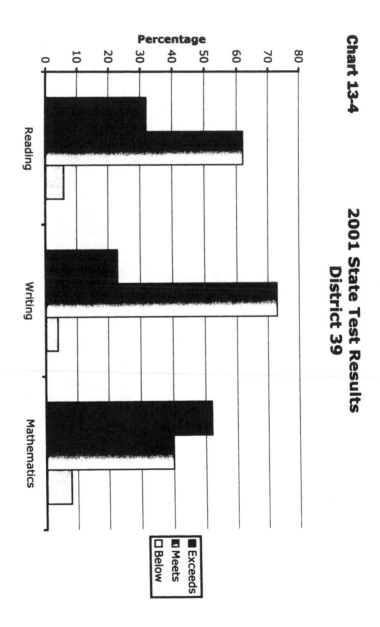

Chart 13-4

2001 State Test Results District 39

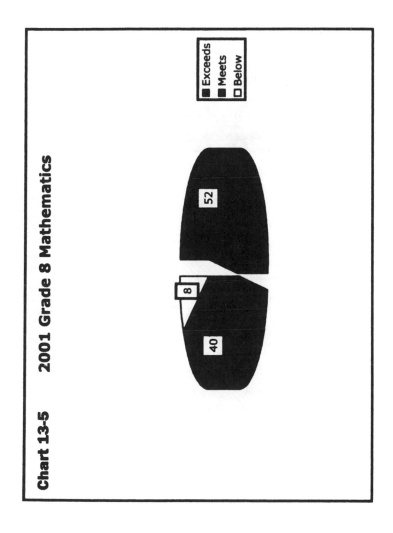

Chart 13-5   2001 Grade 8 Mathematics

■ Exceeds
■ Meets
□ Below

52

8

40

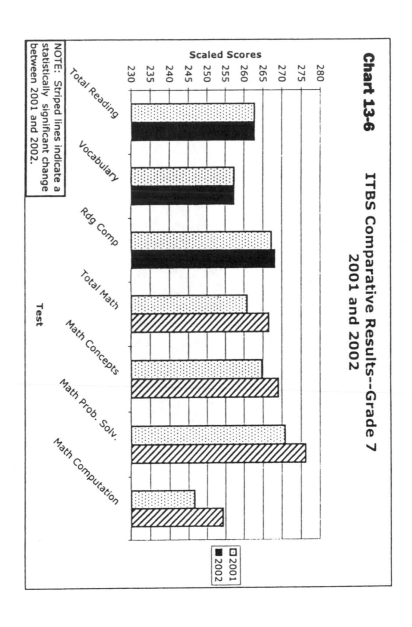

Chart 13-6

**ITBS Comparative Results--Grade 7
2001 and 2002**

NOTE: Striped lines indicate a statistically significant change between 2001 and 2002.

Scaled Scores

Test: Total Reading, Vocabulary, Rdg Comp, Total Math, Math Concepts, Math Prob. Solv., Math Computation

Legend: ☐ 2001 ■ 2002

Use graphs to communicate your message as well. *Remember to use the same scale on each graph, to have a maximum of four lines or bars on each graph, and to clearly label axes and titles.* If you are looking at results over time, use line graphs. If you are comparing groups of students or percentages of students at specific performance levels, use bar graphs or pie charts. *Do not use bar charts to compare results over time, and do not use a line graph to compare results from one group to another!* When using graphs, follow the same rules as for tables: keep them simple and readable.

For example, Graph 13-1 (see the Graphs above) shows how one district's scores, compared to state scores, have changed over time. The lines represent the "percentage of students meeting or exceeding standards." Graph 13-2 tells a more important story for the district in very simple form: it shows the significant improvement of the percentage of students "exceeding state standards" over time. Graph 13-3 shows the percentage of students scoring at each of Illinois' performance levels (exceeds, meets, below, and academic warning). Although this graph is the appropriate use of a line graph—showing change over time—it has so much information it is unreadable. Graphs 13-4 and 13-5 show how bar graphs and pie graphs should be used to compare results from one group to another.

We recommend that your tables and graphs use either scale scores or performance levels. Stay away from the jargon words that are misleading or confusing, such as stanines, grade equivalents, and normal curve equivalents.

2. When you present the results, **be sure to explain how you are using them as well as what they mean**. To use results most effectively, you have to disaggregate groups. You have to compare boys and girls, racial/ethnic groups, low-income students with peers, and the like. Your schools are accountable for the learning of *all* students.

Since the public will not have a clue about significant differences, you need to teach them. The bar graphs in Graph 13-6 differentiate between gains that are statistically significant and those that are not. In Chapter 3 we saw that Excel spreadsheets were a very simple tool to help determine significance.

3. Finally, as with any type of communication, be sure to **have your message points clear at the beginning of your presenta-**

tion. Stick to three or four points and reinforce them. For example, in my most recent Board meeting, here were the points:

* Math scores have significantly increased in each of the past four years at all grade levels.

* Compared to other districts in the state with similar demographics, our district is one of the highest performing, indicating that we are maximizing the value of each tax dollar.

* The decline in eighth-grade reading and writing scores appears to be primarily due to a large gap between achievement of boys and girls.

* To address this problem, our entire staff is committed to becoming reading teachers and to motivating our male students. In addition, we are studying similar schools in other districts to identify programs, practices, and services that have enabled them to close this gap.

Use the Information (aka Data) to improve Teaching and Learning

How you use the results is of critical importance. Assessment *must be used to drive school improvement plans*—both their development and execution! The main goal of School Improvement Planning is to empower teachers at the building level to influence decisions, which will have a positive impact on student learning. This process should include a total analysis of the academic progress of the school.

Some thoughts about School Improvement:

* Teachers need to be part of the decision-making process to ensure that the decisions are executed. Anyone can plan, but implementation takes commitment. You will not have commitment without including teachers in the process from start to finish— from data analysis to delivery. These school improvement teams should be formulated to compile a review process that includes data analysis. Staff development is needed to make these teams effective. In fact, the school improvement teams should also be instrumental in developing building and district staff development plans.

* Pay teachers for this planning; it is the most important task they will accomplish.

* Use hard data to make decisions: local assessments, staff surveys, student surveys, parent surveys, community surveys, state tests, national tests, etc.

* Remember, all change will have positive and negative results. Anticipate the negative results, and use the trust and building skills you learned to overcome them.

* This process will encourage teachers to take real ownership in the entire school process. The school improvement planning process forces teachers to look outside their own grade level and empathize with fellow members.

School Improvement Plans should also:

* Identify problem areas by stating the issue in terms of the hard data from the tests and surveys. Use your compilation of demographics to individualize student academic needs.

* Identify strengths in the curriculum. Celebrate those strengths.

* Develop an evaluation system to assess the effectiveness of instructional strategy. Instructional plans and the prioritizing of instructional time allocations should be discussed.

* Go beyond simple assessment data and work on climate issues such as safety, self-esteem, respect, etc. A general brainstorming session should take place regarding teacher and administrator observations in the areas of teaching and learning, student learning, progress and achievement, and the learning community as a whole. Once building-wide teams have developed priorities, then grade level teams need to be formulated to develop grade level integrated action plans. These plans should address deficiencies that current year students demonstrated in the previous year's assessments.

In this chapter we've seen how to lay out an effective School Improvement Plan that will result in meaningful action and change. Chapter 6, "Planning," also offers suggestions related to school improvement plans. The importance of good school improvement planning should by now be more than obvious since we have mentioned it in this book about 600 times.

There are many other things you can do to check your school's effectiveness with assessment. We call this your own internal audit. Ask yourself and your staff these questions:

* Do teachers have ownership in your reporting instrument? Does your report card effectively communicate to parents?
* What kind of communication system do you have with parents? Are parent conferences required? Are they effective? Is there enough time for meaningful dialog? Can parents meet with each teacher alone? Will teachers meet parents in the evening or on weekends to accommodate their schedules? (Ours do.)
* Is there an alignment of local, state, and national tests with the instructional program so that evaluation and improvement can take place?
* Is trend data examined and then used to help determine the emphasis of instructional needs?
* Do you use data to help formulate needs for staff improvement?

What additional strategies can the school administrator and staff use to help students take greater responsibility for their learning?

Here are some suggestions that you, as the school leader, can use to improve test scores. Identify where the two or three worst problems are. Convene a team to examine the data. Find schools or districts like yours that have higher scores. Call them. Visit them. Invite them to your school. Pick their brains and harness their wisdom. Be a real community of learners. Make it a school problem. Insist that the identified problems appear in school improvement plans and that the measure of improvement is the percentage of students improving. Set the percentage high. Provide support, cover, and training for teachers. Reward successes.

School visits can be especially rewarding. One of our top suburban junior high schools—in terms of wealth and academic achievement—wanted to do a better job of meeting students' social and emotional needs. They wanted to develop their students' character as well as their intellect. In short, they wanted to become a middle school. After some extensive research, the staff steering committee recommended that they visit a successful middle school located in deep southern Illinois. Though the junior high teachers were polite, they were mostly skeptical. What could they learn from those downstate bubbas? Meanwhile, downstate at the model middle school, the teachers were more than a bit cynical about their first meeting with the yuppie suburban snobs.

Within ten minutes, the trepidation and attitude disappeared. The six-hour drive proved to be valuable to the junior high staff. They returned renewed and established a powerful partnership. As it turns out, the scores at both schools rose, and fast friendships developed and have lasted. Best of all, students at both schools thrived.

What else can you as a school leader do to improve test scores in your district? The first thing you should do is align your local curriculum with your state's learning standards for both regular and special education students. Unless this step is done, there will be very little chance for improved scores. Likewise, determine if students' basic needs of food, shelter, clothing, and safety are met. One of these years, our governmental and business leaders, along with the media, will realize that it doesn't matter if a child is in a public, private, parochial, charter, or home school. If a child doesn't have proper nutrition, he or she will struggle in school. Children will be left behind unless we as school leaders can provide all students with a secure environment where they eat a healthy meal, get medical attention, and have warm clothing. A stronger family unit, provision for basic needs, and parenting education are the only ways the poverty factor is going to be overcome in our society.

Next, use a local assessment to strengthen your curriculum.

* Use it to test prerequisite skills.
* Make your local test tough so that the state and national tests seem easy.
* Include performance assessment, such as writing.
* Have your teachers score the local assessments; the individuals who do the scoring will become your experts.
* Rotate your experts so that this becomes a training process for new or inexperienced teachers. Be careful to bring in only a few newcomers each year so that quality is maintained.
* Reading, writing, and math local assessments should occur at nearly every grade at the elementary levels. New federal legislation requires testing of reading and math at each grade level in

grades 3-8. It only makes sense to include writing as an annual local assessment.

* Administer the local assessments strategically.

* Do not over-assess students; avoid desensitizing them to the importance of the tests.

Individual Student Improvement Plans (see Table 13-1) provide parents with options for their child that can enhance his/her learning outside the regular school day. Individual student improvement plans should be used to bring the parent along in the learning process and make the parent jointly responsible for the child's learning. These should be used for:

* Students who are working one grade level below where they should be performing.

* Identifying a problem and telling the parent.

* Interpreting present achievement data when available.

* Communicating that the school is using teacher judgment—any student who is failing or close to failing should have an individual improvement plan.

* Background data at parent conferences.

Instruction is still the most important component to improving test scores. While professional development is a key to improvement, the following are general instructional tips to help you improve scores.

* Use a daily warm-up activity to gain student mastery of what has been taught. Put this on the board or give a handout. Remember that a concept has to be revisited multiple times in multiple ways before mastery occurs.

* Practice lessons using the answer sheet or a facsimile so the students can become comfortable with coloring in the circles.

* Use summary review periodically to check retention.

* Encourage parents to ask their children to read. Then also encourage parents to ask their children what they have read. Growth occurs in the stair-step method—one sound, one word, one sentence, one paragraph, one page, one chapter, one section, and one book.

Table 13-1

INDIVIDUAL IMPROVEMENT PLAN

Student Name:_____ Grade: ____ Date: _____

It is the goal of our school district to help your child achieve the highest possible level of success. Presently, your child is achieving significantly below grade level in the following subject/s:

_____

Your cooperation is requested in assisting your child to enhance his/her achievement level. The primary determination for the need for this plan is based on teacher judgment. Additional resources, such as achievement tests, state tests, exit tests, classroom tests, and daily assignments may have been consulted.

PLAN FOR IMPROVEMENT

The teacher and the parent understand that all items checked below will be addressed in an effort to reduce the child's identified deficiency:

____ The school and home will work together to improve study skills and organizational abilities.

____ Using teacher suggestions, parents will work on (English) (Reading) (Spelling) (Writing) (Math) (Science) (Social Studies) facts.

____ Extra time will be spent on reviewing (Math) (English) (Science) (Social Studies) facts.

____ Child will be encouraged to read a library book for at least 15 minutes per night.

____ Positive reinforcement will occur at home and school when success is achieved in the deficit area.

____ Deficiencies on tests will be identified by the teacher and communicated to the student and parent.

____ Teacher and parent will discuss summer activities to improve the identified deficit area.

____ The child may be retained or placed in an expanded or modified program (final decision by the end of May).

____ Special instructional accommodations are reflected on an attached sheet.

____ Other: _____

I understand and agree with the above plan.

Teacher Signature: _____ Parent Signature: _____

INDIVIDUAL IMPROVEMENT PLAN (p. 2)

Quarterly Report Card Grades in Identified Areas of Deficiency:

Subject	1st Qtr.	2nd Qtr.	3rd Qtr.	4th Qtr.
English				
Reading				
Math				
Social Studies				
Spelling				
Writing				
Science				

Dates of Review with Parent: _____

_____

Revised September 22, 1998

* In math, if a student is behind on the learning of the basics in addition, subtraction, multiplication, and division, we must not only inform the home that the child is behind, we must also ask the home for help on the development of skills. If we get one parent in every class to help, we achieve success. Homework is valuable here too. We need to provide the students with the resources to improve in these areas.

The administering of tests often leads to students not being able to maximize their potential. The principal's and teacher's attitude are the most important aspect of successful test taking. Remember when administering tests:

* Make sure you give the allotted time to administer tests. Test scores are greatly lowered when lesser times are given.
* Encourage students to check their answers when they finish, before time is up.
* Secure a quiet environment. If any time interruptions occur, the teacher should remain calm and reassure the class that it will get its allocated time.
* Have extra pencils so that sharpening does not take place during the test.

* Carefully monitor to make sure each student is filling in the correct answer numbers on the correct test. For example, make sure the student is not doing #1 in math when he/she should be doing #1 in reading.

* Give the students sufficient breaks, and stress the importance of each doing the best they can.

* Make sure students erase any stray marks.

* Maintain proper temperature control in the classroom.

* Limit interruptions—grass mowing, field trips, intercom. Inform all staff of the importance of the assessments.

* Make sure the students have marked the answers dark enough. Also, the corners of the test cannot be dog-eared as this impacts the scanner at the scoring center.

* Rearrange music, art, planning periods, etc. Make the state or national test a top priority in the school.

* Make sure students make up missed tests in a positive test-taking atmosphere.

* Try *not* to change the students' environment. The students should take the test in the regular classroom, with the regular teacher, in the regular seat, with their regular classmates. It is important not to create distractions that will move the student's attention away from the test. The test should be what gets their attention.

* Send a reminder letter home. This letter helps parents understand the importance of the test (See Table 13-2).

Things that teachers can do in the testing classroom to help the assessment environment, make students feel comfortable, and still be legal to the test administration are:

* Answer all students' questions. Be sure they clearly understand the instructions before beginning. However, the teacher should read the testing instructions carefully beforehand. There may be some rule changes.

* Never leave the room.

* Circulate around the room. Check to see if students are on the correct section of the answer sheet, answer questions, make certain they are not just randomly filling in responses, etc.

Table 13-2

DATE

Dear Parent:

From March 9 through March 20, our school district will be giving the annual state tests to students. Because of the importance of these tests, we ask your cooperation with the following:

1. Make sure your child comes to school on time so that classes will not be interrupted.
2. Try to rearrange doctor and dental appointments so that they are <u>not</u> scheduled in the morning.
3. Please make sure your child gets a good night's sleep (9-10 hours).
4. Please make the extra effort to make sure your child gets a good breakfast.
5. If your child wears glasses, please make sure he/she has them at school.
6. Remind your child to ask the teacher questions if he/she does not understand the test directions.
7. Advise your child not to worry about the tests, and express your confidence in his/her ability to do well on the tests.
8. Encourage your child to do the best he/she possibly can on the tests. Your child's individual results will be available next fall.

Sincerely,

SCHOOL PRINCIPAL
or SUPERINTENDENT

* Remove students who are distracting others or are being disrespectful. These students should be tested individually in a different environment than the classroom. If a student has caused problems throughout the year, be proactive and secure another testing area for the student. Use resource people to administer the test.

Check the tests to be sure that students receive appropriate credit for their efforts:

* Be sure that erasures are complete.
* Be sure that marks are dark enough.
* *Never change an answer*—cheating is wrong, and cheaters can and should be fired.
* Erase stray marks.
* Be sure names are completed correctly, the form is properly filled in, etc.
* Be sure that *all* students are accounted for in the totals.
* Be sure the header pages are completed accurately.
* Be sure all testing materials are returned.
* Pack testing materials, and send them out promptly for scoring.

Brainstorming is a way to help teachers cope with the testing environment. This gives teachers the ability to vent a little and relieve some of the stress associated with accountability.

* Allow teachers to share experiences, successes, and problems and to collaboratively develop some solutions.
* Organize it and pay them. Set an agenda if you need to, but don't let the meeting become only a complaint session.
* Set the goal to identify solutions, not problems. With that said, there are times when testing problems need to be identified and reported at the state level.

A key to overall success is to help teachers new to the profession, to the building, or to the grade level. The scores coming from these classrooms count just as much as the scores from experienced teachers' classrooms. Some activities include:

* Set up a mentoring system, especially for state and national tests.

* Monitor the mentoring process carefully so that everyone is prepared for the test. Meetings should also take place between the principal and new teacher.

* Make testing a team effort. Remember than when the scores are reported in the newspaper or on the watch list, everyone is lumped together!

* Provide an internal building support system which sets up buddy mentor teachers and group reinforcement meetings.

Maintain High Standards

Knowing how fads come and go, by the time you read this book "standards-based reform" may have gone the way of "values clarification," "whole language," "new math," and a truckload of other *big* ideas. Most educational leaders, however, are convinced that the "standards movement" is here to stay. We, on the other hand, are not so sure. Notice where it is in this book—almost last. We think assessment and accountability are here to stay; we think standards-based reform will soon be a footnote in the annals of public education.

Don't get us wrong. We like standards. We think they are important if, and only if, you develop them in collaboration with your teachers and community and if, and only if, they translate into high expectations for all of your students and all of your teachers. In other words, we like *local* standards.

We also like standards because we see that they have the power to transform *instruction*. That's right, we think standards can change the way people teach. Unfortunately, most leaders don't get the fact that standards are not just about "alignment" or "curriculum"; they are about delivery of instruction in the classroom. We like standards because leaders can use them to unfetter teachers from texts and empower teachers to use multiple resources to teach the standards.

My (Max McGee's) son had a science teacher who should win the Nobel Prize for both science and teaching. A quarter of the way into the year, she used the following resources to teach the state science standards: two different science books, in-class lab assignments, computer simulations, Power Point presentations (which my son designed), class lectures, small group investigations, home labs, extended student-driven observations, and an engaging sense of humor. Quite literally, my son learned more in the first quarter than he has in any other three years of school (when he also had good teachers). She made the standards very clear, the expectations high, and gave daily homework. That is the first homework he did! Standards can have an enormous impact if we focus on teaching instead of documents.

We dislike—vehemently—state mandated standards based on a theory that they will lead to the types of changes that improve teaching and learning. They don't. In fact, as Richard Elmore points out in *Building a New Structure for School Leadership*,[2] most educational reforms (including standards) are bent by the public schools to fit their existing practices. In other words, we hear a lot about "alignment to standards," but the teachers still teach their curriculum with the same materials they used before they ever heard of standards. No wonder there is not more improvement in public education. State mandated standards—and the millions of dollars to support them—do nothing more than preserve the status quo in many districts and are often too watered down—or dumbed down—to matter in several more.

We hear that standards are implemented in our schools, but we don't see them displayed in classrooms. We hear that standards improve student learning, but we have yet to see a school district's report card with any measure of a state standard. We hear that standards drive instruction, but we will bet you that we can choose a teacher at random from most schools and he or she will not be able to tell us one state standard—not one!

That said, having *high* standards for students is important because, in our mind, high standards mean high expectations! It has been substantially documented that teacher expectations directly impact the learning of poor, minority students.[3] If expectations are tied to standards, we are all for standards. It is not the wording of the standards that matters, then, but having standards.

In Illinois, we have a clear case in point. The Galesburg School District developed local standards about a year before the Illinois State Standards were published. Teachers learned the standards, they were trained in how to teach them, they received ongo-

---

[2] Washington, D.C.: The Albert Shanker Institute, Winter, 2000.
[3] Ronald Ferguson, "Teachers' Perceptions and Expectations and the Black-White Test Score Gap," in C. Jencks and M. Phillips, Ibid., pp. 273-317.

ing support and training, and the report card was aligned to measure the standards. Despite having more than 50% of the students from low-income families, Nelson School had *more than two-thirds* of its students meet state standards over a three-year period. Standards-based reform worked, but ironically they weren't the state or federal standards. They were local standards that translated to high expectations, high support, and high achievement.

Our recommendation to local leaders is to determine your own standards, communicate them, support your teachers in teaching them, and measure progress by them. Assuming that you give a statewide test, you ought to look at the tests to see what standards they are measuring. Working backwards is okay because with your own high standards, your students will move forward and your results will improve.

Summary

Effective school leaders use standards, assessment, and accountability to improve teaching and learning. We recommend that they take the lead in embracing accountability; in other words, accept and articulate responsibility for improving teaching and learning. Effective leaders insist upon high quality local and state assessments. They involve themselves deeply on statewide committees and insert themselves into the decision-making process at the state policy level to fight for sound assessment instruments, practices, and reporting. Successful school leaders are also successful teachers in that they can communicate what test results do and do not tell the staff and public about student achievement. They use results to highlight success and improvement and identify areas where changes in curriculum and instruction might be necessary. Rather than determining the solution to improving results, they work collaboratively to set short- and long-term goals and then they have teachers develop the improvement plans. Finally, they make sure that the standards for student achievement are clear and understood by students, staff, and the public.

Chapter Fourteen

Case Studies
in Real-World Leadership

Jim Rosborg
Max McGee
Jim Burgett

This chapter presents 10 case studies, six from the first edition of
this book and four from this updated, second edition. The situations are real, but we have altered a few of the names and places
for reasons that will be obvious. We aren't about to tell you that
we have all the answers, nor have we found anyone else who has
them all either. What we will tell you is that after a few years in
this business, you will be able to write some unusual case studies
of your own.

 We share these situational stories with you as a way of demonstrating the kinds of skills needed when you are faced with a
problem begging to be solved. Ours is not a one-step, one-stop
business. Almost everything we do requires many skills and usually mandates a coordinated effort on the part of many people.
You will see what we mean when you read the case studies.

 One more comment: your solution to these situations may be
different. Actually, it probably should be different. Different
communities, states, climates, and situations require different solutions. That is what makes our job so interesting. We learn from the
action of others and from the daily need to change and create. We
hope that in this book, and this chapter, we have been able to share
some useful ideas, tips, and skills that will make your job easier as
you make a difference for kids.

Case Study #1

Time to Move to a New School
Without Moving your Address

You have just passed a bond issue to build a new elementary school. In the campaign for the bond issue, the district was up front with the voters that boundary changes would have to take place and they would affect all of the elementary schools in your district. Since no consolidation has taken place requiring the expansion of district boundaries, the boundary changes are going to be done within the district. The problem you are facing is that your district has had the same boundaries for over 20 years. In your research, you have read about other districts where boundary changes had been so emotional that Board meetings had been packed for over two years. You strongly believe in the neighborhood school concept. The community has a strong allegiance to its present elementary school, but it realizes that the present schools are over-crowded. How will the process of boundary changes be implemented? How should the communication take place?

How could this problem have been prevented?
It couldn't have.

What process should the Board of Education and the administration follow to have a successful boundary change?
Set up a School Boundary Committee of parents, teachers, administrators, and community members. Include a representative from the Board of Education, preferably the president. Explain to all parties that a change to the grade level schools is impossible because of the range of school capacity (200-650). A demographic study should take place to identify the enrollment projections and the present and future location of students. Initial materials will need to be provided to the committee (see listing on next page). This committee should study past, present, and future enrollment patterns and formulate the proposed boundary alterations. In addition, a rationale for these changes should be prepared. Communication should then take place with key stakeholders for input. After input, make adjustments before the Board decision is made.

Who are the key players to get this accomplished?
The key players are the Board of Education, the administration, staff members, the media, local government officials, leaders of organizations within the schools, and members of the community committee.

What materials do administrators, community committee members, and Board members need to have?

* Present boundaries of schools
* A district map
* Identification of neighborhoods where the mobility is high
* Location of mass transit systems
* Present bus routes for the schools and community
* The present outline of your schools' usage (classroom maps)
* Present major arteries of transportation
* Present latch key numbers and the numbers on the waiting list
* Present rooms needing to be re-established
* Enrollment projections for each grade level and each school
* Present block-by-block student enrollment

What are some of the general guidelines that need to be followed?

* New boundaries should minimize travel and retain the neighborhood school concept.

* New boundary lines should follow natural community lines wherever possible, i.e., major roadways, railroads, mass transit routes.

* New boundaries should promote a natural student movement plan. For example, you do not want boundaries to send half of the students at Jefferson Elementary School to one junior high school and the other half to another junior high.

* New boundaries should allow all parts of each attendance area to be contiguous. (All homes on one block should attend the same school.)

* New boundaries should seek to keep subdivisions intact.

* New boundaries should reflect projected demographic studies for future growth.

    * New boundary lines must make certain that the student enrollment is within building capacities and that class sizes are within Board policy and agreed contracts.

    * Boundaries in the district may have to be adjusted because of the differences in building sizes.

What should the initial goals include?
The protection of the neighborhood concept, development of equitable classroom sizes, minimization of travel, decreasing the number of students needing to be transferred, the ability of all students in an elementary school to attend the same junior high school, and, in schools with a current increase in new housing, to make the effort to allow these schools to grow without the need of immediate transfers.

How will communication to all the stakeholders take place?
Once the boundary decisions have been made, information must be shared with the parents. This should be accomplished through a press release and a letter to the parents. In addition, administrators and Board members need to attend meetings of the PTA, Mother's Club, Father's Club, Neighborhood Watch groups, and any other school-related organizations.

What are some external resources to help solve the problem?
I (Jim Rosborg) used some excellent resources to develop our plan, particularly a paper prepared for the School District of La Crosse, Wisconsin called "One Solution to a Growing Problem."[1]

    I also used Roger Creighton's *School Redistricting: Policies and Procedures* for planning.[2]

To change boundaries, what knowledge and skills are needed by the leader?

    * A will to collaborate
    * Research time from others
    * Good organizational skills

---

[1] Prepared in July, 1993, by Superintendent Richard Swantz.
[2] Oakland, CA: Oakmore Associates, 1994.

* An excellent work ethic to put in the time to organize the fact-finding and to present the information
    * Patience
    * Good communication skills
    * Knowledge of media relations

Case Study #2

Let's Play Ball!

You receive a call from the election judges at a polling site. The judges are very upset because school-age students are playing basketball at a church playground area across the street. In their minds, these kids should be in school. The judges want you to go there immediately and put the kids back in school. You send your truant officer to the scene. Much to your surprise, you find out that every one of these kids are being "home schooled." You have no jurisdiction over these students under current law. You are frustrated too because after talking to the students, you can see that proper learning is not taking place. What do you do?

How could this problem have been prevented?
Needless to say, if the parents of these children had been supportive of their child's education, making certain that they were in school would have prevented this problem. The school might also have some responsibility by not having motivated the home-schooling student to stay in public school. Another prevention would be for each state to have stricter accountability guidelines for home-schooled students.

What process should the Board of Education and administration follow to deal with this problem?
This is a problem that does indeed require our attention. We have children in our communities who are not receiving an appropriate education. Their parents have learned how to "beat the system." The other side of that is that many home-schooled students receive an outstanding education. So as not to punish the home-schooled children that are receiving an appropriate education, the following things might be done:

* Make the local police aware of the situation at the basketball court.

* Identify the families at risk and discuss ways to keep their students in home or public school.

* Work with state representatives and senators to make home-school situations accountable for academic progress.

* Work with the local truancy programs.

* Consider taking parents to court for not providing an appropriate alternative education.

* Work with the appropriate legal authorities to have a joint plan to deal with children not in school.

* Work to pass a truancy ordinance that makes all families accountable.

Who are the key players to get this accomplished?

The key players are truancy personnel, truancy judges, police departments, Board of Education members, administrators, teachers, parents, and community members.

What materials do administrators need?

* Laws regarding truancy and home schooling

* Numerical estimates of the number of local home-schooled children (These can come either from your district or the agency that collects this data in your state.)

* The compulsory attendance laws of your state

What should initial goals include?

* The main goal should be to get kids back in school who are not receiving adequate schooling in the home.

* As an offshoot, coordination needs to take place between all local agencies regarding truancy. Contacts need to be made with the local juvenile judge, local chief of police, local truancy officials, other administrators, and local government officials. A meeting needs to take place to brainstorm ideas about truancy and problems with home schooling regarding needed instruction. After brainstorming, a plan of action needs to be developed for the area.

What external or internal resources can you use to help solve the problem?
The same individuals identified in the previous paragraph are great resources. Good home-schooling parents are also excellent sources for such vital information. Your local newspaper can be an effective way to share information about kids, home schooling, and schools.

What set of knowledge and skills does the leader need to have to help solve this problem?

* Good organizational skills
* Knowledge of truancy and home-schooling laws in your state
* The ability to work with legislators to work for change
* Knowledge that many good home-school parents will be upset with your efforts to increase accountability for their children

Case Study #3

My Child is Behind

You are in a school district that has had outstanding test scores for the past 15 years, in spite of the fact that you have both high poverty and a high mobility rates. Your district has been honored for the high test scores, and you know you have an excellent staff. You, as the administrator, believe strongly that assessment helps improve student learning. You are proud of the fact that despite an increase in poverty, the test scores have gone up. But now you face a dilemma. You do an analysis of your test scores and see that you do not meet the criteria in two areas of the Adequate Yearly Progress (AYP) component of the recent No Child Left Behind (NCLB) federal law on school accountability. The areas of deficiency are at your junior high level; they are the special education and African-American scores. This is in spite of the fact that your test scores are some of the highest in the state and your scores showed improvement. You have to formulate a strategy to improve results in the identified areas so that you are not sanctioned under the provisions of Adequate Yearly Progress (AYP). What strategies and methods need to take place to alleviate this problem?

How could this problem have been prevented?
This problem could have been prevented if all sub-groups would have met the minimum criteria. Also, you realize that there needs to be some tweaking of the initial rules. This includes:

     * Changing the cut scores at the state level (to meet the intent of the NCLB) to lessen the number of students and schools that do not make the AYP criteria.

     * Ensuring that all new students do not count towards the school's accountability requirements under AYP. The law says new students should not count if they enrolled within one academic year of the test. Make sure your state abides by this provision and doesn't lessen the time. For example, if your state test is in April, the provisions of NCLB might say that any student enrolled after the beginning of the academic year would not be included in the results of the tests for calculation of sanctions under Adequate Yearly Progress (AYP).

     * Professional development activities to make teachers and administrators aware of test-taking techniques, the new testing process, and compliance to the new federal law. Practice tests similar to the state tests also help.

     * Review state and local standards to make sure they correlate with national educational standards.

What process should the Board and administration follow to deal with this problem?
The first thing the district should do is research why the district is not meeting the minimum criteria for Adequate Yearly Progress. What can you do to improve the scores? For example, you may need to look at having more students in special education take an alternate assessment. You may need to inservice your teachers on identifying the appropriate test and making sure you are maximizing scores. You need to be active with the State Board of Education, the U.S. Education Department, and your congressperson on the inappropriateness of special education being listed as a sub-group with the same academic rules as the other sub-groups.

Continuous studies need to take place to improve African-American scores. In our district, much of this has to do with economics and the confidence to learn. We have been able to increase test scores by dealing with the basic need of food, shelter, clothing, and safety before the school day even starts. We have looked at a variety of rewards and awards to help instill self-confidence in the learning process. Our scores were down somewhat this year in this category. We researched the issue. We had an extraordinary number of African-Americans move into our district last year from districts that are experiencing academic difficulty. We know now that we are going to have to make academic adjustments for these students. We are going to have to closely monitor student progress.

Who are the key players?
The key players are students, parents, teachers, administrators, State Board of Education personnel, U.S. Department of Education personnel, and congressional members.

What external or internal resources could be identified to help solve the problem?
Needed materials include the rules and regulations that go along with the No Child Left Behind Act. In addition, school administrators will have to collect data in each of the assessment categories. Strategies explained in Chapter 13 of this text will have to be used. Staff members will be needed to provide input on additional strategies.

What set of knowledge and skills does the leader need to solve this problem?

* A realization that these guidelines are in effect (Study the law and its regulations.)
* Collaboration skills with staff, parents, and governmental leaders
* Articulation skills not only for identifying the problem, but for working towards a solution
* An ear for the details
* The ability to develop a school improvement plan
* The courage to take the necessary step for success

* Research skills on how to improve test results for minority and special education students

* The ability to identify problems and collectively formulate solutions on the local, state, and national level

Case Study #4

Leave All Principals Behind (the Eight Ball)

The principal of a Midwest elementary school just received her state test scores, and she is not pleased. For the second year in a row, scores at her school declined while two other elementary schools in the district showed marked improvement and one stayed stable (see Table 14-1 below).

The superintendent has asked each principal to present his or her school data and school improvement plan to the Board in five weeks. The Board meetings are televised, and the press will be present. Her staff meeting is the next day; she is meeting with her PTA the next week. What will her "main message" points be to her staff? To the PTA? To the Board? Write these message points and one school improvement goal.

| Table 14-1 | Reading Scores (percent meeting state standards)

Reading Scores (% meeting state standards)							
	Midwest		**North**		**South**		**Central**	
Year	3rd	5th	3rd	5th	3rd	5th	3rd	5th
2002	51	47	84	83	69	68	52	50
2001	55	48	85	82	62	65	48	43
2000	62	55	85	80	60	65	40	33
% Low Inc	20		9		32		57	
Size	420		365		490		560	

How could this problem have been prevented?
Clearly, every school with declining scores has a different story. Generally, though, scores do not decline because of external factors. That's right—it is not more new kids, changing neighborhoods, state mandates, outdated textbooks, lack of technology, etc. that leads to a drop in test scores. It may be due to high teacher turnover, elimination of a critical program, reduction in instructional time, or just ineffective teaching. Our experience is that decline does not happen overnight and that there are several warning signs. Decline often occurs because of benign neglect like not worrying about curriculum alignment, leaving staff development up to individual choice, ignoring standards, clinging to outmoded practices, and maintaining low expectations in the name of "developmentally appropriate" education.

The leader must act decisively to ensure that all students are learning to read, that teachers share common training experiences, and that instruction and curriculum align to standards. He/she needs to take a hard look at the effectiveness of the six-week dinosaur unit or the three-day outdoor education program to see how much this time commitment contributes to education. Above all, the successful leader has to insist and be certain that expectations are high and that instruction matches these expectations. For example, if second-grade teachers believe that students cannot be taught to write a good paragraph with supporting detail, scores in grades three and above will suffer. If kindergarten teachers believe it is not "developmentally appropriate" for students to learn their letters, master their sounds, write every day, learn new words, and attempt to read, every student will pay the price.

Who are the key players?
The key players are those who teach the children—all staff members. We mean *all*. In a case of declining test scores, all teachers need to have a sense of responsibility, accountability, and ownership. Another key player is that individual who can communicate test results in a clear, understandable, and non-threatening but straightforward manner. From reading this book, you can tell that we think *you* should be that person. Finally, never underestimate your parent leaders as key players. Engaging key parents as partners in the improvement process—beginning with their input on what is not working well—is of critical importance.

**What knowledge and skills are necessary to
solve the problem?**
Clearly, a knowledge of what the data does and does not tell the
school leader is critical. The leader must have a basic understanding of statistics. He or she must also be an exceptional communicator. Declining results get a lot of attention, and the leader will
perish if he or she does not have a communication plan based on
distinct message points. The leader must also be able to distinguish between good and lousy instruction. This is not as easy as it
sounds. For example, we find that few leaders are well versed in
reading instruction. When visiting classrooms, they may mistake
reading assessment (asking questions about what students read) for
reading instruction (teaching students how to comprehend what
they read). Finally, the leader must be a collaborator willing to
share leadership. The leader does not teach children; the staff does,
and so do parents. To engage the teachers, paraprofessionals, and
parents in fundamental change leading to school improvement, he
or she will have to collaborate with all groups.

**What internal resources can our school principal use to solve
the problem?**
The most important resources are her staff members. She must
first explain what the numbers say, give them the opportunity to
pour over the data, and charge them with the task of identifying
the problems that contributed to the decline. Teachers have the
most insight into student learning, yet they are often left out of the
process.

She should also make it very clear that improvement is the responsibility of all staff. A drop in third-grade scores is not only a
third-grade problem. It is a problem for all teachers in grades K-3.
A decline in average ACT scores cannot be "fixed" by simply
changing high school curriculum; working with the grade school is
essential. Without a solid foundation in elementary and middle
school, high school students flounder.

Another important internal resource is the test data. Looking at
questions missed, patterns of errors, the achievement of disaggre-
gated groups (boys, girls, low-income students, students new to
the district, etc.) will give her clues to first identifying and then
solving the problem.

What external resources can our principal use?

The most important external resource is a colleague in the district. After reviewing Table 14-1, she should make her first calls to the principals of schools that have been improving. Also, an administrator from her central office or someone in the state agency should be able to help her identify schools similar to hers that have a record of improvement rather than decline. Once she knows these schools, she needs to take a staff member or two and visit them.

She should also enlist the help of parents. Parents want their schools to succeed. They have a personal stake in the schools' success. Including parents in the school improvement planning process will provide some powerful support and able assistance.

The rest of the story? Our recommended solution.

Main Message Points

First and most important, the main message points must be identical for each group. As a leader, the principal needs to set the tone of accountability by being accountable herself. Our recommendation is that she acknowledge the decline in scores, specify improvement goals, outline strategies to accomplish them, and articulate how she will evaluate progress toward improvement. Specific message points would be:

* I am concerned that student test scores at Midwest have declined for the past five years.

* Although there are other measures of our students' success, I am holding myself accountable for working with staff and parents to improve these results, beginning today.

* My goal is to see an improvement of at least 15 percentage points during the next three years.

* Having examined the drop in scores and discussed the problem with staff and parents, I believe that the contributing causes are that we are not serving our struggling readers, are not providing adequate training for teachers, and we are neglecting the role of our parents. To address these issues, we will use a multi-faceted approach to improvement that will include assuring that each child has the support necessary to learn to read at grade level, that teachers have access to high quality ongoing training on site, and that parents are involved with their child's education.

* In addition to using state test results to evaluate our progress on an annual basis, we will use standard measures to ensure that all students are learning, that parents are involved, and that teachers are using the training they receive. Student measures will include teacher assessments, portfolios of student work, and quarterly local assessments.

Note that none of the message points blame anyone. Whereas most leaders are quick to find fault with the test, the administration, the lack of funding, or even the students, our leader looks ahead, holds herself accountable, and outlines a plan concisely and in plain English. We are sure that her leadership will result in real improvement, while a leader who blames students and others will continue to experience poor scores and increased frustration.

A School Improvement Goal...

As you have read in previous chapters, stating an improvement goal in measurable terms is a critical core leadership skill. As a leader, our principal needs to be the first to be accountable to the Board, to the public, and to her staff. We would advise her to write goals such as these:

* Increase the percentage of students meeting state standards by 15 percentage points in the next three years
* Develop and implement a local assessment instrument to track student progress in reading and mathematics each quarter
* Identify and replicate the reading intervention program that has proven so successful at South School
* Have 90% of Midwest's teachers participate in professional development activities that will enable them to align instruction with state standards and district curriculum

And a Final Thought.

This case study is a crash course in leadership. Our principal can improve teaching and learning by being action-oriented, collaborative, and forthright.

Case Study #5

A story of Sinking Morale

It is mid-November and the teachers have worked without a contract since July 1. Morale is seriously sagging, or "in the toilet" as one senior teacher recently shared with a group of parents at a PTA meeting. Where the teachers' lounge used to be filled with lively conversation, most of the staff have retreated to their rooms to have lunch with two or three friends. Whenever a group does congregate, constant complaints about the Board and central office administration are heard. You notice that teachers are starting to "work" the parents for support for what could be a strike in the near future by portraying themselves as "victims" of the Board. Though you have personally heard from some parents who support the teachers' position in the labor dispute, you have heard from several more that they are disturbed that the teachers' morale is interfering with instruction. Said one, "My son complains that his teacher is 'like really depressed' all the time and has told us she might go on strike. She spent half an hour going on and on about how she can barely afford to live on what she gets paid.... We pay really high taxes here, and I expect to send my son to school so he can learn something, not just listen to whining every day."

Even their work ethic seems to have changed. Most teachers are not coming in early or staying a minute past contractually required hours. You can't even get volunteers for your school's holiday party committee! One of your trusted confidants even told you that if your next staff meeting runs even a minute past 4:00 (the contractual time the school day ends), most of the teachers will get up and leave.

What are some strategies and tactics you can use to improve morale?

How could this problem have been prevented?
Unlike test scores, morale issues may be out of the hands of the leader. More often than not, however, the first step in preventing a morale problem is looking in the mirror. As you can probably guess, we believe that active collaboration, constant communication, thoughtful planning, and active advocacy set a tone of high morale. We also contend that your staff looks to you as a bell-

wether of morale. If you do not take care of yourself (physically, mentally, and spiritually), if you lose trust, if you behave badly, if you don't treat people well, your morale will slump and so will theirs.

If there are clearly identifiable external tensions such as negotiations, a hostile parent group, or a feisty Board of Education, the only way to improve morale is to act. Your staff must see you as the champion. Even if you are management, you must show that you are working hard toward a fair settlement. Though the Board is your boss, you must show your staff that you are in charge, that you are knowledgeable, prepared, calm, cool under fire, and that you maintain a real sense of class. You cannot improve morale with external rewards or words—only actions will help.

Who are the key players?

The key players are a few staff leaders as well as a network of school leaders. Leaders need to count on their "critical friends," those teachers who will tell them the truth no matter what. They also need to be able to find a trusted group of colleagues with whom they can commiserate and share problems and solutions. Finally, in difficult times, your family and faith become key to both your survival and your success. Rely on them!

What knowledge and skills are necessary to solve the problem?

The critical skill set is the ability to be trusting and trustworthy. You cannot solve a morale problem by building trust, but you can help by demonstrating it through your actions. Finding colleagues whom you can trust to give you help and keep your confidences is imperative to working through those times when morale wanes.

What internal resources can you use to solve the problem?

As with the previous case, the most important resources are the leader's staff. The leader needs to use key staff to identify the causes of a problem and to identify possible solutions to it. When the rest of the staff knows that you are seeking input, that you are collaborating, and that you are taking their concerns seriously, morale will improve.

Find staff that is self-actualized; that is, staff that does realize that it is responsible for its own morale. Seek its help in communicating this to others.

What external resources can the leader use?
Because staff morale is inexorably tied with your morale, your external resources of your family, your exercise class, your church, and your friends will be critically important in improving morale. When facing difficult times at work, many leaders hunker down. They have the bunker mentality; even their appearance changes. They withdraw to the safety of their office, they walk with their head bent, and they think survival instead of success. Be conscious of your posture and presence. Reading a good book is a nice escape from the drudgery and renews and recharges your drained batteries. It also gives you something to talk about besides doom and gloom.

An additional resource is your fellow leaders. Many of us are often too proud to admit that we are facing serious problems at work and too proud to seek the counsel of other superintendents or principals. We believe that in tough times you need to reach out. As the saying goes, "Do lunch or be lunch." We agree! Treat another superintendent or two to lunch and ask them what they would do if they were in your shoes. Open yourself up and you will be surprised at how many of them have faced similar circumstances and can impart some wise advice.

The rest of the story? Our recommended solution.

Strategies and Tactics
Whenever we discuss this case study, the responses invariably involve "morale boosters" that range from flowers to Happy Hours. School leaders write letters to staff, buy gifts, create spirit days, and basically knock themselves out to improve morale. Like a sugar buzz or caffeine rush, morale may improve for a few hours, but it generally slumps a day or two later and you and your staff are more drained than ever before. The most important lesson to learn about morale is that we are all responsible for our own morale—period.

Ironically, we strive to teach students that they are responsible for their own feelings, that they must be intrinsically motivated, that sincere praise matters, and that external rewards are not important. When faced with morale problems, though, administrators often revert to activities like those described above, things we would never do with students. Real leaders do not change during tough times; they stay the course and maintain a presence in the face of adversity. The most important strategy for improving the morale of the staff is to remain stable and strive to improve your own morale.

The initial strategy that we recommend, then, is that you take care of yourself first. Like the airplane safety briefing, put the oxygen mask on yourself first, then on your child. Staff looks for strength in its leaders. When morale sags, you must be stronger and more positive than ever before. You cannot let the turkeys—those impinging conditions—get you down. You have to cook them up and serve them with a side of cranberry sauce.

A second strategy is to listen. It's not necessary to respond to complaints, but you must listen to them. Empathize and sympathize. To help staff work through tough times, you need to be there for them and not try to take care of them. They need a leader who listens.

The third strategy is to take decisive action to impact the conditions that are affecting morale. Staff morale will improve when it sees you acting to change things rather than attempting to mollify or bolster their feelings. The teachers need to see the principal not as one of them but an administrator who is trying to solve the labor dispute. They need to see you working for a settlement. Make no mistake, we are not recommending that you challenge the Board, but we are recommending that you insert yourself in the process by talking with negotiators from both sides. We do not recommend that you try to solve the problems but that you ask questions and seek to understand the causes of the dispute, and then help the negotiators reframe the discussion around issues from a different point of view.

The most important strategy, and fourth, is to improve morale by continuing to do what you do best. That is, lead. Teaching, learning, and students must always take precedence over any other issue in any other conversation. Like Lewis and Clark, you may face your own Rocky Mountains to cross, but even those are temporary obstacles and setbacks on a journey to achieve a grand vision. Not dwelling on the immediate problem but focusing on the short- and long-term goals will make an enormous difference in improving morale.

A Final Thought.
Anyone who has been a leader knows the cycles of morale. The lowest loops of the cycle are the few weeks before winter break, when it seems like you will never see the sunlight, and at the end of the school year, when responsibilities are stacked up like planes over O'Hare Airport on a nasty day. Morale is lower than a hellgrammite's heel. Ride it out. Be a *positive* presence in your building. Let people know that you appreciate them, show them how you cope, and keep a good sense of humor. Though you will not see spirits soar, we guarantee that you will feel a collective improvement.

Case Study #6

Going, Going, Almost Gone!

Many districts are bulging at the seams. Put yourself in our situation. You have used every closet, corridor, and office for instructional space. You have classes in the auditorium, in the cafeteria, even on the stage. You desperately need a new school to eliminate the overcrowded conditions. You have also done your homework and have on your desk the results of a comprehensive "Five Year Strategic Plan" that took almost two years to complete and involved more than 300 citizens. The mandate is clear—build a new middle school. You have two basic problems: (1) you can't get the voters to approve a bond issue due to a poor economic environment, and (2) the property you have tagged for the school is about to go on the auction block to become a subdivision. The thought of again reconvening the study groups to look at optional sites activates the Mixmaster inside your stomach. You remember how much collaborative work it took to agree on this site and how happy everyone was when the decision was announced. You also remember the problems in finding a suitable alternative site. The district was able to give the owners of the land you want a payment that legally held the property until funds were available. That agreement is running out, and the owners want to put the property back on the market. It will sell in a heartbeat since it is prime property for residential development.

How could this problem have been prevented?

If any of the previous three bond issues had been passed, the property would have already been purchased. Even if state construction grants were pending, the property would have been available for future construction. The property wasn't on the market until two years ago, so previous Boards could not have bought it. It is, by far, the best location for the new school since it is across the street from the existing high school and offers the district many, many unique opportunities to share parking, athletic facilities, and academic space.

Who are the key players?

The key players in this situation were the Board of Education, superintendent, the district's legal personnel, and members of the B.E.A. (Business Education Alliance).

What process did the Board of Education and administration follow to purchase this property?

Unfortunately, the options for the Board are few. It would be political disaster for the Board to expend funds they do not have to buy property for a building that the voters have not yet approved. Many feel that this action would hurt the efforts to ever get a bond issue passed. The district does not have the $250,000 it would take to make the purchase, and it does not have the authority to borrow the money. This situation must be solved by creativity.

The Board directs the superintendent to take the problem to the community leaders and see if there is a way they can "hold" the property until the bond issue passes.

The superintendent meets with a small group of leaders who are working hard to pass the bond issue and, late one night, a brainstorming session results. From this session it is determined that the school should not purchase the land until the voters give approval. The group decides that it needs to find a way to purchase the land for the school and hold it for the school until it can be legally purchased. Then, if the bond issue doesn't pass by a certain time, resell the property.

Within 48 hours, a group is formed and initiates a Legal Liability Corporation, called the "LLC," which will sell "shares" for $2,500 each. If $250,000 is raised, the property will be purchased by the LLC, held for the school district for up to seven years, and sold back to the district for the purchase price. Shareholders would invest their principal in the future of the district and would forfeit interest on their investment. When the district is able to purchase the land from the LLC, the shareholders will recover their principal and the district will be able to purchase the land for the set price of $250,000. Within three weeks, all shares were sold, and the land was owned by the LLC! All legal and financial services were donated and the only costs were the taxes on the land, which were paid for by the school's Foundation.

What external or internal resources could be identified to help solve the problem?
The district used its legal services to initially research the issue. They utilized information from the State Board of Education, the regional Office of Education, and the minds of several local business leaders. People who worked on this issue included some industry CEOs, a bank president, a lawyer, an accountant, a school superintendent, and a farmer.

What knowledge and skills does the leader need to solve this problem?
    * How to solve problems creatively
    * Knowledge of the law and how to access legal and financial information
    * Collaboration skills with local leaders, government agency personnel, and others
    * The ability to compromise and take a risk
    * Salesmanship

The rest of the story? Our recommended solution.
The bond issue for the middle school finally passed and the property was purchased within 18 months of the formation of the LLC. For many voters, the LLC indicated strong support for a new school and probably helped pass the bond issue. After the sale of the property to the school district, the 50-plus shareowners voiced

their support for the district, and many of them said to "keep the money." When the books were closed and the LLC dissolved, over $50,000 had been donated to the Business Education Alliance!

Case Study #7

Bipolar Case Study

This is an actual case study. For reasons you will find very obvious, the names and places have been changed. My appreciation to those involved in providing this information and to the respected attorney who shared his valued opinions.

Assistant Principal Randy Shocker has a teacher, Joel Emokay, with 20 plus years of experience and an excellent record. Over the past few months, however, Randy has noticed what he considers some uncharacteristic behavior from Joel. At times he receives a large volume of notes from this individual and many are written between 2 and 4 a.m. Randy then has periods of time when he received no notes, calls, or communications. He notes that at these times Joel seems withdrawn and subdued.

Randy shares these concerns with his principal, Mrs. Dowhatever. The principal, being a wise and trusting individual (?), decides to let Randy handle this situation on his own.

Randy begins to take notes and starts noticing some behaviors that he fears might end up costing Joel his job. Randy decides to set up a private meeting with Joel to share his concerns and observations. Randy tells Joel that he is not trained in mental health assessment, but he thinks that he (Joel) may well be suffering from a bipolar disorder. Joel is offended and feels that he is having no problem whatsoever. Randy then refers to some of the other behaviors he has witnessed, some of which he states border on the bizarre. Joel remains highly offended and ends the discussion. At this point, all Randy has managed to do is to anger Joel.

Randy, however, still wanting to help, continues to "handle the situation" as directed by Principal Dowhatever.

He next calls Joel's spouse who grudgingly admits that there may be a slight problem, but nothing serious. She readily admits that if help were to be obtained it would have to come from someone other than her. The phone call is short and semi-sweet.

Knowing that the family is quite religious, Randy calls the pastor of Joel's church and relates some of the incidents and tells the pastor that the individual is coming close to crossing the line and doing something for which he might be dismissed. The pastor agrees to meet with the family and also tells Randy the name of the family physician. The pastor says he will try to get the teacher to see this family doctor.

Yep, you guessed it. Randy phones the physician and confidentially relates his concerns as well as his fear that Joel is reaching the point that he will say or do something that will cost him his job.

Was Randy within his "ethical" boundaries? Did he cross ethical lines by contacting family, pastor, and physician, even though he felt that the individual was close to doing something that would cost him his job? How far can or should an administrator go to try to help an employee when the person does not want the help. What privacy concerns have been sidelined? What would you have done?

What happened?
Oddly enough, the follow up to this situation is almost as strange as the situation. No one complained about privacy issues. No one sued. No one "went after" Randy. The pastor convinced the family to see the doctor. The doctor, with the heads-up from Randy's call, made a referral to a mental health facility for a 30-day stay for treatment. Randy got help and all is well. Mrs. Dowhatever and Randy dodged some potentially big bullets.

What are the legal concerns with this case study?
I contacted a respected school attorney to review this case. He almost had a seizure when he read it. Here are his comments.

"This situation crosses the line from issues of ethics to issues of law. Here you have an assistant principal who has a good heart but is not cognizant of the serious legal issues involved in his actions. A better approach would have been to treat the teacher's issues as performance-based and not address any medical issues, unless the teachers in the district, or the union, raised the issues.

"In any event, to go to the spouse and, certainly, to the pastor and physician, and accuse the teacher of having a serious medical disorder borders on slander and will compromise any disciplinary action taken against the teacher in the future. The assistant principal may properly have been subject to discipline for his actions in this matter. Of course, he also suffered from a failure of leadership as the principal and the principal's supervisor should have become involved if the situation if it was as serious as the assistant principal believed."

How could a situation like this be handled differently?
First, talk to your administrative superiors or team and discuss not only the concerns, but the liabilities. If your administrator gives you direction to handle an issue that you feel is potentially liable, contact an administrative peer, your professional organization, or some third party source to share your concerns.

In any case, if handled correctly, the schools administrative team should agree to contact the district's attorney for direction and suggestions. When you are dealing with mental health, stress, job performance, and potential, rather than actual, situations, you are skating on thin ice.

What type of skills and knowledge are needed to handle a situation like this one?
Probably first and foremost is the desire to balance what you can do legally with what needs to be done morally. The desire to help Joel is commendable. Helping Joel is directly related to providing the students with a competent and healthy teacher. All that is good and fine, but the skill set needed in this situation involves an understanding of our inability to diagnosis medical problems, of a person's right to privacy, and who to share information with. Personally I feel the most needed skill in this situation is understanding the need for legal advice before taking action.

A final thought…..
We learn from our mistakes, and then sometimes we don't. If Randy and Principal Dowhatever think that this solution was handled well, and use it as a template for the future, they are tossing

live grenades in a game of catch. At some point they *will* find themselves in big trouble. A better idea would be to pick up the phone and get some suggestions from a respected school attorney. There are ways to help an individual that don't compromise the law, set the district up for a potential law suit, and possibly even harm the individual involved more in the long run. And, remember, *always document* every step, and every conversation.

This is one of those case studies where doing the wrong things resulted in the right outcome, but that can be very dangerous.

Case Study #8

Hazing Case Study

This case study actually happened. The name of the school and any indicators of location or names have been changed. The concept is real and the solution was not only effective, but a model for other school districts. The challenges for the administration were many and were serious.

For the past two years the format of Homecoming at Anytown High School have been adjusted to promote good sportsmanship and conclude the week's activities with the big game. In the past, the homecoming events were at night which gave students an opportunity to get together in groups. The annual "TP" party, when the kids covered the town with rolls and rolls of toilet paper were also an unapproved, non-school related tradition held on one of the nights of homecoming. Unfortunately there were also rumors in the past of students being subjected to physical abuse. All of these things prompted the faculty to move all homecoming activities to daytime hours. There were the traditional activities including float building, hallway decorating, competitive games, all of which led to an afternoon movie prize for the winning class. Anytown High School could really be in Anytown, anywhere.

Thursday night was the volleyball game, and Friday the football game. On Thursday the gym was a haven of positive school spirit, with young men wearing colored wigs and cheering on the lady athletes. After a victorious evening, the school officials were looking forward to the football game on Friday night. Unfortunately, a tragic situation arose on Thursday evening which would end up affecting many families in the community.

A few hours after the volleyball match, some AHS athletes took turns driving by a house which contained four younger team members and began yelling profanity toward the students and their families. Later that evening when the four kids drove away from the house to join in the TP fun, their car was blocked by two vehicles full of the same kids that were yelling the profanities. The car was quickly swarmed by the older athletes who dragged out the younger kids while calling them obscene names. They lined up the four kids while dousing them with syrup and vinegar. One began pelting them with the syrup container and others threw water balloons. The police broke up the hazing incident before it would have progressed to the use of tuna and dog excrement, which was found in one of the vehicles. Within minutes of police intervention, a police officer contacted school officials and the police halted all toilet papering activities.

The news of this hazing event had profound impact on school operations for the next few months. By the time the administrative team arrived at the high school on Friday morning, they had received countless messages from parents wanting to know exactly what the school was going to do to correct the situation. The administrative team spent the day interviewing the four students who were victims of the situation and the eight students who did the alleged hazing. The administration was given a list of names from a parent and also a list from the police department. The school has a reciprocal reporting agreement with the police department.

Talk about hazing! The school administrators were in a perpetual haze from the incident, from the parents and, of course, from the friendly press.

There were lots of questions: Was this a school activity? Is it ethical for the school to discipline for something that was not on "school time" or "school premises"? Eight students from one team would essentially ruin the season; was that fair to the other team mates not involved?

Not an easy one. Or is it?

Who are the key players in this case study?
Certainly the high school administration, the district leadership, the President of the Board (or other board members), the coaches involved, and the students/parents. The implications of this incident require a close involvement with both the local police and the press. The potential for widespread media involvement and the legal implications demand that the district's attorney be a key player from the start to finish. An issue of this magnitude dictates a well devised plan of action, a committee of key players acting as a "command detail," and a carefully crafted chain of command.

How did the district resolve this particular situation?
At the end of the day, the district considered a recommendation that the eight perpetrators be released from their teams, per their coaches, for the rest of the year. As student-athletes they signed an athletic code of conduct. This hazing activity was a breach of that agreement. The decision was backed up by the administrative team. At the next Board of Education meeting, fifty or so guests were in attendance to question the ruling of the coach and administration. The Board of Education backed the decision, and the dismissal of the eight students from the team was affirmed. The newspapers had a hey-day with the decision.

What did the district learn from this incident?
The district has since looked at ways to prevent this type of behavior from happening in the future. While hazing can be difficult to define precisely, it is clear that it almost always includes new members showing subservience to older members, lowering the self-esteem of the newcomers. Definitions could include a variety of terms including but not limited to, committing an act or coercing a student to commit an act that creates substantial risk of harm. Hazing usually involves compromising the victim's safety and/or dignity. One of the biggest concerns with hazing is that most victims do not report it. Many victims are unwilling to disclose the abuse. Many families are likewise afraid to report it to the local authorities. The need to belong to a group outweighs the need to disclose the information.

Some individuals believe that hazing is a rite of passage and that hazing is not bad. The reality is that hazing is a criminal activity, and, at the time of this writing, 43 states have anti-hazing laws in place.

What are the legal considerations of this case study?
A well respected school attorney was asked to review this case study and suggested the following.

"Now, just add to this scenario that the entire event was videotaped and is being played every hour on CNN and Fox News!

"Clearly, the school district could adopt a policy governing extracurricular activities which prohibits hazing at all times and places. Here it did so and properly applied the policy to the involved athletes. As the scenario notes, the wording of the policy is important (actually, the wording of most policies is important).

The more difficult question arises if the students involved were not athletes; could they have been suspended for off-campus conduct? The normal rule of thumb is that a sufficient "nexus" must exist between the school and the off-campus activity. The existence of such a "nexus" is always a question of fact dependent upon the circumstances of each situation. Here such a nexus appears to exist. The misconduct was tied to the school's homecoming activities and directly impacted the school's homecoming activities. Disciplinary action by the school's administration would appear to be justified if the Board's policy and student handbook specifies that students can be disciplined for off-campus activity if a sufficient nexus exists between the misconduct and the school and its programs and activities."

A final thought….
Proactive leadership, a well crafted set of policies, clear and easily understood codes of behavior, and a sense of awareness of past and potentially negative practices can help prevent this type of situation. However, if something like this does happen,a good administrator begins the response immediately but takes the time to listen and involve the key decision makers and advisors. Mess this up and you have a nightmare second to none. An incident of this level involves tactical planning and careful action.

A rookie administrator should seek help from those who can see the big picture, rely on experience, and stay cool all at the same time.

Case Study #9

"Signs, Signs, Everywhere a Sign..."

You are a high school principal. Parent teacher conferences are scheduled, and you notice that the parents of one of your students, for whom you are particularly concerned, have scheduled an appointment with you. In the past, this student has spoken openly about his beliefs that there is nothing wrong with drug use as long as it is dome where "no one can be hurt by it." This student is often off task, and he frequently talks about "partying" and the weekend. Although the student has not explicitly said that he uses drugs, it has been reported to you of him drawing pictures of mushrooms and other drug related artifacts.

On the day of the conference, you are pleased to see that both of his parents have arrived. To your surprise, they are happy with his grade, which is a low C. They say that his ADHD often makes it difficult for him to achieve and they are happy to see that he is doing well. You mention that he has told you that he is, in fact, happy with a C. Also, he has expressed his lack of concern with school and grades because he is planning to be a mechanic. The student's parents confirm that he has told them the same, but they are concerned because he is failing auto mechanics class.

It is obvious to you that their child must be preoccupied with something outside of his ADHD, so you carefully push the issue. You mention to the parents that you have noticed that the student loves to draw. In fact, you show them a picture sketched on the top of his note sheet. The picture portrays a leprechaun smoking a pipe as he sits on a mushroom. Both parents agree that the picture "looks like their child." At this point, the parents convey that their son has many beliefs that they do not support which include heavy smoking, and a lackadaisical attitude towards life and school. You try to converse with them by sharing that he is often off task and preoccupied with weekend and evening party plans, even when the week has only begun. The mother appears concerned, but the father simply states that he does not want to talk about it. Both parents thank you for your time and leave.

How could this problem have been prevented?

The parents seem to have relinquished parental responsibility and control long before their son entered high school. Keeping closer tabs on their son and addressing his problems when they began may have prevented the current situation. Also, past teachers and administrators may share some responsibility for not reporting his behavior when it first began.

What process should the Board of Education and the administration follow to deal with this problem?

This student is not the only student with this problem. Many high school students are tempted by drug use, gang involvement, and sexual activity. Their parents have either learned to ignore the problems, accept the problems, or, perhaps, they honestly do not know how to identify the problems. In order to help parents to help their children the following things might be done:

- Form a student referral program in which teachers may anonymously express concern for a student.
- Form a student referral program in which students may anonymously express concern for another student.
- Educate teachers on the signs of potentially hazardous practices most commonly entered by teens.
- Work with local law enforcement to stay updated on the latest gang signs and drug terms.
- Develop a "warning packet" to be sent home and made available at conference time. This packet should contain the gang and drug information obtained from the police. In order to avoid making serious false accusations, make the material available for all parents to use as they wish. In addition to communicating the warning signs to parents, each packet should contain a list of agencies that may be contacted in order to get help.
- Form parenting groups to discuss the problem and allow time for developing strategies.

Who are the key players to get this accomplished?
The key players are police departments, administrators, teachers, coached, counselors, parents, and students.

What materials do administrators need?
- Frequent dialogue with local law enforcement officers.
- Knowledge of treatment centers' locations, requirements, costs, availabilities, etc.
- Appropriation of printing costs.

What should initial goals include?
- The main goal should be making parents, administrators, and teachers aware of new drug and gang fads so they are able to identify students who are potentially in danger.
- Also, schools (and parents) should enforce rules prohibiting the display of drug and gang signs so that students understand that their behavior will neither be ignored nor accepted.

What external or internal resources can be used?
The individuals identified in the "key players" paragraph are great resources. Also, it is important to include students with good intentions rather than only asking help from "good" (high achieving and/or well-behaved) students. Other possible sources are those books that may be located via an Internet search.

What set of knowledge and skills does the leader need to have to help solve this problem?
- Awareness that drug and gang problems do affect school achievement.
- Acceptance that an increase in gang and drug problems could ultimately affect AYP (Adequate Yearly Progress); student gang involvement, and that drug use affects teachers, administrators and the community.
- The ability to openly address existing problems.
- The willingness to work with law enforcement officers.

Thanks goes to graduate student Jamie Rakers
for input into this case study.

Case Study #10

"Home Alone"

You are an elementary principal. A student in your school has received passing grades in the last two quarters, but the third quarter grades at progress report time are all failing remarks. You have knowledge that her single mother works long hours. Your student has previously explained that she is responsible for taking her ADHD medicine in the morning and getting herself dressed. In addition, she has spoken of being home alone after school. You have talked to the mother about her progress report grades and she pleads that her daughter has no motivation.

Recently, you have seen this situation escalating in the classroom and at school. The student continually strives for attention at inappropriate times during class. She has become a distraction to other students. She recently has been caught cheating on a test. When you confront her with the situation, she admits she was wrong. She begins to cry and explain that she wants to do well in school, but she does not know how to study. You know that she is not maximizing her academic potential, but the factors at home inhibit her success. If she continues with her current pattern, she will put herself in jeopardy of not passing the fourth grade. What do you do?

How could this problem have been prevented?

Obviously, if the parent of this student had been supportive of her child's education and made certain she was studying correctly, this problem could have been prevented. The parent has remarked that her daughter has had little to no interest in school in prior years; as a result, a previous teacher could have noticed the situation and prevented it from escalating to its present point. Another prevention method could have been placing the student under adult supervision before and after school. For instance, a before and after school program could have been an ideal place for this student to receive correct study habits.

What process should the Board of Education and administration follow to deal with this problem?

Chances are this is not an isolated situation. Some parents may not be aware that the time period after school is often decisive in a student's educational progress. If students are left to monitor themselves, they are unlikely to choose to study or to work on homework. Even when students desire school achievement, they may be unaware of how to study. Parents too, may be unaware of how important it is to teach study skills and to give their child structure for the hours immediately following the school day. In order to help parents to protect their children and to aid them in academic progress the following things might be done:

- Make parents aware of the before and after school program throughout the school year.
- Educate the parents on the necessary study habits a child must possess to be successful.
- Accommodate the before and after school program to the parents' work schedules.
- Emphasize the importance of study habits in the classroom and at home.
- Keep an open communication with parents.

Who are the key players to get this accomplished?

The key players are administrators, teachers, before and after school program coordinators, parents, and students.

What materials do administrators need?

- Information providing the parents with the correct study habits for at home.
- Handouts explaining their before and after school program.
- Informing the teachers of the importance of notifying students and parents of the importance of after school studying.

What should initial goals include?

- School counseling and support for the student.

- The main goal should be to make parents and students aware of the importance of study habits outside of the classroom setting.
- Also, schools should provide the parents with the opportunity to place their child in before and after school programs.

What external or internal resources can you use to help solve problem?
The same individuals mentioned among the key players are integral resources. Students should be involved, so that the other key players understand their situations. The school newsletter can provide information on the importance of working with your child at home to ensure academic success.

What set of knowledge and skills does the leader need to have to help solve the problem?
- Knowledge of the child's situation at home.
- The ability to work with the before and after school program.
- Knowledge that some parents may feel that they are invading the privacy of their lives.
- Cooperativeness and communication with parents on the importance of after school study habits.

*Thanks goes to graduate student Nathan Rakers
for input into this case study.*

Case Study #11

"Bobby and Bib Overalls"

It was a quiet Thursday afternoon in April, about an hour after lunch. Mr. Erlinger walked into the middle school office and asked if the principal was in. The secretary replied yes, but he was on the phone. Mr. Erlinger then proceeded to walk past the counter and headed directly for Mr. Burke's office.

Mr. Erlinger was a short man and he was wearing bib overalls. His right hand was tucked inside the overalls. The secretary, Mrs.

Ebersol, noticed his hands and the anger in his eyes. She politely said, "You need to wait in the lobby until Mr. Burke can see you."

"He will see me know, that son of a bitch."

Mr. Burke quickly ended his call, gave Mrs. Ebersol a quick look, and raised two fingers. Mr. Burke then stood and asked Mr. Erlinger to have a seat.

"I don't want to sit." was the response.

"Well, how can I help you?" replied Mr. Burke.

With his right hand still neatly tucked in his overalls, Mr. Erlinger said, "Are you the guy that called DCFS and had them come to my house and threaten to take away Bobby?" (Bobby is his sixth-grade son, the oldest of five children.)

"Mr. Erlinger, I won't talk to you until you have a seat and we can discuss this calmly."

"I'm not sitting."

"Well, then you will have to make an appointment and come back when you are ready to talk in an appropriate manner."

Just then the police arrived. They asked Mr. Erlinger to raise his hands, which he did, and they asked if he had anything in his pockets. He replied that he only had a wallet and a comb. They asked if they could frisk him, and he agreed. Indeed, he only had those two items. The police then asked if Mr. Burke wanted him removed, and he said no as long as Mr. Erlinger was willing to talk calmly. Mr. Erlinger agreed. The police left.

Mr. Burke then said that DCFS reports are confidential, but if he had reason to believe that something improper was happening between Bobby and Mr. Erlinger he would indeed make such a call, not just because he was required to do so, but because it was the right thing to do.

"Nothing wrong is going on and I'm going to find out who called and make sure they know that what goes on in my house is none of their damn business," Mr. Erlinger said.

Mr. Burke asked, "Is that a threat?"

Erlinger replied, "No, that is a fact, because I treat my kids right."

The two men talked for several minutes more. Mr. Erlinger apologized for barging in. Mr. Burke told him that if DCFS had made a contact they would do an investigation and that if the report was made in error, nothing would happen, but if the report was valid, then Mr. Erlinger needed to think hard about his behavior. Mr. Burke talked clearly and with compassion to Mr. Erlinger, realizing he was not fully aware of how DCFS worked. The men shook hands and Mr. Erlinger apologized once more. When he left the office the police were in the lobby. They watched to make sure he left the building.

The Follow-up.
This is a wonderful example of having a plan ready. Mr. Burke's raising his two fingers could have meant just about anything to anyone except his secretary. To her it meant to get the police here immediately, without sirens. Mr. Burke then did what he needed to do: calm Mr. Erlinger down and keep him contained, to control him until the police came. Once he knew the situation was safe, the principal calmly talked to Mr. Erlinger and did his best to get him to understand the circumstances.

The Rest of the Story?
Mr. Burke had indeed called DCFS based on information that indicated possible sexual contact between Bobby and his father. He didn't fall victim to intimidation nor did he allow Mr. Erlinger to discover any information. He handled it properly.

Everyone involved knew what to do and the "crisis plan" worked flawlessly.

The police maintained extended observation on the Erlingers for several days. Within weeks the family moved overnight. They never contacted the school to have the records updated or forwarded.

What have we learned from this case study?
A code to get the police worked and may have been instrumental in containing the anger of the upset parent. Remaining calm and working hard to calm and contain the parent was the focus of the administrator. Being reasonable and rational throughout the situation brought it to a peaceful conclusion. The end result of this case study was not the best since the family disappeared and no resolution to the concern of abuse resulted. It should be noted that DCFS and the police were immediately informed when the family moved.

Authors' Biographies

For photos and more biographical information, please check the website: http://www.superintendents-and-principals.com.

Jim Rosborg

Dr. Jim Rosborg, has recently been appointed as Program Coordinator for the External Graduate Programs at McKendree College and instructor of graduate classes in Education. In June of 2005, Rosborg retired after eleven years as superintendent of the 3,750 student Belleville Public School District #118, Belleville, Illinois. Under Rosborg's leadership, Belleville #118 had some of the highest district scores in the state of Illinois. In addition, District #118 schools received Golden Spike Awards, State and National Blue Ribbon Schools Awards, and, most recently, the Northern Illinois University's Spotlight Awards for the academic achievement.

The collaboration between Rosborg and key stakeholders also led the District to receive the national AFT-Saturn/UAW Collaboration Award in 1999. Rosborg himself is a past recipient of the Illinois Master Teacher Award, the Illinois State Board of Education "Those Who Excel" Award, the Illinois State Board of Education "Break the Mold" Award, the Boy Scouts of America's Russell C. Hill Award for outstanding contribution to character education, and the 2004 Illinois Superintendent of the Year Award. Rosborg has published articles on dealing with children with AIDS in the classroom and the need to adjust the 2002 No Child Left Behind Act for successful implementation.

Dr. Rosborg graduated from Hoopeston High School in Hoopeston, Illinois, in 1968. Rosborg received his undergraduate degree from Southern Illinois University at Carbondale, a master's degree from Southern Illinois University at Edwardsville, and completed his Doctorate work at Southern Illinois University at Edwardsville in 1994. Rosborg taught math and history and served as a counselor and coach for 13 years at Belle Valley District #119, as well as serving 20 years as an administrator in Belleville District #118. Rosborg has been married for 30 years to his wife, Nancy. Together they have three children Mike (27), Kyle (24), and Carol (22).

Max McGee

In June of 2007 Max was chosen President of the Illinois Mathematics and Science Academy. Previously, after completing a three-year term as State Superintendent, Glenn "Max" McGee was the Superintendent of Wilmette School District 39. He is also Chairman of the Golden Apple Foundation, a member of the Board of Directors of the Great Books Foundation, and a member of both the Governor's Educational Excellence Task Force and the Task Force for Education Accountability.

Dr. McGee has served as a substitute teacher, middle school teacher, principal, and superintendent of three suburban districts. He is an avid writer who has published numerous articles and speaks at national conferences. He recently presented at several national conferences including AASA, NASB, the American Education Research Association Conference, and the International Reading Association Annual meeting. He also is a regular speaker on leadership at conferences throughout Illinois.

Dr. McGee's recent research on high-achieving, high-poverty schools that have closed the achievement gap has garnered state and national attention for identifying how schools and communities can help all students succeed. In 2004 the *Journal for the Education of Students Placed at Risk* published this study about Illinois' Golden Spike schools. His mission is to make an "enduring difference" in the lives of all children and share his passionate commitment and support for Illinois' educational leaders.

Dr. McGee's real passion is his family. He and his wife Jan, who is the Executive Director of the Associated Colleges of Illinois' Center for Success in High Needs Schools, have three children and an energetic grandson, Trent. Max has retired from running marathons, but is still an avid and successful triathlete, having won his age group in three races in 2005.

Jim Burgett

Jim Burgett is a nationally recognized speaker and consultant in education. He was named the "Illinois Superintendent of the Year" by the American Association of School Administrators and "Administrator of the Year" by the Illinois Association for Educational Office Professionals. He has received numerous honors and recognition for his leadership and skills as a motivator. Jim serves on many boards for the State of Illinois, various professional organizations, the Editorial Board for an educational publisher, and several community organizations.

Jim is the recipient of the Award of Excellence from the Illinois State Board of Education, was named a Paul Harris Fellow by Rotary International, and is currently President of his local Community Foundation Board.

After earning a B.S. degree in education, with a minor in chemistry, at the University of Wisconsin-Platteville, Jim earned his M.S. and C.A.S. degrees at Northern Illinois University. Jim has continued his educational training and currently writes and presents Administrative Academies for several states.

Education has been the cornerstone of his career. Jim has been a teacher of grades five through twelve and a principal of elementary, middle school, and high school. During his 38-year tenure, he served as the Superintendent of the Elizabeth Community Unit School District, the River Ridge Community Unit School District, and the Blue Ribbon Highland Community Unit School District, all in Illinois. He retired from Highland in 2004.

He is frequently published by many professional journals, speaks across the country to a variety of organizations, and has keynoted at most major educational conferences in Illinois.

Jim Burgett is known for his practical leadership. He consults many districts, leads strategic planning sessions, and has been a leader in such areas as school construction, administrative standards, and effective teaching strategies.

Jim's wife, Barbara, is a medical records specialist for a senior citizen service complex in Highland. Jim and Barb have three children and five grandchildren.

Acknowledgments

The authors wish to acknowledge the following people for their assistance in the research, development, and production of this book:

Jim Rosborg

Bill Porzukowiak, Tom Mentzer, Jeff Dosier, Evelyn Duncan, Debbie Murphy, Rhonda Brenner, Lynn Clapp, Linda Michael, Chris McMahon, S. Michelle Emmerich, Elizabeth Zeibig, Jennifer Freeman, and the Board of Education at Belleville District #118.

Max McGee

Mike Dunn, Clay Graham, Andy Metcalf, George Schueppert, Ruth Ann Tobias, Pete Trott, Harvey Smith, Carmen Chapman-Pfeiffer, the NIU Center for Governmental Studies, friends at the Illinois State Board of Education, and the District #39 Board of Education.

Jim Burgett

Pat Schwarm, Dennis Brueggemann, Marvin Warner, Darell Bellm, Marie Grandame, Fred Singleton, Bill Hyten, Kent Hammer, and the exceptional Boards of Education and educators I have worked with.

Bibliography

Adler, M., *The Paideia Proposal*. New York: Macmillan, 1982.

Ambrose, S., *Nothing Like it in the World*. New York: Simon and Schuster, 2000.

Apple, M., *Ideology and Curriculum*. London: Routledge & Kegan Paul, 1979.

------, *Education and Power*. Boston: Routledge & Kegan Paul, 1982.

Barnett, S. W., "Long-term Effects on Cognitive Development and School Success," *Early Care and Education for Children in Poverty*. S.W. Barnett and S. Boocock, eds. Albany, NY: State University of New York Press, 1998.

Beauchamp, G.A., *Curriculum Theory*. 3rd ed. Wilmette, IL: The Kagg Press, 1975.

Bennett, W.J., ed., *The Book of Virtues*. New York: Simon and Schuster, 1993.

Berry, R.M., and others, *Collaborative Professional Development Process for School Leaders*. Washington, DC: The Interstate School Leaders Licensure Consortium (Council of Chief State School Officers), 2000.

Blanchard, K., S. Johnson, and E. Harvey, *The One-Minute Manager*. New York: William Morrow, 1981.

Blanchard, K., and N. V. Peale, *The Power of Ethical Management*. New York: William Morrow, 1988.

Blanchard, K., B. Hybels, and P. Hodges, *Leadership by the Book*. New York: William Morrow, 1999.

Bloom, B., ed., *Taxonomy of Educational Objectives: The Classification of Educational Goals*. New York: David McKay, 1956.

------, *Human Characteristics and School Learning*. New York: McGraw-Hill, 1976.

Bobbitt, J.F., *The Curriculum*. Boston: Houghton Mifflin, 1918.

------, *How to Make a Curriculum*. Boston: Houghton Mifflin, 1924.

Bolman, L. G., and T. Deal, *Leading with Soul*. San Francisco: Jossey-Bass, 1995.

Bruner, J.S., *The Process of Education*. Cambridge, MA: Harvard University Press, 1977.

-----, *The Culture of Education*. Cambridge, MA: Harvard University Press, 1996.

Burgett, G., *How to Create Your Own Super Second Life*. Santa Maria, CA: Communication Unlimited, 1999.

Burke, K., *How to Assess Authentic Learning*. Arlington Hts., IL: Skylight Professional Development, 1993.

Carnegie, D., *How to Win Friends and Influence People*. New York: Simon and Schuster, 1936.

Clayman, C., *Monitoring Your Health*. Pleasantville, NY: Reader's Digest Association, 1991.

Cook, W. Jr., *Strategic Planning for America's Schools*. Arlington, VA: American Association of School Administrators, 1988.

Covey, S., *The Seven Habits of Highly Effective People*. New York: Simon and Schuster, 1989.

------, *Principle-Centered Leadership*. New York: Summit Books, 1991.

Creighton, R., *School Redistricting: Policies and Procedures*. Oakland, CA: Oakmore Associates, 1994.

Cuban, L., *The Managerial Imperative and the Practice of Leadership in Schools*. Albany, NY: State University of New York Press, 1988.

Daley, T.D., and M. Jamula, *School Crisis Response Handbook for Education*. Reading, PA: New Century Solutions, 1998.

Diamond, M., and J. Hopson, *Magic Trees of the Mind: How to Nurture Your Child's Intelligence, Creativity and Healthy Emotions from Birth through Adolescence*. New York: Dutton, 1998.

Dewey, J., *The School and Society*. Chicago: University of Chicago Press, 1900.

------, *The Child and the Curriculum*. Chicago: University of Chicago Press, 1902.

------, *Democracy and Education*. New York: Macmillan, 1916.

------, *Experience and Education*. New York: Macmillan, 1938.

DuFour, R., and R. Eaker, *Professional Learning Communities at Work: Best Practices for Enhancing Student Achievement*. Bloomington, IN: National Educational Service, 1998.

Eaker, R., and R. DuFour, R. Burnette, *Getting Started: Reculturing Schools to Become Professional Learning Communities*. Bloomington, IN: National Educational Service, 2002.

Edwards, J.G., "State Farm to Limit New Home, Car Policies in Nevada." *Las Vegas Review Journal*, June 21, 2002.

Einstein, A., and L. Infeld, *The Evolution of Physics*. New York: Simon and Schuster, 1938.

Eisner, E.W., *The Educational Imagination*. 3rd ed. Upper Saddle River, NJ: Merrill Prentice Hall, 2002.

Elmore, R., "Psychiatrists and Lightbulbs: Educational Accountability and the Problem of Capacity." Annual Meeting of the American Educational Research Association, April, 2001.

-----, *Building a New Structure for School Leadership*. Washington, DC: The Albert Shanker Institute, Winter, 2000.

Erikson, E., *Childhood and Society*. New York: Norton, 1963.

Etzioni, A., *Modern Organizations*. Englewood Cliffs, NJ: Prentice-Hall, 1964.

Fiedler, F.E., and M.M. Chemers, *Improving Leadership Effectiveness: The Leader Match Concept*. 2nd ed. New York: Wiley, 1984.

Freire, P., *Pedagogy of the Oppressed*. New York: Harper & Row, 1971.

Gagne, R., and L.J. Briggs, *Principles of Instructional Design*. New York: Holt, Rinehart, and Winston, Inc., 1974.

Gardner, H., *Intelligence Reframed: Multiple Intelligences for the 21st Century*. New York: Basic Books, 1999.

Gebelein, S.H., and others, *Sucessful Managers Handbook: Development Suggestions for Today's Managers*. Minneapolis: Personnel Decisions International, 2000.

Giroux, H.A., *Ideology, Culture, and the Process of Schooling*. Philadelphia: Temple University Press, 1981.

Glenn, J., F. Withrow, and others, *Preparing Schools and School Systems for the 21st Century*. Arlington, VA: American Association of School Administrators, 1999.

Goodlad, J., *A Place Called School: Prospects for the Future*. New York: McGraw-Hill, 1984.

------, *Educational Renewal: Better Teachers, Better Schools*. San Francisco: Jossey-Bass, 1991.

Goodlad, J., and T.J. McMannon, eds., *The Public Purpose of Education and Schooling*. San Francisco: Jossey-Bass, 1997.

Grissmer, D., A. Flanagan, J. Kawata, and S. Williamson, *Improving Student Achievement: What State NAEP Scores Tell Us*. Santa Monica, CA: Rand, 2000.

Hart, B., and T. Risley, *Meaningful Differences in the Everyday Experience of Young American Children*. Baltimore: P.H. Brookes, 1995.

Harvey, E., and A. Lucia, *Walk the Talk—and Get the Results You Want*. Dallas: Performance Publishing Co., 1995.

Herzberg, F., B. Mausner, and B. Snyderman, *Motivation to Work*. New York: Wiley, 1967.

Hirsch, E.D., Jr., *Cultural Literacy: What Every American Needs to Know*. Boston: Houghton Mifflin, 1987.

Hirst, P., *Knowledge and the Curriculum*. London: Routledge & Kegan Paul, 1974.

Hoy, K.W., and C.G. Miskel, *Educational Administration: Theory, Research, Practice*. 6th ed. New York: McGraw-Hill, 2001.

Hutchins, R.M., *The Higher Learning in America*. New Haven: Yale University Press, 1936.

Hunter, M., *Mastery Teaching*. El Segundo, CA: TIP Publications, 1982.

Illich, I., *Tools for Conviviality*. New York: Harper & Row, 1973.

James, J. *Thinking in the Future Tense: A Workout for the Mind*. 2nd ed. New York: Touchstone Books, 1997.

Jencks, C., and M. Phillips, eds., *The Black-White Test Score Gap*. Washington, DC: Brookings Institution Press, 1998.

Kane, T., and D. Staiger, "Volatility in School Test Scores: Implications for Test-based Accountability Systems," in *Brookings Papers on Education Policy 2002*. D. Ravitch, ed. Washington, DC: Brookings Institution, 2002.

Kane, T., D. Staiger, and J. Geppert, "Randomly Accountable," *Education Next*. Spring, 2002.

Karoly, L.A., and others, *Investing in Our Children: What We Know and Don't Know about the Costs and Benefits of Early Childhood Interventions*. Santa Monica, CA: Rand, 1998.

Katzman, J., and others, *Testing the Testers 2002*. New York: The Princeton Review, 2002.

Keenan, N., and others, *Collaborative Professional Development Process for School Leaders*. Washington, DC: Council of Chief State School Officers, 2000.

Kotlowitz, A., *There Are No Children Here*. New York: Anchor Books, 1992.

Kozol, J., *Savage Inequalities: Children in America's Schools*. 2nd ed. New York: Harper Perennial, 1992.

KSA Group, Inc., "Business, Educators Find Power In Baldrige to Improve Schools*." Work America,* vol. 15, no. 4, April 1998.

Lewis, J., Jr., *Implementing Total Quality in Education to Produce Great Schools*. Westbury, NY: National Center to Save Our Schools, 1993.

Likert, R., *New Patterns of Management*. New York: McGraw-Hill, 1961.

Lynch, K., *The Hidden Curriculum: Reproduction in Education, a Reappraisal*. London: Falmer Press, 1989.

Marx, G., *Ten Trends: Educating Children for a Profoundly Different Future*. Arlington, VA.: Educational Research Service, 2000.

Maslow, A., *Motivation and Personality*. New York: Harper and Row, 1987.

Maxwell, J., *The 21 Most Powerful Minutes in a Leader's Day*. Nashville: Thomas Nelson, 2000.

McGregor, D., *The Human Side of Enterprise*. New York: McGraw-Hill, 1960.

McNabb, M., and others, *Technology Connections for School Improvement. Planner's Handbook*, Oak Brook, IL: NCREL, 1999.

Murphy, J., "Principal Instructional Leadership." *Advances in Educational Administration I* (Part B), 1990.

Neuman, S.B., "Access to Print: Problems, Consequences, and Instructional Solutions," White House Summit on Early Childhood Cognitive Development, 2001.

Newberry, A., *Strategic Planning in Education: Unleashing our Schools' Potential*. Vancouver, BC: EduServ, Inc., 1992.

Newman, F.M., R. Rutter, and others, "Organizational Factors that Affect School Sense of Efficacy, Community and Expectations." *Sociology of Education*, vol. 62, no. 4, 1989.

Oakes, J., and M. Lipton, *Teaching to Change the World*. Boston: McGraw-Hill, 1999.

Oliva, P.F., *Developing the Curriculum*. 5th ed. New York: Addison Wesley-Longman, 2001.

Ornstein, A.C., and F.P. Hunkins, *Curriculum: Foundations, Principles, and Issues*. Boston: Allen and Bacon, 1998.

Peale, N.V., *The Power of Positive Thinking*. New York: Prentice-Hall, 1952.

Phenix, P., *Realms of Meaning*. New York: McGraw-Hill, 1964.

Phillips, D.T., *Lincoln on Leadership*. New York: Warner Books, 1992.

Piaget, J., and B. Inhelder, *The Psychology of the Child*. New York: Basic Books, 1969.

Pinar, W., ed., *Contemporary Curriculum Discourse*. Scottsdale, AZ: Gorsuch Scavisbrick, 1988.

Plato, *The Republic*. Translated by R. Sterling and W. Scott. New York: Norton, 1985.

Ramey, C.T., and S.L. Ramey, "Early Intervention and Early Experience." *American Psychologist*, vol. 53, no. 2, 1998.

Rogers, C. and H.J. Frieberg, *Freedom to Learn*. 3rd ed. New York: Merrill, 1994.

Rothstein, Richard, "Finance Fungibility: Investigating Relative Impacts of Investments in Schools and Non-school Educational Institutions to Improve Student Achievement," from *Improving Educational Achievement: A Volume Exploring the Role of Investments in Schools and Other Supports and Services for Families and Communities*. Washington, DC: Finance Project, 2001.

Schmoker, M.J., and R.B. Wilson, *Total Quality Education*. Bloomington, IN: Phi Delta Kappa Education Foundation, 1993.

Sears, J.T., and J.D. Marshall, eds., *Teaching and Thinking About Curriculum: Critical Inquiries*. New York: Teachers College, Columbia University, 1990.

Segal, A., "The Importance of Non-School Investments for Improving School Readiness and Educational Outcomes," in Rothstein, R., *Improving Educational Achievement*. Washington, DC: Center on Education Policy, 2000.

Sergiovanni, T., *Moral Leadership: Getting to the Heart of School Improvement*. San Francisco: Jossey-Bass, 1992.

Shipley, J., and M.C. Wescott, "Baldrige Education Criteria: 'Flavor of the Month' or the Road to World Class Schools." *Quality Network News*, vol. 10, no. 4, September/October 2000.

Skinner, B.F., *The Technology of Teaching*. New York: Appleton-Century-Crofts, 1968.

Snow, C.E., M.S. Burns, and P. Griffin, eds., ***Preventing Reading Difficulties in Young Children***. Washington, DC: National Academy Press, 1998.

Spillane, J.P., and R. Halverson, *Distributed Leadership: Toward a Theory of School Leadership Practice,* Annual Meeting of the American Educational Research Association, Montreal, 1999.

Stenhouse, L., ***An Introduction to Curriculum Research and Development***. London: Heinemann, 1975.

Stogdill, R.M., ***Stogdills's Handbook of Leadership: A Survey of Theory and Research***. 2nd ed. New York: Free Press, 1981.

Strickland, D.S., "Early Intervention for African-American Children Considered to be at Risk," in S. Neuman and D. Dickinson, ***Handbook of Early Literacy Research***. New York: Guilford Press, 2001.

Strike, K.A., E.J. Haller, and J.F. Soltis, ***The Ethics of School Administration***. New York: Teachers College Press, 1988.

Swantz, R., "One Solution to a Growing Problem," paper prepared for the School District of La Crosse, Wisconsin in July, 1993.

Taba, H., ***Curriculum Development: Theory and Practice***. New York: Harcourt Brace, and World, 1962.

Thomas, M.D., and W. Bainbridge, "All Children Can Learn: Facts and Fallacies," *Education Research Service Spectrum*, Winter 2001.

Thorndike, E.L., ***The Measurement of Intelligence***. New York: Columbia University, 1926.

Tanner, D., and L. Tanner, ***Curriculum Development: Theory into Practice***. New York: Macmillan, 1975.

Toffler, A., and H. Toffler, ***Creating a New Civilization: the Politics of the Third Wave***. Atlanta: Turner Pubs., 1995.

Tyler, R., ***Basic Principles of Curriculum and Instruction***. Chicago: University of Chicago Press, 1949.

Wasik, B.A., and R.E. Slavin, "Preventing Early Reading Failure With One-to-one Tutoring: A Review of Five Programs," *Reading Research Quarterly*, 28, 1993.

Whitehurst, G.H., "Research on Teacher Preparation and Professional Development," Remarks to the White House Conference on Preparing Tomorrow's Teachers, 2002.

-----, Remarks at the White House Summit on Early Childhood Cognitive Development, 2001.

Wiles, J., ***Curriculum Essentials***. Boston: Allyn and Bacon, 1999.

Ziglar, Zig, ***See You at the Top***. 3rd ed. Gretna, LA: Pelican Publishing Company, 1978.

Index

"What do we live for, if it is not to make life less difficult for each other?"

George Eliot

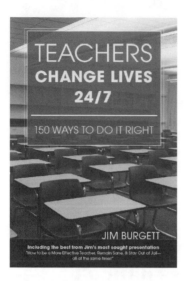

Table of Contents

At last, veteran master teacher and honored administrator Jim Burgett shares his most sought stories from his keynote/workshop "How to Be an Effective Teacher, Remain Sane, and Stay Out of Jail—All at the Same Time!" combined with his popular "150 Time-Tested (and almost guaranteed) Ways to Be an Effective Teacher and Change the World."

Jim's passion is infectious and fun. His joy of life is at the core of why he excelled teaching science, coaching basketball, and moving up the administrative ladder. "What teachers do doesn't end at 3:15," he says. "It is felt every day of their students' lives. Teachers change lives 24/7."

ISBN 0910167915
150 pages
Trade Paperback
$17.95

For more details...
- ✦ sample chapter
- ✦ more content info
- ✦ Jim's bio
- ✦ testimonials

**www.superintendents-
and-principals.com**

TEACHERS
CHANGE
LIVES
24/7

Jim Burgett

Illinois Superintendent of the Year
Illinois Administrator of the Year

THE PERFECT SCHOOL

✓ Jim Rosborg
✓ Max McGee
✓ Jim Burgett

Authors of
*What Every Superintendent and Principal
Needs to Know*

Ever wonder what a **PERFECT SCHOOL** would be like? What a model for a new school—or the rebuilding of an old one—would include?

Here's the vision, with practical how-to steps, plus lots of related fun from three of Illinois' top K-12 leaders, who have a combined 100+ years in the classroom and at the top.

Table of Contents

A Perfect School?
The Perfect Teacher and
   Perfect Staff
The Perfect Parent
The Perfect Principal
Service Makes or Breaks the
   Perfect School
Infuse Character, Build
   Characters
Perception is Reality
Eliminate the Weakest Link
The Devil is in the Details
Gathering Data to Help
   Improve Student Success
Bridging the Academic Gap
Financing Education
Total Curriculum

ISBN 0910167907
246 pages
Trade Paperback
$24.95

For more details...
✦ sample chapters
✦ both covers
✦ authors' bios
✦ testimonials

www.superintendents-and-principals.com

Testimonials
about the 2003 (1st edition) of this book

Doing the right thing is a big part of this book, not just in Burgett's chapter on Civic Leadership and Ethics, but in every chapter on nearly every page are reminders about leadership behavior. You can find almost any topic that presents a challenge to school leaders. From accountability to zero tolerance, from band instruments to wellness, a tip is in the book. If you want to become a better principal or dean, or perhaps see the superintendency in your future, you should read this book.

Illinois Principals Association Newsletter, *August 2003*

What Rosborg, McGee, and Burgett have written could not have come at a better time. They have focused their collective experience to provide school administrators with practical, no-nonsense advice on how to lead every school to educational excellence.

Dr. Walt Warfield, Executive Director,
Illinois Association of School Administrators

This book is great. It should be required reading for all aspiring educational leaders.

Dr. Donald L. Kussmaul, President-Elect,
American Association of School Administrators

What Every Superintendent and Principal Needs to Know is a comprehensive blueprint for how to succeed as an educational leader. This is a must read for anyone in the business of doing what's best for kids!

Chad Allaman, Principal, Illini Central Grade School, Mason City, IL

What Every Superintendent and Principal Needs to Know should be required reading for any administrator! It would be difficult to duplicate the collective experiences, wisdom, and perspectives of the authors in any graduate or post-graduate program. I found the sections on ethics, buildings and grounds, planning, and increasing test scores very insightful and motivating. I highly recommend this hard-to-put-down book!

Dr. Lane Abrell, Principal, Plainfield High School, Plainfield, IL